Following the Human One

Following the Human One

The Way to Fulfillment and Flourishing

ROBERT L. MONTGOMERY

WIPF & STOCK · Eugene, Oregon

FOLLOWING THE HUMAN ONE
The Way to Fulfillment and Flourishing

Wipf & Stock
An Imprint of Wipf and Stock Publishers
199 W. 8th Ave., Suite 3
Eugene, OR 97401

www.wipfandstock.com

PAPERBACK ISBN: 978-1-5326-1836-9
HARDCOVER ISBN: 978-1-4982-4388-9
EBOOK ISBN: 978-1-4982-4387-2

Manufactured in the U.S.A.   AUGUST 23, 2017

Dedicated to
the aboriginal people of Taiwan,
who made me ask,
why don't all people receive the gospel like them?

Contents

Preface

INCREASING NUMBERS OF PEOPLE around the world seek to be followers, as I do, of the most important person in history, Jesus Christ. One measure of the importance of Jesus Christ is the measurement of the years based on his birth. Even thought many scholars prefer to use BCE or "Before the Common Era" and CE or "Common Era," this division of eras is still based on the birth of Jesus Christ. This is why I will use the traditional designations of BC for "Before Christ" and AD for *Anno Domini*, "Year of our Lord," as many scholars studying from a secular perspective still do. I have respect for secular studies and have carried out secular social scientific studies of religion where I seek to avoid injecting my theological views. However, in this book, although I use social scientific perspectives, I am writing from my theological viewpoint.

Following Jesus Christ is never done perfectly, partly because no one has a conception of Jesus Christ in their minds that conforms to the reality of Jesus Christ. In other words, every one who claims to follow Jesus Christ is following what they know of Jesus Christ, which is never complete. Many times over the last two thousand years the followers have misrepresented their Lord, as I have. But he whose favorite name for himself was "the Human One" ("the Son of Man") continues to call us to follow him into new life in fellowship with God. He stated, "I am the way, the truth, and the life. No one comes to the Father except through me" (John 14:6).

This statement troubles some Christians and non-Christians who are thinking only of verbal affirmations of belief in Jesus Christ, but this is placing more emphasis on a verbal affirmation than necessary. First of all, our verbal affirmation is of our imperfect concept and can only be made with words, which are all symbolic. More importantly, this thinking is not in line with the deep meanings in the Bible and of Jesus' own sayings. Jesus himself discounted verbal affirmations when he warned against simply calling him "Lord, Lord." What was important was doing "the will of his Father in heaven" (Matt 7:21, 22). As we know from Christian history, there are many affirmations of Christian faith that have been combined with bad or even evil intentions and actions.

The affirmation of faith in Jesus Christ can be and often is an important basic first step in the Christian life, but we need to grasp a deeper truth from the words of Jesus about coming to the Father through him. This truth follows from what is said in the prologue of the Gospel of John: that Jesus, as the Word, was with God in the beginning of all things and that all things came into being through the Word (John 1:1–3). Even earlier, Paul stated in his Letter to the Colossians (all his letters were earlier than the Gospels): "All things have been created through him and for him. He himself is before all things and in him all things hold together" (Col 1:17). These words may be from an early Christian hymn. The deep meaning is that being in the way of Jesus Christ is moving in accordance with not only our creation as human beings, but with the creation of all things. Just as all things came into existence from God through Jesus Christ, the image of God, so all things return to God through him as we fulfill what it means to be in the image of God. That makes "his way" both our destiny and the destiny of the universe. Thus coming to the Father through him is not simply a matter of what people say they believe, but is a matter of how people live under the grace of God throughout human history, the grace that became incarnate in Jesus Christ. Obviously, people before Christ and since he came have not known the name of Jesus. Peter stated to his Gentile host, Cornelius, "I truly understand that God shows no partiality, but in every nation anyone who fears him [God] and does what is right is acceptable to him" (Acts 10:35). People often forget this "liberal" statement by Peter. We could say that in these cases "doing what is right" is walking in the way of Jesus that leads to God. Paul stated to the Athenian intellectuals that God made all people "so that they would search for God and perhaps grope for him and find him—though indeed he is not far from each of us." He then added, "God has overlooked the times of human ignorance . . . " (Acts 17:27, 30). In both cases Peter and Paul proceeded with preaching the gospel. Sharing the gospel is the ongoing joyful task of Christians, but that doesn't mean that hearers have been entirely ignorant of or outside of the way that leads to God.

To add to this perspective, to keep believers from pride in their own knowledge of the way of God, Paul writes:

> When Gentiles who do not possess the law, do instinctively what
> the law requires, these, though not having the law, are a law to
> themselves. They show that what the law requires is written on
> their hearts, to which their own conscience also bears witness;
> and their conflicting thoughts will accuse or perhaps excuse
> them on the day when, according to my gospel, God, through
> Jesus Christ will judge the secret thoughts of all. (Rom 2:14–15)

Christians believe that Jesus is the personification of the law, so it could be said that Jesus may be written on the hearts of some who do not know his name. Clearly the Scriptures show that the way to God through Jesus Christ is not limited to a human mental knowledge and verbal affirmation. One of my main purposes in this book is to show how human beings have built-in longings that are only fully satisfied by Jesus Christ. This is the "groping" Paul speaks of to the Athenian intellectuals (Acts 17:27). It is the task of Christians to help people crystallize their longings and find their personal and communal fulfillment as they follow Jesus Christ.

What we can say here is that Jesus calls his followers to make him our focus and make our mission to help people of all nations to be drawn to Jesus Christ, as he said in speaking of his death on the cross (John 12:32). Thus they will actively fulfill their human destiny, a destiny given from creation and written into human nature and into the universe itself. In the last chapter, I call this the Great Circle of Love that comes from God, proceeds through creation, human history and human nature, and returns to God. Before we get to the last chapter, I have much more to say about Jesus. Here I would simply say our focus should be to follow Jesus and to continually think about what that means, as stated in Psalm 1:2, "And on his law they meditate day and night"—Jesus being the personification of God's law. As to what should be our central concern, when Peter asked what would happen to his friend John, Jesus said, "If it is my will that he remain until I come, what is that to you? Follow me!" (John 21:22). "Follow me" is the first and last word of Jesus to his followers.

I became a follower of Jesus Christ through my believing and loving parents. Later in life I came to see what a powerful effect following him could have on a group of people when I went to live and work among the aboriginal people in Taiwan. I came to wonder then why could not all people hear his call and follow him as the aboriginal people did, so openly and enthusiastically? I started on a pilgrimage to try to answer this question, a pilgrimage that has lasted up to the present. I embarked on a study, using both social scientific and historical studies, of receptivity to the Christian gospel around the world. It turned out that I was really studying receptivity to Christianity or Christians, not simply Jesus Christ, by numerous diverse peoples because it was through Christians that people obtained their perception of the gospel and Jesus Christ. And in many cases they rejected Christianity because of Christians. As I studied why Christianity spread and did not spread, I had to look at the whole period since the coming of Christ. I also had to look at other religions because I discovered that Buddhism and Islam in their various forms had likewise spread more widely than other religions and had also experienced both acceptance and rejection, as well as many changes within them.

Initially, I noted that the aboriginals in Taiwan had not been dominated directly by Western colonial powers or White Christians, as had the aboriginal people of America, my homeland. On the other hand, the less responsive majority society in Taiwan, as well as other traditional societies I knew (I had grown up in China), were very conscious of Western domination in their history. They were also very conscious of the Opium War (1841) forcing China to buy opium, as well as all of the "unequal treaties" forced on China by the so-called Christian West. These experiences were taught in Chinese schools. In fact, the major imported item to Taiwan in the nineteenth century was opium. I became convinced that association with domination was a great hindrance in the spread of the gospel or of any religion. Of course, Jesus Christ, although having great authority for me and other Christians, never tried to dominate others in the same way as the rulers of this world. However, after beginning my studies of the social factors affecting the spread of religions,[1] my attention was drawn by two of Rodney Stark's books to the fact that religious content was a major factor in causing religions to spread.[2] It may seem paradoxical, but as a Christian missionary I wanted to give full attention to the social factors I thought many Christians overlooked. I credit Rodney Stark with encouraging me to give attention to the influence of religious factors on the spread of religions. That is when I discovered that the three most widely spreading religions each have a central special human being: Buddha, Jesus, and Muhammad, in historical order. As far as I know, no one else has made special note of this fact. I concluded that a "special person" with certain special characteristics was the key cause, though not the only cause, for the spread of a religion.

1. Montgomery, "Receptivity to an Outside Religion," 287–99; "The Spread of Religions and Macrosocial Relations" 37–52; *The Diffusion of Religions*; *The Lopsided Spread of Christianity*. These were my first four publications attempting to explain the spread of religions. After encountering Rodney Stark's writings, I wrote *Why Religions Spread*; "Conversion and the Historic Spread of Religions," 164–89; and "Special Persons and the Spread of Religions," 369–93.

2. Stark, *The Rise of Christianity*, 4; *One True God*. 1.

For Christians, we know that the special person is Jesus Christ, and though we Christians believe he is divine, we also believe he is fully human. Jesus has demonstrated unusual power to draw forth love and loyalty, as have the special persons who founded Buddhism and Islam, as we shall see. This made me want to examine the basis of the drawing power of Jesus, as well as of Buddha, Muhammad, and other special persons. This is basically the experience that led me to tackle the very special and distinct Way of Jesus in this book.

It has long puzzled me why the scholarly world, though strong on descriptions of the world's religions, has not paid more attention to *why* religions have spread. The founders of religions are clearly important to why they have spread. Perhaps the neglect in seeking to explain the reasons for their spread (or non-spread) is because comparing religions, especially their founders, who attract love and loyalty from hosts of followers, is too sensitive a subject. Most scholars try to be objective and want to be considered tolerant toward all religions. Many have no attachment to any one religion's founder. Furthermore, awareness of the strong feelings of millions of people may cause scholars to avoid any focus on the importance of the central human being when examining the three most widely spreading religions. Also, often those who are uncommitted to any religion may be relatively unaware of the personal power found in the founders of religions. Whatever the case, many scholars have largely overlooked the power of a special human being to attract followers. Belief in the special power of Jesus Christ to draw people certainly does not discount the power of other "special people," especially the founders of other religions such as Buddha and Muhammad.[3]

My studies of the spread of the three religions—Buddhism, Christianity, and Islam—and knowing my own attraction to Jesus Christ convinced me that the major reason Christianity has been able to spread to include approximately one third of the population of the world is because of the *person* of Jesus Christ. (Jesus Christ is the title most often used by Christians, meaning Jesus the Messiah.)

I also came to the conclusion that Christians and Christianity have often been a major hindrance to the spread of Christianity. I wrote about this as the work of the Opposition.[4] Although I do not think we should give much attention, especially speculation, to the Evil One (who in any case has been defeated), I do not object to saying "the Evil One," as Jesus probably says in the Lord's Prayer, "Deliver us from the Evil One." (I understand that

---

3. This was the special focus in my article in "Special Persons," 369–93. Chapters 3 and 4 contain a great deal of material from this article.

4. Montgomery, *The Real New Age,* 70–181.

it is just as well to translate the word as "evil" rather than "evil one" because of all the superstitions regarding Satan and evil influences.) After my studies I desired to state as simply as possible what was the particular source of the power of Jesus Christ to attract people in spite of the poor representations (or witness) we Christians have given of him. I believed that anything that can be done to understand him and the reason for his impact on billions of people is for the good of the world and especially for those who love and want to follow him. This is a particularly important task because of the spread of freedoms in the world and with now the spread of the "faith option," which I believe is consistent with God's desire to be chosen (or for us to realize that we are chosen). It is also consistent with the nature of faith as a non-coerced, trusting, faithful, and loving relationship to God. In this way, my pilgrimage through my studies of the spread of religions is what led to the present book.

Anyone can see that this book is written from my faith perspective that God has not given up on creation, and especially on human beings. Rather, God wants a loving interaction with God's creatures, made in God's image. Specifically, I believe God came into history as a human being to redeem what God loved, that is, restore us to what God originally made us to be—human beings made in the image of God. This fact needs continuing and increasing exposure to all people, with careful sensitivity to the circumstances, remembering that the best exposure is in human lives and human communities that follow the Human One in the Way of fulfillment and flourishing. The importance of following the one who identified himself as the Human One and carried out the work of the Suffering Servant is especially important in a world that is increasingly the arena of human beings in action and interaction.

Introduction

MY CONCLUSION FROM MY studies mentioned in the preface was that the *key factor* in the spread of the three most widely spreading religions is their elevation of single human savior figures.[1] In other words, without the founders, although aided by other religious and social secular factors (the latter distinct from the founders themselves), the religions would not have spread as they have spread. Other religions without distinctive founders having the *special characteristics* of the founders of the three most widely spreading religions have not spread nearly as widely or to as great a variety of social groups. I became convinced that there is something built-in to human beings that make them responsive to such figures. Human beings need leaders and they usually recognize this fact. This is consistent with my belief as a Christian that human beings are created to be attracted to other human beings and especially to special human beings, and this helps to account for why God became incarnate in order to draw human beings into fellowship with the triune God. I believe that the love of God to which human beings respond is supremely expressed in the person and work of Jesus Christ. At the same time, although created to be receptive to God, human beings are also resistant to God, even making use of the gifts of God as barriers to God. Christian views of Jesus Christ and of God can be distorted. But it is especially the deeds of Christians that have misrepresented the Christian message. In short, the resistance of Christians to God distorts the gospel and hinders the reception of the gospel of Jesus Christ by others. Many times it is not individual Christians who cause others to resist Christianity, but the

---

1. Montgomery, *Why Religions Spread*; "Conversion," 164–89. "Special Persons," 369–93. In the last article cited I particularly focus on the place of the three founders of Buddhism, Christianity, and Islam.

association of Christians and Christianity with various kinds of behavior, such as coercive power exercised on the societal level. People in whole societies, as well as individuals, have often perceived Christianity as being imposed upon them, which is very different from the approach of Jesus Christ to people and the world. Without giving further introductory words, I give below a brief summary of the chapters of this book.

In chapter 1 I take up a discussion of the name Jesus chose for himself, which is in the title I use for the book. This name draws attention to his identification with human beings, but at the same time draws attention, perhaps unrealized in the thought of many, to his divinity. I believe the name "the Human One" also draws attention to what I believe is God's purpose for humankind: to be made over into the image of God through Christ. The doctrine of the incarnation is a mystery and so is the name "the Son of Man" or, as translated by Walter Wink and others, "the son of the man."[2] I seek to show that the very ambiguity and different meanings of the name are important to understanding the revelation of God to humanity.

In an attempt to be "up front," I set forth in chapter 2 the larger theological-philosophical view of reality in which I believe human beings live and with which I approach the subject of the drawing power of Jesus Christ. Following this overview of my basic view of reality, in chapter 3 I discuss the confused human scene of religions, heroes, morals, and authorities that reveal the built-in human longings for what I interpret as incarnation and atonement that is fulfilled in Jesus Christ. Chapter 4 examines how human longing for special human beings is fulfilled in the three religions that have spread more widely than other religions. Without depreciating the important founders of Buddhism and Islam and their special gifts, as a Christian, I see the drawing power of Jesus Christ as the most powerful of all. The contents of chapters 3 and 4 is very similar to the argument published in my article in *Pastoral Psychology*.[3] I wrote this article when I was developing my thought found in these two chapters so that the material is very dependent on this article.

In spite of the built-in longing of human beings that finds fulfillment in the outreach of God in the incarnation and atonement of Jesus Christ, there has been a major problem expressed in various ways human beings have resisted God. Chapters 5 and 6 consider some of the ways human beings have resisted and continue to resist the outreach of God to humanity. This is in accordance with the vision of human beings given in the Bible and seen in human history. A central point of these two chapters is that the

2. Wink, *The Human Being*, 19–31.

3. Montgomery, "Special Persons," 369–93.

resistance of Christians to God creates the greatest opposition to the message of the gospel.

Following the background treatment of the first six chapters, the rest of the book looks particularly at Jesus Christ as believed in by early followers, throughout history, and in the present. First, the book would not be complete unless it reviewed the extraordinary claims by his followers about Jesus Christ resulting in so many people being drawn to him. Chapter 7 discusses the person of Jesus based on the names his followers used for him. Christ cannot be separated from what he did, so chapter 8 discusses the claims of his followers regarding the work of Jesus Christ. I use statements from the Bible without argument about who said them or wrote them, even in the case of the statements attributed to Jesus. Although I accept the Gospels as a true representation of what Jesus said and did, what is important in the argument of this book is that the New Testament represents the witness of the early Christians to what they experienced with Jesus and believed about him.

From the perspective of human history, the two thousand years since Jesus Christ is a very short time, but many highly significant events have taken place. As a Christian and judging by the last words of Jesus, I believe the leading significant event in history has been the spread of the gospel of Jesus Christ, which may be only in the beginning stage of a longer period than simply the time since Jesus came. This history is taken up in chapter 9, which describes the spread of the gospel up to the present through four recognizable periods. I believe we are now in the early stages of the fourth period, which could be followed by other important distinguishable periods or simply a long period.[4] Rather than give a description of the history subsequent to Jesus life on earth, I primarily give a Christian philosophy for understanding this history.

The drawing power of Jesus Christ cannot be understood without consideration of Jesus Christ in the personal and communal life of human beings. This is the subject of chapter 10. Chapter 11 deals with the special authority of Jesus Christ that is to be realized by his followers. The claim to this authority is when Jesus said, "All authority in heaven and on earth has been given unto me" (Matt 28:18). The chapter considers the meaning of the important reality of the authority of Jesus Christ for the followers of Jesus Christ.

A question is floating in the world that is awaiting an answer by many people. In chapter 12 I discuss the question that Jesus asked his

4. This chapter draws particularly from my books, *Why Religions Spread*, *The Real New Age*, and from my article, "Conversion and the Historic Spread of Religions," in *The Oxford Handbook of Religious Conversion*, 164–89.

disciples—"Who do you say that I am?" (Matt 16:15; Mark 8:29; Luke 9:20)—as the most important question human beings can answer. In some ways, belief about the particular person who represents God in his life, death, and resurrection is prior to and more crucial than belief in God. I became convinced that the basic religious issue for human beings is not whether they believe or do not believe in God ("Even the demons believe—and shudder"; Jas 2:19), but rather whether they believe God has acted in a particular way, especially to save us through Jesus Christ. The question as to who Jesus is may be avoided or answered in an outwardly correct way, but with the wrong understanding, as by Peter of old. But it is a question that I believe is inescapable in the end and must be answered throughout life. It is the faith option that is becoming clearer in human history, which I believe is God's purpose for history.

Chapter 13 is the final chapter. In it I discuss an overall perspective with which to view the meaning of the appearance of Jesus Christ in human history. I find the Great Circle of Love as a helpful way to view what the triune God has done, is doing, and will do through Jesus Christ and the Holy Spirit.

I wish to acknowledge the excellent help of the editor of my first manuscript, Cynthia Bright. In addition, I wish to thank the good work of Matt Wimer, Nathan Rhoads, and Jana Wipf at Wipf and Stock. All my editors were a great help in improving the clarity of my writing, but, of course, I take full responsibility both for the ideas expressed and the way they are expressed. In addition, I appreciate very much the encouragement and help of Lewis Rambo in getting published in *Pastoral Psychology* and *The Oxford Handbook on Religious Conversion*. I have already made it evident that Rodney Stark had a strong influence on my thought in recognizing religious content as a causative force. Christian Smith also had a large influence on my thought about human believing, personhood, and secularization. In regard to the name "the Human One," I am especially indebted to Walter Wink for his study both of the name the Son of Man and of "the Powers." Daniel Boyarin contributed greatly by his study of Jewish thought contemporary with Jesus to understanding references to both the Son of Man and the Messiah.

Chapter 1

The Favorite Name

THIS BOOK CONTAINS IN its title the favorite name Jesus used for himself, the Son of Man, which can be translated "the Human One," as in the Common English Bible translation. Bruce Chilton translates the title as "One like the person."[1] In some ways it is strange to start this book with a discussion of this name. The Son of Man is not the name the early Christians normally called Jesus Christ. This is easily verified by looking at the New Testament epistles and the Book of Acts. However, Stephen at his death in Acts 7:56 says that he sees the Son of Man "standing at the right hand of God." This is an important exception to followers not referring to Jesus as the Son of Man, but Stephen's vision recalls both the vision of Daniel 7:13–14 and the saying of Jesus at his trial. Stephen's vision emphasizes the importance of the Daniel passage to both Jesus and the early Christians. He also followed the example of Jesus in asking him to receive his spirit and to "not hold this sin against" those stoning him. It is only in the gospels, which were written after most of the epistles, that we frequently hear Jesus calling himself with the name meaning "the Human One." This means that the Son of Man was the name the gospel writers remembered (or were told) that Jesus constantly used for himself. I do not have a clear answer to why the followers of Jesus did not continue to use the name the Son of Man or the Human One to refer to Jesus. It was certainly not because they did not believe in the humanity of Jesus. See Paul's sermon to the Athenians, when he referred to "a man whom he [God] has appointed" (Acts 17:31). I can only conclude that "Jesus Christ" or "Jesus the Messiah" served best to emphasize that Jesus was the "Fulfiller of the promises to God's people for a Deliverer."

---

1. Chilton, *Rabbi Jesus*, 157–58, 160, 172.

After consulting biblical scholars, I came to believe the favorite self-designation by Jesus could have meanings related to both humanity and divinity, and even to a broader meaning in which redeemed humanity is included, as we shall see. Thus, in many ways the name the Son of Man is very strange and its meaning less clear than his other names, but I believe its very ambiguity had an important meaning for Jesus and also has for us today.

In the case of the most important name Jesus used for himself, it is difficult to believe that his followers who affirmed his lordship over their lives would have made up such a name as the Human One (the Son of Man). It is also difficult to believe that they would imagine that the Messiah would suffer, given all the images they had of a conquering and ruling Messiah. The Bible makes clear the disappointment of the disciples and their failure to understand Jesus, a failure that continued even after the resurrection of Jesus and, we could say, continues among us Christians today.

I had always thought of this favorite name for himself as a way Jesus used to identify with humanity. However, in looking into the work of scholars of the Bible, I discovered that this name contains a great deal more meaning than I had realized. Yes, Jesus' choice of this name shows his identification with humanity, but also, surprisingly, his identification with divinity. Yet, very consistently with the whole approach of Jesus: it asserts these dual identifications without a dominating or imposing approach. I believe he was even reaching out to humanity in an inclusive approach. Some have sought to make the point that Jesus never declared himself to be divine in the synoptic gospels. They are looking for a kind of self-projection uncharacteristic of Jesus—"I am divine." Nevertheless, the divinity and humanity of Christ became Christian doctrine, proclaimed in such early Christian writings as the letters of Paul and later in the Gospel of John.[2] Thus, significantly, the title the Son of Man (the Human One) is ambiguous or carries a double meaning of both humanity and divinity, just as the doctrine of the incarnation refers to both the divinity and humanity of Jesus. Furthermore, it points towards our redemption to become truly human and also like God, as the biblical scholar Walter Wink has pointed out.[3] In this way the favorite name of Jesus for himself was a very suitable way for Jesus to introduce and affirm the incarnation and also the redemption of humanity. The name is

2. Ehrman, *How Jesus Became God*, 235, 244–46, 282. Ehrman does not admit the historicity of many statements in the New Testament, which I accept, but he recognizes that the early followers believed Jesus was divine very early on and that belief in the resurrection was basic to the initiation of the Jesus movement.

3. Wink, *Human Being*, 257–60. Wink wrestles with the numerous studies of the name the Human One but in the end admits its mysterious nature.

mysterious, even an enigma, but the incarnation is also a mystery beyond rational explanation. Recent scholarship supports the mysterious and ambiguous meaning of the name the Son of Man or the Human One. Contrary to much thought, scholars have shown that some Jewish thinking before, during, and after the time of Jesus had no difficulty in believing in a secondary divine figure associated with God. This was new to me until encountering the studies of the Jewish scholars Daniel Boyarin and Peter Schäfer.[4]

Where did the name the Human One, chosen by Jesus so deliberately and carefully, come from? Jesus took the name from a general ancient tradition that Chilton calls the "throne and chariot tradition."[5] This goes back to Moses' encounters with God, Elijah's ascent in a chariot of fire, and Ezekiel's heavenly visions. Ezekiel refers to himself continuously as "son of man" or "mortal one," but he has numerous visions in which he sees the redemption of Israel from the perspective of God. Wink notes that Ezekiel, in his important and very mysterious first vision, sees God "in a human form."[6] In general, Ezekiel clearly refers to his own mortal humanity. Nevertheless, "the throne tradition" in which certain human beings are elevated very close to God is brought to a climax in the apocalyptic visions of Daniel and specifically in Daniel 7. For me, this can be seen to be the most important reference for "the Son of Man" used by Jesus, because he used it in his trial. There "the Son of Man" is associated with "clouds of heaven," a phrase used both independently and with "the Son of Man" in the gospels. We read in Daniel 7:13–14:

> As I watched in the night visions, I saw one like a human being
> [a son of man] coming with the clouds of heaven. And he came
> to the Ancient One [God] and was presented before him. To him
> was given dominion and glory and kingship, that all peoples,
> nations, and languages should serve him. His dominion is an
> everlasting dominion that shall not pass away, and his kingship
> is one that shall never be destroyed.

Although not an accepted interpretation by everyone, I believe that later in the chapter "the son of man" or "the human being" is referred to in the plural as "the holy ones, who will possess the kingdom forever—forever and ever" (7:18), and to that is added: "The kingship and dominion and the greatness of the kingdoms under the whole heaven shall be given to the people of the holy ones of the Most High; their kingdom shall be an everlasting kingdom, and all dominions shall serve and obey them" (7:27).

4. Boyarin, *Jewish Gospels*; Schäfer, *Jewish Jesus*.

5. Chilton, *Rabbi Jesus*, 48–51.

6. Wink, *Human Being*, 25.

Here is a very significant expression of the triumph and dominion of the redeemed, but it is a triumph and dominion that is very different from that understood by most people. Both Jews and Christians have often forgotten that the triumph over all expressed by "every knee shall bow" (Isa 45:23; Phil 2:10) is not the triumph of earthly power, but the triumph of truth, love, and justice. I believe Jesus was expressing this at his trial when he selected the passage from Daniel 7 referring to the Human One to answer the question of the high priest. When asked by the high priest, "I put you under oath before the living God, tell us if you are the Messiah, the Son of God," Jesus said to him, "You have said so. [In Mark 14:62 Jesus says, "I am."] But I tell you, from now on you will see the Son of Man [the Human One] seated at the right hand of Power and coming on the clouds of heaven" (Matt 26:63–64).

Both Mark and Luke record similar uses of the Daniel passage by Jesus at his trial. I believe that Jesus is explaining how his destiny is identified with the destiny of the redeemed people of God. He also placed on those questioning him the responsibility for designating him as Messiah. He clearly did not want to accept their concept of the Messiah while at the same time asserting his own view of his role and destiny, which was to reveal the conquering love of God—the love that will be shared and shown by all the redeemed in the unfolding of time.

The "little apocalypses" of Matthew, Mark, and Luke, harking back to Daniel 7, make reference to "the Son of Man coming in clouds with great power and glory" (Mark 13:24, cf. Matt 24:29–31; Luke 21:25–28). The connection with Daniel 7 might be missed by many, but also surely exists in the reference to the Son of Man who "will sit on the throne of his glory" and judge those who did not see the Son of Man when he was hungry, thirsty, a stranger, naked, sick, and in prison (Matt 25:31–46). What is highly significant is that when the passage in Daniel is considered in its totality, it is clear that the references to "son of man" and "holy ones" are to a redeemed Israel, but also to a divine figure who is given a throne alongside God. Jesus was declaring his destiny and also the destiny of the redeemed. His coming meant the coming of the redeemed of God. Thus, I believe in his trial Jesus was actually issuing an invitation to all people to join him as the redeemed people in "coming with the clouds of heaven." This is the eschatological vision of Jesus Christ: his coming means the coming of redeemed humanity with him. And to be redeemed is to become (begin to become in this life) like Jesus Christ, who is divine and fully human. It is important to recognize that this vision was caught by the apostles: a double final revelation is coming—the revelation of Jesus *and* the revelation of the children of God (Rom 8:19; 1 Pet 1:6–7).

I believe that this double revelation—Jesus Christ and redeemed humanity—has a double fulfillment or realization: one in history and one at the consummation or end of history in the "new heaven and new earth." At that time, we will become like him—truly human—"for we will see him as he is" (1 John 3:2). The image of God, according to God's original intention for humanity (Gen 1:27), will be then fully restored. All of this gives great significance to the choice of Jesus to constantly refer to himself as the Human One, a name used primarily in the synoptic gospels and not in the letters of the New Testament or the early preaching. Thus, his followers did not refer to Jesus as the Son of Man, but they did believe or came to believe that Jesus would be seated at the right hand of God, just as the Human One in Daniel and as affirmed by Jesus in his trial. Clear examples are found in the Letter to the Hebrews: (1) "When he had made purification for sins, he sat down at the right hand of the Majesty on high" (1:3); and (2) in the passage that challenges believers to "run with perseverance the race that is set before us, looking unto Jesus the pioneer and perfecter of our faith, who for the sake of the joy that was set before him endured the cross, disregarding its shame, and has taken his seat at the right hand of the throne of God" (12:1–2). Furthermore, the followers of Jesus believed that he was the very image of God (Col 1:15; Heb 1:3), which is what they knew Genesis says we were made to be (1:26, 27).

One of the scholars who confirmed to me the importance of the Daniel 7 passage to Jesus and early Christians was Boyarin, who wrote of the binitarian views in Jewish thinking that saw a human within God, a "younger god," if you will. Boyarin stated, "I see it [the binitarian view] very much a living part of Israel's religion both before and long after, explaining both the form of Judaism we call Christianity and also much in non-Christian later Judaism as well. If Daniel is the prophecy, the gospels are the fulfillment."[7] If one accepts Boyarin's views, it helps us to believe that Jesus saw the incarnation represented in the name he so often chose to use for himself.

In addition to the incarnation, the second part of what I will emphasize is important to know about Jesus Christ, the atonement, is not expressed in a single name, such as the Human One, but by a host of passages in the Bible referring to the suffering and death of Christ by which he accomplished the atonement. Nevertheless, the Human One also is associated with suffering. Just after the confession of Peter, Jesus says, "The Son of Man must undergo great suffering, and be rejected by the elders, the chief priests, and scribes, and be killed, and on the third day be raised" (Luke 9:22). I believe it is the suffering of Jesus for humanity that particularly speaks to the universal

---

7. Boyarin, *Jewish Gospels*, 52.

human longing for compassion. In the gospels a great turning point took place after the confession of Peter. He began to reveal to his disciples his coming suffering and death by the religious leaders, but the disciples did not understand him. Suffering, of course, was contrary to what they felt was the role of the Messiah, and Peter said as much. Eventually, they came to understand the importance of his suffering and the name Messiah (Christ) became among Christians the most common title attached to the name Jesus, as seen in Acts and the epistles. Nevertheless, Peter and the disciples were told not to tell anyone that he was the Messiah because of the misconception of what the Messiah was to be like (Matt 16:21; Mark 8:30; Luke 9:21). This became "the Messianic Secret." It is not that the image of the Suffering Servant of God was lacking in Jewish thought, as shown in Isaiah (52:11—53:12). In fact, we can believe that Jesus embraced the image of the Suffering Servant there.

To emphasize that the suffering Messiah was only in the later understanding of his immediate followers, Jesus after his resurrection had to explain to his followers on the road to Emmaus "that the Messiah should suffer these things and then enter his glory" (Luke 24:26). This message was also conveyed by the evangelist Philip to the Ethiopian eunuch, who asked specifically about the Isaiah passage (Acts 8:32–33). We also note that the assertion that the Messiah "must suffer" was an important part of the witness of Paul, given before King Agrippa (Acts 26:23), not to mention throughout his letters. Contrary to the prevailing view, Boyarin states, "The notion of the humiliated and suffering Messiah was not at all alien within Judaism before the coming of Jesus, and it remained current among Jews well into the future following that—indeed, well into the early modern period."[8] As we shall see, the suffering of Jesus becomes an extremely important part of the expression of his compassion and of his drawing power.

It is not so much my purpose to set forth the *what* of the doctrines of the incarnation and the atonement, as well as of the Trinity, with which they are closely associated. In other words, it is not my purpose to make a Bible study or make a theological statement per se. Rather, I am primarily interested in looking at the *why* of the incarnation and the atonement in meeting human longing. I will first consider, in chapter 3, the person and work of Christ from a perspective that takes in the experience of all human beings, who appear to long for an incarnation of the Divine or some tangible and visible representation of the transcendent. Perhaps less obvious, but nevertheless present among all human beings, is the longing for compassion. Both of these longings, though present among human beings in general,

8. Ibid., 132.

were expressed more clearly in the story of the people of Israel recorded in the Hebrew Scriptures than in general human history. In other words, the Hebrew Scriptures or Old Testament makes clear the felt need for the incarnation and the atonement of Jesus Christ. The period of preparation taking place before the coming of Christ clarified (1) the need for a Savior, particularly as this was expressed through the expectation for a Messiah; and (2) the need for forgiveness and reconciliation with God, seen clearly for example in Psalms 51 and 32. The need for forgiveness and reconciliation was expressed clearly by the prophets, but also seen in the sacrificial system. In spite of many warnings the people of God repeatedly failed to live as God intended. In particular, the nature of the salvation brought by the Messiah was misunderstood and in many ways is still misunderstood by both Jews and the Gentile followers of Jesus, of whom I am one.

I should say that as a Christian, my belief in Christ's full divinity and humanity (incarnation) and in the redemption through Christ (atonement) is based first on my experience through the gift of the Holy Spirit. But I must add that my belief and understanding are far from complete. In other words, I follow my conception of Jesus Christ, but that conception is far from perfect and that is why I need to constantly to improve my conception of Jesus Christ. It will only be complete beyond this life. Both my belief and understanding are circular experiences needing constant renewal and expansion. I look to the Bible for my belief and understanding, which means listening to the interpreters of the Bible, especially those from my community of faith and understanding, the Presbyterian-Reformed tradition and community. Some statements in the Bible about the incarnation of Jesus are rather clear, as in the statement in John 1:1, "the Word was with God and the Word was God," along with 1:14, "And the Word became flesh and dwelt among us." I find support in the earlier lyrical affirmation in Philippians 2:5–8—probably older than Paul's quotation of it—which includes both the incarnation and the work of the atonement (notice that they are made models for Christians): "Let the same mind be in you that was in Christ Jesus, who, though he was in the form of God, did not regard equality with God as something to be exploited, but emptied himself, taking the form of a slave, being born in human likeness. And being found in human form, he humbled himself and became obedient to the point of death—even death on a cross."[9]

In addition to the above passages, we have the very strong statements of the cosmic Christ (meaning that the cosmos was created through Christ) in Colossians 1:15–20 indicating the divinity of Christ. Also, Hebrews 1:3;

9. For Ehrman's discussion of the incarnational understanding of Christ in Phil 2:5–8, see Ehrman, *How Jesus Became God*, 254–66.

12:1–2 indicate his divinity and his elevation to the right hand of God, as in Daniel 7. While the incarnation of Jesus Christ as being fully divine and fully human is fairly easily stated (not easily understood) and either believed or rejected, the meaning of the atonement has historically been stated in a variety of ways with different aspects of it being emphasized. I am not interested here in seeking to sort out the different aspects of the meaning of the atonement, but only wish to state the basic message of the Christian gospel that Jesus Christ suffered and died on our behalf so that we could be reconciled to God the Father, the one who sent Jesus into the world out of love for us and all creation (2 Cor 5:16—6:2). It is not God who was hostile to human beings, but human beings who were (are) hostile to God and resistant to God's appeals. It is important to remember, when thinking of our reconciliation with God, that Christ and the Father are one (John 5:19–24; 14:6–11; 17:20–24) and that God did not need his attitude toward us to be changed since it was always one of love from the creation of the world.

After accepting both the divinity and humanity of Christ and the atoning power of his death followed by his resurrection, I am particularly interested in why it was so important for Jesus to affirm his humanity so strongly and why it was so important for him to sacrifice himself on the cross. I am proposing that the historical and personal effects of an uplifted and single central Savior expressing compassion for all human beings, as did Jesus Christ who was so "lifted up" (John 12:32), give us a great deal of understanding of the *why* of his incarnation and atonement. It was his "lifting up" that draws all people to him and through him to our Creator.

I know that no one can be argued to faith and that faith in Jesus Christ as Savior is not based on reason or a rational and empirically based demonstration. (Forget the word "proof," because even in science little is proved, but rather is demonstrated and accepted over time.) However, I believe strongly that this faith is reasonable and "makes sense," and has supporting empirical evidence found particularly in the human longing for an incarnation of God and for compassion that brings deliverance in and from the world. It fits with a pattern of thought and desire that has been built into human beings and is found in human consciousness. The mystery of human consciousness and its experiences and longings, which include prayer, visions, inspirations, joyful worship, coincidences, and even near-death experiences (NDE), can barely be touched by science, but are nevertheless known as very real to people and certainly have real consequences.[10] My contention is that the capacities and propensities of the human brain, while

---

10. See Alexander's *Proof of Heaven* as an example of an NDE and a probing of human consciousness.

still mysterious, are consistent with how a loving God would have created us and enabled us to develop in evolution (mysteriously and anonymously directed by God) in order that we could recognize and believe in God, especially in what God has done and does to relate to us.

Today people continue to be puzzled by and yet attracted to Jesus Christ, especially wondering why it is necessary for the Creator of the universe to become a human being among human beings in the midst of human history and to suffer and then rise from the dead as he did. I do not expect that a faith in this event and in the person of Jesus Christ can be the same as intellectual acceptance or assent to the argument that I will make, but I hope that there will be enough agreement with my argument for people to find support for a personal faith in Jesus Christ as God's intervention in human history for our salvation. Even more, my hope is that, whether for the first time or for the thousandth time, readers will know something of the "burning of the hearts" (Luke 24:32) experienced by the two followers on the road with Jesus as he explained why it was necessary for him to do what he did. It is really a story of a Person that we will be considering, a story that "fits" with human need, desire, and experience.

At the close of this chapter on the name Jesus most often used for himself, I must recognize the influence on me of Wink's *The Human Being*, which is deeply scholarly, theological, and psychological. I am not ready to follow him in all of his views, as best as I can understand them. Probably I do not want to follow his thought that the church's theology in effect abandoned what Jesus was conveying in his favorite name for himself.[11] I believe the hymn in Philippians 2:5–8, mentioned above, and other passages on the humanness of Jesus—for example, Hebrews 5:7–8—show a deep realization of Jesus as the Human One in his sufferings. But even here I can see that Wink is right in how the church in its life, particularly after the fourth century, misunderstood and misused the last verse in the Philippians hymn: "So that at the name of Jesus every knee should bend, in heaven and on earth and under the earth, and every tongue should confess that Jesus Christ is Lord to the glory of God the Father." The church and many of us Christians have failed to follow or understand the Human One in his noncoercive yet loving way, nor have we taken seriously enough what Wink calls "the Dominion System" that opposes the Human One.

It is appropriate to close this chapter with Wink's words:

> Despite our best efforts, however, the Human Being will forever remain shrouded in mystery. We cannot say definitely what the Human Being is or means, for the nature of a powerful, living

11. Wink, *Human Being*, 193–97.

symbol is that we *cannot* [italics his] reduce it to words, as if our explanations were more meaningful than the symbol itself. When what we say about a symbol becomes more important than the symbol, the symbol has ceased to live. So the inability to define the Human Being is due not just to our inadequacies, which are obvious, but to the nature of archetypes, which are by definition unknowable, except by their effects. Therefore, everything said in this book must of necessity have "as it were" inscribed beside it.

Nor does wishing the Human Being to manifest itself as a "powerful, living symbol" make it happen. For this reason I must warn against turning the real experience of the darkness surrounding God into a mere idea. *God is* [italics his] "in the likeness, as it were, of a human being." But God is much more: non-human, totally other, incomprehensible, incalculable, un-fathomable, all of these, none of these—yet capable of being experienced, at least fractionally, by everyone. Are we not all children of the Human One, and therefore made for commu-nion with the Mystery and each other?[12]

12. Ibid., 195–96.

Chapter 2

Broad Perspectives about What Is Reality and What Is a Person

ESTABLISHING A VIEW OF REALITY: THE NATURAL AND SUPERNATURAL

ALTHOUGH THEY MAY BE looked at empirically as human beliefs about Jesus Christ, the incarnation and atonement of Jesus Christ are Christian theological concepts in which I and other Christians believe along with a personal commitment to Jesus Christ. In order to be clear at the beginning of this book, I place these beliefs within my views of total reality and human experience. My beliefs with my commitment are based first on my interpretation of the Bible learned within my Presbyterian faith tradition, but at the same time I see them as an expression of what I believe is classical Christianity. I also seek to incorporate into this theological and philosophical perspective whatever knowledge I have gained from secular studies of the natural world, especially in history and the social sciences and my own experience.

To place the incarnation and atonement of Jesus Christ in the context of reality as a whole, I begin with the faith perspective that God is real and that the rest of reality is God's creation. I hasten to add that evil is also a real force within creation, but it results from the misuse or distortion of God's good creation. In some sense, then, evil is less real than creation itself, and evil is certainly not equal to God in power or in any sense a divinity in competition with God—though nevertheless more powerful than human beings without God and capable of intervening between human beings and God. There is no question for me but that evil is a real force in the world. The references to evil in the Bible in personal terms such as "the Evil One" or "Satan," especially in the gospels (not as much in the epistles), are clear, but I recognize the danger of thought about a personal Satan and devils as a distraction possibly causing Christians to fall into the temptation of seeing evil figures and their influence in the wrong places and missing the real influences of evil. This might be particularly true in seeing "the devil" in individuals and not in social and cultural influences. One thing is clear: the influence of evil is extremely deceptive and beyond human ability to clearly identify and resist with human intelligence and strength. In fact, evil almost always appears in the guise of good, even as "serving God." Nevertheless, classical Christianity (and my belief) is not in any sense dualistic with evil on a level of reality and power with God. It has been defeated by Christ on the cross but, like a snake that has been killed, continues to move—perhaps one reason the snake, a creature of God, is used to represent the Tempter, in addition to being crooked, not straight. I accept the deep theology carried in the "primitive language" of Genesis!

God's creation originally and basically consists of two related realities that are spoken of in the Bible as "heaven and earth," with the heavenly realm and beings and the earthly realm and beings in parallel existence. This twofold reality, when placed alongside other references to supernatural beings and to life beyond the grave, means that creation consists of what may be spoken of as both "the supernatural" and "the natural." This view is not unique to the Bible or the Christian faith but is held by many religious people throughout the ages. However, the Christian faith has distinctive views of the supernatural. Regarding the incarnation, God took created human life into God's self as Jesus Christ and so the resurrected Jesus Christ is in the heavenly realm to which followers will go at the resurrection and in which they are promised they will see Jesus and become like him, God's self being invisible (1 John 3:2).

The supernatural is a mysterious reality that exists in some sense alongside and even within the natural, but also exists apart from the natural creation. The supernatural probably exists outside of the space and time dimensions that we know, but whatever the case, the supernatural was created by God. In contrast to the supernatural, the natural consists of nature throughout the universe and in human historical existence. The supernatural realm is largely unknowable by human beings; but nevertheless, human beings may have consciousness of its existence through faith and experiences arising from faith, such as in prayer, worship, and special experiences of individuals in which they are "transported out of this world" (2 Cor 12:1–7). I would add that at least some near-death experiences could be added, but basically the knowledge of the supernatural realm is for Christians based on the revelation found in the Bible, especially in the coming of Jesus Christ and his resurrection and return to God, the Father.

Other beings, commonly known as angels, exist in the supernatural realm, and human beings enter this realm after death. Ultimately there will be a new creation that encompasses both the supernatural and natural realms. Although the supernatural may impinge on the natural at particular times, the supernatural is not available for examination; and human beings are not encouraged to seek any interaction with any beings, including both angels and the human dead, who exist in the supernatural. We are to communicate only with God, who exists beyond the supernatural and with the resurrected Jesus Christ, our Mediator, who has been brought into the supernatural, where we will meet him, our incarnate Savior, as recreated human beings. The most important fact about supernatural reality is that the resurrected Jesus exists in it, in and with the triune God, but will one day be encountered by human beings after life on earth and in the new creation of all things. If time and space are collapsed in supernatural reality (as impossible to conceive of as infinity), then the new creation may be consciously experienced by human beings immediately after death, but this is speculation. I believe, from the perspective of the living on earth, the dead are waiting or "asleep" until all human beings and all creation experience the resurrection in the consummation of all things. This means after death we may be immediately conscious of the resurrection and recreation of all things. Most importantly, life after death should be thought of in terms of resurrection, not an immortality of disembodied souls floating around. Resurrection after death has the major meaning for me of continued personal identity along with the personal identity of others.

Some of the most important passages in the Bible related to life after death are: (1) the gospel passages of the appearances of Christ after his resurrection; (2) 1 Corinthians 15, in which Paul discusses the resurrection of Christ and of believers; (3) the comforting words of Jesus to his disciples, particularly in John 11:25–26 and 14:1–3; and (4) the statement in 1 John 3:2, just mentioned: "What we do know is this: when he is revealed, we will be like him, for we will see him as he is." Thus, followers expect to both see Jesus and be transformed to be like him.

All of the above is a matter of faith based on an interpretation of the Bible, confirmed by the faith of those I trust in the historic church together with my own experience. For the present time in which we live, while the supernatural may be believed in and contemplated, only the natural creation is subject to direct observation and scientific examination. While awareness of the supernatural realm is important for living, human beings must also live in the natural realm (God's creation), which is sacred. Examination of the natural realm by secular scientific means is an important for caring for it and improving human life within it. I say "*secular* scientific means" because our ideas, religious or merely traditional, are not to be trusted. Nevertheless, our faith should inspire our study, love, and care of nature. Of course, one of the effects of evil is when human beings do not carry out their responsibility for stewardship of the natural realm, or misuse what they have learned about it. Important implications exist for what human beings are as creatures of God in the distinction between the natural and supernatural realms of creation.

THE NATURAL AND SUPERNATURAL IN HUMAN BEINGS

Human beings are *both* natural, that is, belonging to nature, and supernatural, that is, having an existence that is beyond nature. While this would appear to be an untenable and foolish affirmation to many modern secularized human beings, the implication of the existence of a supernatural aspect of human life has been important in human history. The concept that human beings were created in the image of God, as stated in Genesis 1, has had an enormous impact in world history, leading to concepts of human rights and human equality, as stated in the Declaration of Independence of the United States in 1776 and affirmed in the United Nations Universal Declaration of Human Rights in 1948. It is the religious foundation of our secular government, which ultimately is based on the concept of human equality before God and the human dignity of every individual.

Of course, the Bible quickly makes clear that the image of God in human beings is marred and distorted, though not destroyed. But what does being made in the image of God mean? A major element in being in the image of God is the capacity to think about God and, beyond that, to commune or interact with God, as portrayed in Genesis 3 and throughout the Bible. The capacity to commune with God is closely related to capacity to have a loving relationship with other people. Furthermore, this capacity does not cease with death because human beings are eternal, though in what form is still a mystery. Now we can see why human beings are both natural and supernatural, because to communicate with God and to live beyond death gives a supernatural aspect to human lives. If human beings were natural only, they would be simply animals with high capacities. There is no way to prove the twofold nature of God's creation as being both natural and supernatural, and there is no way to prove the parallel twofold nature of human beings. Nevertheless, this book is based on the faith perspective that the reality created by God includes both the immanent natural world and the supernatural transcendent world (which interpenetrates the natural world) and that human beings are related to both.

While I have emphasized above that human beings are both supernatural and natural, I want also to emphasize that the serious examination of nature, including human personhood, without reference to the supernatural as a causative force, while always incomplete, is important to gain an understanding of human life in the world. The phrase "without reference to the supernatural as a causative force" refers to all secular methods of study and observation. I am thinking especially of the natural and social sciences; but I also include other academic fields, since philosophy, history, and literary studies may examine human life without reference to God and contribute important insights to a full appreciation of the nature of human beings and of life in the world. Nevertheless, even in secular studies, God and the supernatural may be referred to—almost have to be referred to—because of the importance of religion and concepts of and faith in the Divine in human life. In secular studies, the concepts of and faith in God and the supernatural can only be seen as human concepts and faith, but they nevertheless have major effects on human life. A religious perspective alone, as we have seen in human history, may be subject to many errors and misunderstandings in viewing the natural world.

Once God is referred to as a causative force beyond human concepts or acts of faith, the study becomes theological. In other words, secular knowledge can only look at the human side, while theological knowledge looks at both the divine and human sides; but it must be remembered that both perspectives are human and fallible—a fact that many religious thinkers forget. (Some theologians seem to apply the concept of sin to everything except their own theological thoughts!) I believe the distinction between a theological approach and knowledge and a secular approach and knowledge is important in order to avoid an unwarranted and unnecessary control of knowledge by flawed theological thought over secular knowledge of nature and history. This does not deny the need of human beings for theological knowledge apart from natural or secular knowledge. In fact, theological knowledge is necessary for a full-orbed knowledge of God's total creation, but theological knowledge is partial and can be seriously flawed simply because it is human. Of course, it is also true that secular knowledge can also be flawed, but the secular scientific method includes a provision for ongoing correction. Theological knowledge, by its nature, has no built-in means of correction other than by new interpretations of revelation. Interpretation, proclamation, and fulfillment in behavior of revelation are major tasks of the church.

Thus, there is a special theological reason to let secular studies be secular and not theological, even though, in the end, theology must incorporate valid secular studies, while secular studies cannot incorporate theology, except as human thought that may have profound effects in human life. The reasoning is as follows: the supernatural part of human beings has "fallen" and exists in a broken condition. This means that although human beings have the capacity to communicate with God, their understanding of God, especially the self-disclosure of God and God's disclosure about all reality in the Bible (the written Word) and in Jesus (the living Word), is highly flawed. It is not that the revelation of the Bible and Jesus Christ are highly flawed, only the human understanding and interpretation of them.

Furthermore, human consciousness and experience of the supernatural, though it may be real, is also incomplete and faulty. All revelation, even though from God or God's Word, can only be known through human partial and flawed interpretations and experiences. In other words, as Paul said, "For now we see in a mirror, dimly" (1 Cor 13:12). Beyond partial and flawed interpretations of God's revelation, one of the most serious and dangerous failings of sinful human beings has even been to claim to have direct divine knowledge and even to speak with the authority of God. It is all right to speak as "a representative of God," but it should always be qualified as partial and spoken in love. There is an authority that goes with those representing God, especially those "set aside" (ordained) to speak for God by the church, but individuals and groups, including church councils, claiming to speak for God have made false and misleading statements of the "truth." It is for this reason the secular disciplines that consider only the natural world are important ways of limiting and correcting some of the false conceptions and viewpoints human beings have developed on the basis of what they *claimed* to be their religious knowledge or even their experience of hearing God's voice. Actually, secular studies that look only at God's creation in nature may be considered as a gift from God, giving human beings an opportunity to learn about and to care more adequately for God's creation to the benefit of humanity. True, science cannot lead us to God, but a secular approach can at least partially protect us from human misconceptions and misrepresentations of God and the harm resulting from them. After all, nature itself, as God's creation, is sacred, not secular. Even the secular is not ontologically secular, but sacred. Science, because it treats God's natural creation with great respect, has been able to produce much knowledge about nature that has in turn made possible great improvements in human life.

I rest my case for the value of a secular approach for the historic contributions of secular government and secular science that have come into contemporary thinking after centuries of misrule and ignorance, when both governmental and religious leaders justified their views and actions by their perceived divine guidance, divine right to rule, or religious knowledge. At the same time, it must be said that science, when essentially deified as the only source of true knowledge, thereby becoming the ideology of scientism, does have severe problems when it comes to providing the only basis for understanding human life and personhood, especially for how to live a full-orbed and flourishing life.[1] Sadly, the impressive record of scientific learning and technology has converted some people to the ideology of scientism and the lifestyle of secularism. The fact is that science cannot account for human experience with the supernatural. What can be said is that science can show that the capacity of the human mind is consistent with what a loving God would create. The failure of scientism when made a political philosophy is accurately described by Paul Froese as the "plot to kill God" carried out by atheistic Communism in the Soviet Union, which was obviously a failure.[2] At the same time, the return of religion, especially a monopolistic religion, to dominance in society is not constructive for a healthy society.

WHAT IS A PERSON?

As a demonstration of the fact that human beings as they exist are consistent with what a loving God would create, I turn to important social scientific studies by Christian Smith.[3] Smith writes as a sociologist, but one who appreciates moral and theological implications that may be drawn from an empirical study of personhood and of the human capacity for faith.[4] He does not (cannot) show as a sociologist that persons are creatures of God, but he does show that persons have capacities and characteristics that are thoroughly consistent with what a God seeking fellowship with persons (the God we see in Genesis 3) would create. This is because persons have the capacity for self-transcendence.

1. Stenmark, *Scientism*.
2. Froese, *Plot to Kill God*.
3. Smith, *Moral, Believing Animals*; *What Is a Person?*
4. As I read Smith's *What Is a Person?*, I became aware of his perspective of critical realism. This philosophical view has been used by social scientists not satisfied with the extreme empiricism of some social scientific approaches. This philosophy was developed by the Indian and British philosopher Roy Bhaskar (1944–2014). The main advantage of this perspective as I understand it is that it validates non-empirical causative forces in society—not necessarily the supernatural, but beliefs in the supernatural. I am recommending consideration of this philosophical view because of the importance of non-empirical causation. Even without adopting this view, scientists have long held that beliefs, even if false, may have empirical consequences.

What do we know about personhood apart from the Bible? We assume that persons whom we observe every day are real human beings and are not to be regarded as just animals. However, the tremendous variety among human beings and the degree to which they are affected by sociocultural forces have made it difficult for social scientists to define human beings or to recognize a common human nature that belongs to persons. Furthermore, making it particularly difficult to understand personhood, human beings have inner qualities and hidden sources for some characteristics that are not subject to direct observation. These include both natural and what I believe are supernatural capacities and characteristics. Outward expressions of inner human capacities such as people praying or expressing their faith or acting morally for the good of others may be observed, but many of the inner sources of these capacities and motivations are hidden from direct observation. This has made social scientists reluctant to even discuss human nature or human personhood.[5] The result for some social scientists has been that human beings as persons have been overlooked as real causative forces in the world, and human nature has been considered only a philosophical or religious concept. Although I believe a full understanding of personhood does require a religious or faith perspective, there is much that can be learned through observation or a scientific approach (not referring to persons as creations of God) that is consistent with and supportive of the view that persons have a supernatural connection. In other words, the connection to the transcendent itself cannot be observed, but what we know about human beings fits well with the assumption that there is such a connection.

As noted, Smith performed a great service by thoroughly examining faith and personhood from a non-theological perspective that nonetheless shows that our best understanding of persons is consistent with recognizing a supernatural aspect to human life.[6] It is not that Smith either proves or demonstrates scientifically the divine link of persons to God. Such a demonstration would amount to a coercion of faith, in that human beings would have no other choice but to accept the reality of God. Clearly, from what we know from the Bible, that is not the kind of faith God desires—it indeed would not *be* faith. Smith shows that human beings, at bottom, are all really believers, meaning that human beings "are all necessarily trusting, believing animals, creatures who must and have beliefs that cannot themselves be verified except by means established by the presumed beliefs themselves."[7]

---

5. Smith, *What Is a Person?*, 2.

6. Smith, *Moral Believing Animals*; *What Is a Person?*

7. Smith, *Moral Believing Animals*, 54.

In addition, and in part because human beings are believing animals, they are also moral animals. Our beliefs shape "our selves, our lives, and our worlds as we know them" and from these "basic life and world definitions and maps our moral definitions derive—our sense of good and bad, right and wrong, worthy and unworthy, just and unjust, noble and shameful."[8] It is difficult to imagine a God that human beings would honor and respect that did not have moral standards to which human beings could refer. The universality of morality among human beings is consistent with there being a link to a God of moral standards, which is exactly the kind of God revealed in the Bible. Even if one argues that the moral sense and capacity of human beings is a product of evolution, it makes sense that a God of moral standards would have overseen such a development.

Scott Allison and George Goethals, in their book *Heroes: What They Do & Why We Need Them*, argue: "It is likely that our brains were designed to prepare us for good and evil, to identify each, and to emotionally respond to each. Moreover, as human beings continue to evolve biologically and culturally, our notions of good and evil will also continue to evolve."[9] This is certainly no proof that human beings are created in the image of God, but it is consistent with what the God of the Bible would do in creating human beings.

Smith deals most fully with personhood in his book *What Is a Person?: Rethinking Humanity, Social Life, and the Good from the Person Up*. First, Smith describes the emergence of thirty specific human capacities that are found in persons.[10] These range from "existence capacities" of subconscious and conscious awareness through "primary experience capacities," "secondary experience capacities," "creating capacities," and "highest order capacities." These capacities interact in individuals, but most important to see at this point is that there is in persons a "centering, interior focal point of personal being, consciousness, and activity."[11] This centering means that persons are centers of subjective experience, durable identity, moral commitment, and social communication. Beyond simply forming a center with powers or potentiality, the centers in persons are centers with purpose.[12]

This understanding of personhood allows us to see that persons have inner capacities and characteristics that give person identity and that are causative forces in the world. For me, this is consistent with the Christian

8. Ibid., 57.
9. Scott and Goethals, *Heroes*, 162.
10. Smith, *What Is a Person?*, 25–99.
11. Ibid., 62.
12. Ibid., 78–88.

belief that individual identity with its God-given capacities will be recreated in a new form in the resurrection. This is in contrast to a dualistic belief, found in Greek and other thought, that denigrates bodily identity, believing only in a bodiless existence after death. It is also consistent with the biblical (Hebrew) conception of the unity of spirit and body, a view supported by modern studies of neuroscience that shows the close relationship of the physical brain to conceptions of God and to both spiritual and moral life.

It increasingly appears that religious thought and behavior are part of normal brain function. This is consistent with the studies of the brain by Andrew Newberg and Mark Robert Waldman in which belief in God, prayer, and related spiritual perspectives is seen to have effects in the brain.[13] This is not a proof for God, but for me it is consistent with a belief about what kind of persons God would make and then recreate—persons who would seek and thrive in a loving relationship with their Creator. Such a belief points toward the resurrection as involving a "bodily identity," even if we do not understand the nature of the new body. The Apostle Paul takes up this question in 1 Corinthians 15:35–49.

It is very important for the purposes of this book that Smith makes clear the fact that human life is far from perfect but rather can be characterized as "broken," both on the individual and social levels.[14] There is a long list of words in every language to characterize all that is bad and evil in human life. This understanding of human brokenness is essential to understanding both the failings of Christianity and of all humanity, including resistance to God's self-revelation in the Human One, to be considered in chapters 3 and 4.

Given the individualistic viewpoint of many in the world, particularly in the United States, Smith goes to great lengths to show that human beings do in fact exist and act within social structures.[15] These structures have three basic features: (1) human social relationships, (2) patterned systems comprised of parts, and (3) temporal durability. Smith states:

> Note that at the most fundamental level, it is the needs and interests of human persons in a world of endemic objective and subjective scarcity and relentless competition that generate social structures that organize and regulate life. Structures are not the products of, for example, the "requisites of the social systems," as structural functionalism would have it. Instead they derive through human activity from the real, concrete requirements

---

13. Newberg and Waldman, *How God Changes Your Brain.*

14. Smith, *What Is a Person?*, 75–78.

15. Ibid., 317–83.

and desires of human persons, given their natural capacities and limitations. It is human persons, and not social systems, who are the ultimate actors in this account. Structured social systems are only the emergent products of ongoing personal interaction. Once emergent, those irreducible social structures can and do function to exert their level-specific causal influences on the persons existing simultaneously at the lower, personal level.[16]

If this argument is not easy to follow, the point is that individual persons, because of their needs—including the need for contact with the transcendent supernatural—create social systems; and these systems, with their organizations, institutions, and cultures—including religious—then act upon persons in an ongoing circular pattern in which the systems themselves are changed by the persons they influence, often only partially. This circular pattern may sometimes make people feel that they are beings conditioned purely by outside forces, but the outside forces are themselves human creations. Again, this understanding of human persons in societies is thoroughly consistent with a view of God as essentially social, interacting both internally in the Godhead and with creation, especially human beings. Furthermore, God created human beings to live in peace and harmony with one another. This understanding is thoroughly consistent with God's establishment of the church and of Jesus gathering, organizing, and sending forth his disciples to establish loving communities. Again, studies of human evolution point to the creation of supportive communities as the direction in which human beings evolved, which is what a God known in the Human One who loved constructive and joyful sociability would have overseen.

Perhaps the strongest statements supporting the theological understanding of the twofold nature of human beings are Smith's arguments relating personhood to dignity. In spite of the tremendous diversity of human life from infancy to adulthood and from those with highly developed capacities to those with very undeveloped and underdeveloped capacities, how can we explain the very widespread recognition of human dignity found in all human beings? Smith states that there are only three approaches to explaining the base for the pervasive recognition of human dignity: (1) human beings have dignity-conferring capacities; (2) human beings have theistic origins; and (3) human beings have no special dignity, but are simply sentient beings who experience well-being and suffering.[17] The last answer recognizes nothing special in natural human beings and appears patently false, not to speak of having dangerous implications for human relationships. Although Smith

16. Ibid., 342.
17. Ibid., 446–53.

sees that human dignity can be partly based on recognizing human special capacities, this does not satisfy the granting of dignity to human beings with very low or even no capacities. In the end, the best reason for recognizing human dignity is in the existence of the divine link to human beings. As he says, "My own reasons for believing in dignity are at rock bottom theistic,"[18] with which I certainly agree. I would add to this that concepts of human rights and equality were developed in a context in which the Genesis account of creation of humanity by God was well known.

CONCLUSION

Although this is a book about the incarnation and atonement of Jesus Christ, I believe it is important to approach the subject from the perspective of all reality and all humanity. This requires taking into account *both* the best social scientific and historical studies of human personhood and the all-encompassing theological perspective of the Bible. The incarnation and the atonement in the Bible are about a Person and the response to that Person is by other persons. It is important, therefore, to have some understanding of what reality is and of the persons who live within it. I use the term "some understanding" since I do not expect total understanding from anyone; and many thinkers continue to debate what is reality is and what is personhood.

First, it is important to understand the twofold nature of reality and of persons living within that reality. Human beings are natural, fully participant in the natural world; but human beings are also supernatural, with capacities to think about and communicate with God and with a destiny that extends beyond the natural world. Looking at the natural person with the help of Smith, there are certain natural capacities of human beings that are highly consistent with there being a connection of persons with God.[19] Here are a few highly significant ones.

As Smith points out, human beings have the capacity for truth seeking, which leads to believing or having faith in certain realities.[20] My belief is that God is seeking a relationship with human beings based on their faith, which incorporates awe and love. Supporting this belief is the recognition that human beings also have a capacity for moral awareness and judgment, which is consistent with coming to know a God who has revealed moral standards or expectations for human thought and behavior. Among the important moral realities of which human beings are aware is the dignity

18. Ibid., 452.

19. Smith, *Moral Believing Animals; What Is a Person?*

20. Smith, *Moral Believing Animals*, 5.

of every human being whatever their condition or stage in life might be. This is especially consistent with the consciousness among human beings of their divine origin. Finally, human beings are clearly social beings, which is consistent with a God who seeks fellowship with humans and who wills humans to live loving one another. There is much more that can be said about personhood, but human capacities, especially the highest order ones identified by Smith, are sufficient to show that what we can know about persons is thoroughly consistent with the revelation in the Bible that persons were created by God and are able to seek after God.

Related to all that has been said above about reality and persons, I believe that human beings consciously or unconsciously long for and seek after God, while at the same time resist God. This seeking after God can be described specifically as human longing for incarnation and atonement that provides: (1) a tangible representation of the divine in order to have direct contact with and an envisioning of the divine, and (2) a sense of mercy coming from the divine that is contacted and envisioned. This longing will be explored in the next two chapters.

Chapter 3

Longing for Incarnation and Atonement in Human Life[1]

HUMANS AS CREATED IN THE IMAGE OF GOD

As I LOOKED AT human religions as a whole in order to find why some religions spread more than others, I found that I had to consider how the incarnation and atonement (or the longing for them) have a place in human life and thought as a whole. I believe that in the world at large, and specifically in human religious life and thought, we may see the work of God in establishing certain human characteristic patterns of thought and behavior. This is based on my belief, affirmed in the Bible, that all human beings were created in the image of God and therefore have a supernatural aspect to their lives. That is, human beings were made with the capacity to think about and relate to God and to the created transcendent realm that is above and yet interpenetrates the natural realm. This created capacity gives an inner longing for contact with the realm that is "above and beyond." It is also true, as we see in the Bible and human history, that the image of God in human beings can be described as badly marred, distorted, or broken. Human beings do not live up to the image and the patterns God intended us to fulfill, and as followers of Jesus Christ we do not represent him (witness to him) very well. Nevertheless, all human beings live under God's common grace and have the capacity to know something about God and respond in some way to God, although this response will be highly partial and unclear. In fact, as already noted, human beings, including followers of Jesus Christ,

---

1. Chapters 3 and 4 draw from my thought already expressed in the article "Special Persons and the Spread of Religions."

have a built-in tendency to resist God and to seek to escape from God, as we shall see.

All of this means that much that is good and true may come from sources outside of Christianity, namely, from human beings simply because they are human. It also means human beings are capable of much evil and—specifically for Christians to note—human history since the coming of Christ, and in the development of so-called Christian cultures and societies, has been shot through with a complex mixture of both good and evil. Thus, good and evil can come from both Christians and non-Christians, even though I believe God has brought and is bringing much good to the world through the gospel of Jesus Christ that has been carried within Christianity. This certainly has not always been accomplished by official representatives of Christianity (of which I am one as an ordained minister).

In this chapter I am shifting from broad theological, philosophical, and sociological perspectives to perspectives that are narrower. I am considering only the human side of religions. This is a task belonging especially to the social sciences and religious studies, but the results of such attempts can enrich theological understandings.

LONGING IN RELIGIONS

This book is basically theological in approach since it is written from a faith perspective and is about the incarnation and atonement of Jesus Christ at the center of the Bible. However, I am coming to the subject in this chapter from a perspective that seeks to include all humanity, especially the needs and longings of human beings, as well as the resistance to those longings that exist within all human beings, including followers of Jesus Christ. In my studies of the spread of religions I focused on the three most widely spreading religions—Buddhism, Christianity, and Islam—and sought to make use of social scientific perspectives on the human side of religions. This led to my developing an overall theory for why religions have spread.[2] Many factors have affected the spread of religions, including both religious and secular social factors, but my studies of the spread of religions found that human longings found especially in religions were most crucial and these longings were supremely fulfilled by the special persons who were the

2. Montgomery, *Why Religions Spread*. Using a social scientific perspective, my theory included three religious content factors and four secular (non-religious) social factors, but I found that the central religious factor discussed in this book was an essential factor for the spread of religions, whereas the secular social factors were factors that could either facilitate or hinder the spread of religions.

founders of Buddhism, Christianity and Islam. In this chapter I will trace my movement toward this theory and in the next chapter look more specifically at the three most widely spreading religions.

Like human nature, religion has been notoriously difficult to define. This is because, like human nature and human society and culture, the wide diversity of religious thought and activity defies attempts to make an inclusive definition. There is no single religion, only religions. Yet in spite of the wide diversity of religions, including religious expressions within the major religions that are given names (consider the many versions of Buddhism, Christianity, and Islam), religions have certain commonalities that make it possible to speak about *religion* in the singular. Religion has entered the debate regarding whether human beings have a religious nature. Even though human beings may have a religious approach to life, in that they live by believing in some authority and by accepting and living by notions of right and wrong, it is obvious that we live in a world in which people can deny the existence of God and not participate in any religion and still live a life that appears to be normal and at least relatively happy. Such people may claim that they are not religious and that they have no religious nature. They are the famous "nones" who answer the question "What is your religion?" with "None." Here I state my own religious perspective: Even though these "nones" have only appeared in large numbers in recent centuries (surprisingly, first in a Christian context and then spreading around the world in the form of secularization), I believe a non-coercive God would not have it any other way. In other words, God wants human beings to choose him without being coerced, including by other human beings. In fact, I believe God is not looking for simply belief in his existence ("even the demons believe—and shudder"; Jas 2:19) but trust and love. By its nature, this kind of faith cannot be coerced. Nevertheless, still human beings create "virtual gods" if not supernatural gods. Science has become such a virtual god for some people, even though good science does not require such adoration.[3]

It is important to know something about the world's religions in order to know what people think and feel. More than that, human religious and even anti-religious thought tell us something about the longings of human beings. Here I will give a brief definition of religion that makes it possible to recognize the commonalities of religious phenomena, but then turn to a discussion of the aspects of religion that are important for the argument of this book about the incarnation and atonement of Jesus Christ.

In spite of the modern tendency, particularly of some intellectuals, to state and even advocate the fading away of religions, religious belief and

3. Ibid., 293–341.

activity of some kind continues to be pervasive among human beings. As Stark recognizes, "godless religions" (e.g., belief in a non-personal transcendent reality as in Buddhism) may exist primarily among intellectuals.[4] Including such religions, Stark defines religions as "explanations of the meaning of existence based on supernatural assumptions and including statements about the nature of the supernatural."[5] In other words, a belief in the supernatural, possibly understood simply as the transcendent, is key to understanding religions. It is possible to replace *supernatural* with *non-empirical*, but in both cases what is meant is that which is beyond the ordinary experience of human beings.

"Explanations of the meaning of existence" may seem to place too much emphasis on the intellect, but it does express the universal human desire to find meaning in life. I would add that emotional feelings and numerous social practices of various kinds are usually important in religions. Religion also brings to mind the spiritual, which is both transcendent and immanent; but here I want to point to other important aspects of religion that may be seen in its historic manifestations and are important for the argument of this book. These aspects are often overlooked because of the spiritual and transcendent core reference of religion. The first aspect of religion that I am referring to is the tendency in religions for people to seek tangible and visible expressions of what they believe. My attention was brought to this fact by Stephen Sharot's study of world religions, in which he used the distinction between elite and popular religion for his analysis.[6] All of the world religions, including the three that spread most widely, have incorporated and expressed varieties of popular religion while maintaining official elite versions. Popular religion is very apparent in tribal religions but is seen most clearly in traditional and hierarchical societies that distinguish clearly between elite and popular statuses, the latter represented by a large underclass. Elite religion defines the current order of nature and society as being anchored in the transcendent cosmos. In this way elites are aided in the maintenance of order and continuity in their rule.

Arend Th. van Leeuwen defined this type of rule as an ontocracy.[7] In an ontocracy, rulers are seen as being at the apex of a pyramid-like structure and as having a direct connection to the transcendent cosmos. This metaphorical structure is often displayed literally in monumental structures pointing upward. In other words, the status quo for the elite is considered

4. Stark, *One True God*, 9, 10.

5. Ibid., 15.

6. Sharot, *Comparative Sociology of World Religions*, 3–19.

7. Leeuwen, *Christianity in World History*, 165–73.

part of the natural order of things. Orthodox doctrine, continuity, overall harmony, and official organization are typical elite religion concerns. Secular knowledge and skills are developed and used by religious specialists supported by the elite to preserve knowledge through literature and to display impressive religious rituals and monuments. The elite forms of religion often become the focus of comparative religious studies.

In spite of the power and display associated with elite religion, popular religion has remained strong throughout history. In contrast to elite religion, popular religion arises from the life of uncertainty and misery of the people at large. It therefore has the thaumaturgical goal of finding relief from suffering and misfortune and the fulfillment of practical needs for healing, but also for having children, crops, and all that contributes to survival and good fortune. Popular religion incorporates family and clan rituals and community rites and festivals to obtain divine approval. At the same time, in contrast to the secular tendencies of elite religion, popular religion is typically drawn to the search for an expression of spiritual power, partly because the people at large lack secular power and have limited resources to deal with life's problems. Festivals also express social solidarity and provide some relief to majority populations from lives of toil and suffering and even a certain resistance to the elite who control their lives most of the time. Elites usually tolerate, foster, and even participate in popular religion partly in order to maintain social unity and order among those under their rule. It is no wonder that Karl Marx referred to religion as the "opium of the people." However, although popular religion may contribute to passivity for some people—even whole peoples—religions in the form of millennial, revitalization, and revolutionary or reform movements have been far from passive forces in human history.

Regarding the longing for incarnation and atonement, the central concern of this book, it is important to note that traditional religions, in both elite and popular versions, make use of tangible and visible representations of supernatural sources for help and for power. In their earliest forms, these have been objects such as sacred mountains, trees, groves, springs, and rivers, as well as animals that were often related to figures found in myths passed down the generations. As civilizations developed, the supernatural figures were represented by created tangible figures, often with a human appearance, or by other tangible objects made sacred. Sharot notes, "A general impediment to the development of monotheism was the demand among the masses for *tangible and accessible religious objects* [italics mine] that could be brought into relationship with concrete life situations and influenced through magic."[8] Of course, in Christianity, both icons and statues became pervasive, the former in Orthodoxy during and following the iconoclastic controversy, and the latter in Roman Catholicism as it has spread worldwide.

The religion of Israel was able to shed itself of images after the destruction of Jerusalem and the temple in 587 BC. This followed the previous long period in which Israelites practiced idolatry along with their non-Israelite neighbors. The turn against the worship of idols came about primarily because of the acceptance (witnessed by the inclusion of the prophets and prophetic psalms in the Hebrew Scriptures) by the Israelites of God's judgment pronounced by the prophets against idolatry and the practice of injustice. However, even though having given up the visible representations of God and other supernatural beings, it is significant for our argument to note that the longing for a tangible and visible contact with the God of Israel was often expressed by the people. For example, in Psalm 27:8–9 we read, "'Come,' my heart says, 'seek his face!' Your face, Lord, do I seek. Do not hide your face from me." Again, in Psalm 42:2 we read, "My soul thirsts for God, for the living God. When shall I come and behold the face of God?" To me these metaphorical expressions come from a longing for incarnation. Beyond these expressions we have the examples of encounters with God by Abraham, Jacob, and Moses in some form of human representation (Gen 18:1–20; 32:22–32; Exod 33:11, 17–23).

Beyond these experiences, however, is the development in Israel and later rabbinic writings of the concepts of the Son of Man and the Messiah, which speaks strongly to the need for a tangible human representation of God. These writings were very important for Christian thought, which grew in a Jewish context, regarding both the Son of Man and the Messiah. In that regard, the Jewishness of Jesus and of early Christian thought has received increased attention in recent decades. As noted in the introduction and chapter 1, Daniel Boyarin and Peter Schäfer, both Jewish scholars, have shown the many shared views of both the Son of Man and the Messiah in Judaism and Christianity, so much so that early Christian Jews fit very naturally into their role of being both Christians and Jews. As noted, Boyarin speaks of "binitarian" views in Jewish thinking in which there is a second divine figure.[9] This is seen especially in Daniel 7, so important for the source of the title the Son of Man in the language of Jesus. Whatever scholars may think of this view, we can believe that Jesus must have been familiar with the Daniel 7 passage that provided the vision with his favorite name for himself

8. Sharot, *Comparative Sociology of World Religions*, 40.

9. Boyarin, *Jewish Gospels*, 51–52.

and that the name the Son of Man or the Human One, provided a means of indicting both his humanity and divinity. We may also see in these words the longing for incarnation and the reality of incarnation that existed in some thinking among Jews.

Up to here I have emphasized the longing for incarnation or a tangible representation of God that we see throughout popular religion and also in the faith expressions of Israel. In addition, there may be seen a longing for compassion from "on high" that can bring relief and aid in the midst of the many troubles of life. I am interpreting this longing as the longing that is fulfilled in the atonement of Jesus Christ. The connection of the longing for compassion with atonement is supported by the fact that prayers for help have often been accompanied with sacrifices of some kind. The practice of making sacrifices has been with the understanding that the one or ones sacrificing do not deserve the compassion being sought. Sometimes sacrifices of animals, fruits, or produce were even considered as a means of satisfying the hunger of a divine figure or as a kind of payment for kind treatment in the past, present, or future. Whatever the case, it is clear that in popular religion the vast majority of people sought deliverance from lives of hardship and danger, a deliverance that could only come from a source beyond their own strength and because a power beyond them had some pity on their need.

Thus sacrifices were deemed a means of obtaining favor or pity. We can see that the longing for atonement is also clearly and universally expressed just as the longing for incarnation or a tangible contact with transcendent power. The former implies a sense of guilt and a desire for reconciliation with the Divine. Of course, the tradition of blood sacrifice is ancient in Israel, being associated with the deliverance from Exodus (Exod 13). Furthermore, a Day of Atonement was set aside to be celebrated every year (Lev 23:27–28). Although the sense of guilt was not always highly pronounced in popular non-biblical religions, the desire for compassion in the midst of danger and misery and the practice of making sacrifices to obtain help were quite prevalent.

SPECIAL PERSONS

As I focused on the importance of the tangible and sacrifices in religion in satisfying the human need for contact with God, I also came to see the importance of special persons in drawing people to religions. Thus, alongside the tendency of traditional religions, especially popular religions, to create tangible and visible representations of divine beings (longing for incarnation) and to seek their compassion for the difficult circumstances of life (longing for atonement) is the pervasive characteristic of human beings to elevate certain particular human beings to special, even divine, heights. The adulation of heroes may be seen as one form of this human tendency. When one turns to the numerous societies and religions of the world, the numbers of heroes, many of whom became mythic characters who were worshipped, are too many to count. These heroes-made-gods appear in temples and shrines and on family altars. In Hinduism, many of the divine figures are actually spoken of as *avatars* or "incarnations" from the Sanskrit, meaning "to descend." I came to the conclusion that, to the great disadvantage of Hinduism in spreading widely, it has no single avatar-savior figure. Nevertheless, the avatars in Hinduism contribute to the argument that human beings long for a tangible and visible representation of the Divine in human form.

Mythical heroes who might have some historical basis, such as King Arthur, or known historical heroes, such as Napoleon, are rather well known. However, interestingly and importantly, when looking at modern demythologized and disenchanted societies, still numerous heroes are revered. They could be called secularized gods or idols. Modern societies are also famous for their continuous creation of celebrities or what might be called public idols. Secularized America demonstrates that human beings inevitably seem to be attracted to special human beings—those who are regarded as above ordinary people and often as having special powers to lead large numbers of people and to solve problems. Supplementing these real-life heroes are even movie and cartoon heroes. All of this represents a longing for the incarnation of special power beyond ordinary human power.

Max Weber early recognized in *Wirtschaft und Gesellschaft*—published after his death in 1920—the importance of charismatic authority in human life:

> The provisioning of all demands that go beyond those of everyday routine has had, in principle, an entirely heterogeneous, namely a *charismatic* [italics his], foundation; the further back we look in history, the more we find this to be the case. This means that the "natural" leaders—in times of psychic, physical, economic, ethical, religious, political distress—have been neither officeholders nor incumbents of an "occupation" in the present sense of the word, that is, men [*sic*] who have acquired expert knowledge and who serve for remuneration. The natural leaders in distress have been holders of specific gifts of the body and spirit: and these gifts have been believed to be supernatural, not accessible to everybody.[10]

10. Weber, *From Max Weber*, 245.

Although charismatic figures have been important throughout history, I am noting that Buddha, Jesus, and Muhammad could be said to fit Weber's definition extremely well, especially with his reference to the supernatural. Weber's work with the three types of authority (traditional, charismatic, and rational-legal) gave impetus to the study of authority and personal leadership in human societies, but in general the *social* sciences have neglected the study of persons, particularly special persons. That has been left more to historians and biographers, many of whom are believers in the "great man theory" of history, largely rejected by social scientists.

Allison and Goethals, already mentioned, are exceptions. They produced a study of American heroes and celebrities that shows the importance of such figures in modern life. This attraction to heroes is very much related to the human need for both protection and direction in life, particularly moral direction. These heroes are not only tangible and can be envisioned, but they often accomplish their good deeds through sacrifice, pain, and suffering. Related to the longing for atonement, which in the case of Jesus Christ came through great suffering, the suffering of the hero is the basis for great attraction from people. One thinks especially of the suffering and death of Abraham Lincoln, as well as the suffering of Franklin Roosevelt and Jack Kennedy. Allison and Goethals comment, "The self-sacrificing actions of heroes cement their positive legacies to such a degree that their values, the things that they stand for, become firmly imbedded into a society's social identity. Suffering is the essential ingredient in hero construction."[11] This points directly, of course, to why the atonement of Christ fulfills human longing.

In the religion of Israel, in which there could be no gods beside the one true God (stated officially and most successfully recognized in practice after the destruction of Jerusalem in 587 BC), there were nevertheless important human heroic figures. In addition to patriarchs Moses, Joshua, and Samuel, it is worth noting the portrayal of King David as a hero. The demand for a king by the people was seen as disloyalty to God by the prophet Samuel (1 Sam 8). Nevertheless, though flawed in character and at different times rejected by many of the tribes, the numerous stories about David reveal the emotional attachment of people to him, especially as time passed. In particular, his royal line was designated as the line from which a future Savior would come, the one addressed as the Messiah or the Anointed One.

Of course, it was on the basis of the doctrine of the Messiah that Christianity was built, though the character of the Messiah had to be reconstructed to be very different from the popular notion of what the Messiah would be like—that of a triumphant king. Nevertheless, it was the Messiah

11. Allison and Goethals, *Heroes*, 192.

as the Suffering Servant, symbolized by the cross, that has proven to be a universally powerful attraction to people. It is worth noting that almost all the heroes of Israel suffered on behalf of others, especially for the preservation of God's people, and that some Jewish thinkers recognized that the Messiah would suffer.[12]

The same experience of suffering on behalf of others is true of most American heroes, with presidents Lincoln, Roosevelt, and Kennedy being prime examples of heroic leaders that suffered. They and other heroes, although sometimes having major flaws as did King David, are also important for setting moral standards by which people measure leadership.

MORALITY

In addition to the desire to be in touch with sources of power, a major reason for human beings to look to elevated figures is the human need for moral direction in life and for some type of authority to guide decision making. Morality and religion have an ambiguous relationship. In most traditional religions, worship of divinities and moral questions are dealt with separately. Temples seem to have little to do with justice or right relations. The religion of Israel, however, made a special point of closely connecting the relationship of human beings to God with their relationship to other human beings. A dramatic example is when Joseph says to his master's wife in response to her attempts to seduce him, "How then could I do this great wickedness, and sin against God?"(Gen 39:9). A major message of the prophets of Israel repeated many times is the condemnation of the Israelites for combining the worship of Yahweh with unjust behavior toward others. A classic example is Isaiah 1:12–17, which includes the words, "When you stretch out your hands, I will hide my eyes from you; even though you make many prayers, I will not listen; your hands are full of blood."

In spite of the tendency of all human beings to separate worship and morality, all human societies have conceptions of right and wrong and some means of controlling or regulating human behavior in the direction of what is considered good, at least by those with ruling power (including parents). Modern human beings may live their lives affirming their non-belief in God or simply live as though God were irrelevant to their lives, but they can hardly escape having ideas of right and wrong and thus may be said to be moral creatures. "Moral awareness and judgment" and "forming virtues" are among the highest order human capacities that Smith identifies.[13] In

12. Boyarin, *Jewish Gospels*, 129–30.
13. Smith, *What Is a Human?*, 54.

fact, Smith devotes a chapter in his discussion of the relation of personhood to "The Good."[14] There is not room or need here to present his argument regarding the good, but certain points may be emphasized. The most important fact is that morality in human life is a reality, but not simply a passive reality. Morality, even if skewed, is a strong force in all human life. Smith makes three points about the reality of morality:

> First, human beings exist as a specific kind of creature, as persons possessing particular, natural characteristics, capacities, interests, purposes, and limitations. Second, the good for human beings consists of persons realizing or achieving the essential nature of their true human personhood as fully as possible. Third, morality—both personal and social—concerns the dispositions, relationships, attitudes, desires, practices, and institutional structures that do and do not help persons to achieve the good.[15]

It is important that the term "limitations" and the phrase "do and do not help" be recognized as being related to the common moral failures of human beings. It should also be remembered, as already noted and made clear by Smith: human persons are "broken" in many respects and morality is an important area in which human beings are broken, often without their knowledge or recognition.[16] A clear distinction certainly exists between, on the one hand, moral knowledge or sense (the knowledge or consciousness of how one ought to behave and society ought to be) and, on the other hand, the energy actually to do the right and work for establishing what is right and just in social relations and society at large. The point for this book is that even though human beings are very much aware of moral brokenness, especially of others (!), one of the ways in which human beings obtain their moral sensibility is through the figures they revere or worship.

Related to heroes mentioned above, the recognition of heroes and their opposites, villains, is very much related to the shaping of morals. Allison and Goethals point out, "Most of us make bad moral choices as well as good ones. We need all the help we can get to act effectively and morally. Heroes blaze the trail toward competence and morality, and villains remind us of the dark side."[17] In other words, alongside the heroes are villains, who also perform an important function in clarifying good and evil. Allison and Goethals list eight characteristics of both heroes and villains.[18] Heroes are

14. Ibid., 384–433.
15. Ibid., 399–400.
16. Ibid., 410.
17. Allison and Goethals, *Heroes*, 207.
18. Ibid., 161.

smart, resilient, strong, selfless, charismatic, caring, reliable, and inspiring. Villains are also smart and resilient, but then are violent, greedy, mentally ill, immoral, egotistical, and vengeful.

Even if American heroes are not literally worshipped (although the Lincoln Memorial might give someone from a traditional society the impression that worship takes place there), heroes provide standards for making moral judgments about the self and others. The need for these moral standards, with the meaning they give to life, contributes to the longing human beings have for incarnation, but included in the desired incarnation is the concrete representation in persons of what a high moral life should be like. With this longing is associated the longing for compassion, namely, atonement for not attaining the moral standards that are recognized as needed.

AUTHORITIES

Yearning for heroes and clarification of the standards of morality is closely related to yearning for authority in life. As just seen, the longing for incarnation and atonement is expressed in the human tendency to seek tangible and clear sources of authority and authoritative persons to set standards for behavior and for some means of attaining these standards. For most people the highest authority is God, but God cannot be seen. Human beings first experience authority from their parents, but soon they encounter authority figures in society beyond their immediate families. In addition to personal authority figures, as human beings developed writing, authority over behavior was granted to written laws and admonitions. Civil laws were developed, but sacred scriptures were given the highest authority over behavior even if governmental authority had the most direct effect.

All sources of authority, including scriptures, require human interpretation and application to life. Thus, authority figures become necessary to interpret and apply the authoritative scriptures and laws regarding their meaning for religious thought and moral behavior. These authority figures may have the backing of tradition, an institution, or the force of personality, or some mixture of all three, but the authoritative human figure finds recognition and acceptance among human beings because a tangible person fulfills the longing for a tangible and immanent source of authority. In addition, however, the authoritative figure only gains authority through recognition of the legitimacy of that authority. It is here that the behavior of the authoritative figure, especially if that figure is to have religious and moral authority, is crucial. The authoritative figure that shows both high moral standards and compassion is the figure to which people are most powerfully drawn. This shows the presence of the longing for both incarnation and atonement.

As scientific thinking became more prominent in Western society, scientists and intellectuals gained considerable authority, to some degree eclipsing the authority of religious figures. Think of Einstein. This authority is based on the tangible nature and effect of scientific findings and the scientific method. Nevertheless, scientific findings are obtained by human beings and must be interpreted by human beings, which makes them subject to constant alteration, correction, and elaboration. In addition, science is an ambiguous source for good or benefit to humanity. It can produce both extremely beneficial and extremely harmful results. Scientific figures, therefore, occupy a somewhat ambiguous position of being either heroes, for example in discovering cures for diseases, or "mad scientists" who create destructive instruments and forces. It is no wonder, then, that religious figures continue in modern societies as sources of religious and moral knowledge, but they are joined by others, including political figures, which speak to the need for inspiration, motivation, and commitment to the good. The yearning for incarnation and atonement may be disappointed, but continues to seek fulfillment in some kind of authority figure or system or both.

LONGING FOR THE ABSOLUTE OTHER

One of the most important arguments regarding human longing was made by the German scholar Rudolf Otto in the first part of the twentieth century and continues to ring true.[19] Otto identified in all religions the human longing for contact with a something that could be described with a number of words, but which in the end could not really be described at all because it was beyond all words. He created the word "numinous" from the Latin *numen*, meaning a deity, especially one occupying a particular object. This reality only could be sensed as *numenous*, but it attracted the one sensing it and at the same time could create great dread and awe. Another term used for this reality was *mysterium tremedum*; however, the term that probably is most recognizable to people is "the holy," from the title of his classic work *The Idea of the Holy*. Holy refers to what is separate or other, and God is absolutely separate or other. Human beings are both drawn to and fearful of and resistant to God, which is the point I am also making.

The Bible, of course, contains numerous accounts of people encountering some representation or representative of God that was both fearful and yet compellingly attractive. Jacob's encounter with the divine representative

19. Otto, *Idea of the Holy*.

in a wrestling match from which he went away wounded, yet blessed, is memorable (Gen 32:22–32). Of course, Moses' encounter with the burning bush, where he heard the voice of "I am" sending him on his divine mission, is likewise famous (Exod 3:1–12). One of the most mysterious accounts in the Bible is when Moses is told that he cannot see the face of God; then Moses is told to stand in the cleft of a rock, where he is covered by God's hand, after which it is taken away and Moses is able to see the back of God (Exod 33:17–23). In Isaiah 6:1–3 we have the famous account of the call to Isaiah, when Isaiah "saw the Lord sitting on a throne, high and lofty." The seraphs called to one another saying, "Holy, holy, holy," which has become the title of a favorite hymn. The New Testament contains a number of accounts of the followers of Jesus encountering awe-inspiring events, such as the transfiguration of Jesus (Mark 9:2–8), the post-resurrection appearances in all four gospels, and the revelation of Jesus to Saul, who became Paul (Acts 9:1–9). What strikes me about the biblical accounts that fit Otto's description is that they center on anthropomorphic representations of God or of the actual figure of Jesus. This is consistent with the longing for incarnation.

Otto speaks of divination as the gift given to prophets through the Spirit to hear the "voice within," but then he adds, "We can look, beyond the prophet, to one in whom is found the Spirit in all its plenitude, and who at the same time in his person and in his performance is become most completely the object of divination, in whom Holiness is recognized apparent. Such a one is more than a Prophet. He is the Son."[20] The Son is preeminently the Human One, but also one who is glorified at the right hand of God (Dan 7:13–14).

CONCLUSION

This chapter is meant to present a broad theoretical background for the longing of human beings for incarnation and atonement. A theory of special persons, discussed above, contributes to the general background of the longing of human beings. The longing for incarnation is seen in the human desire for a tangible representation of God, but more than that, this tangible representation is best seen in a special person with special gifts that put persons in touch with transcendent supernatural realities, especially supernatural power. The longing for incarnation is manifested particularly in the attachment and loyalty of people to immanent and tangible figures that can be envisioned and who are heroic and authoritative. They may be considered divine, semi-divine, or simply above-ordinary people. They may have been mythic figures who help to account for the meaning

20. Ibid., 182.

of life or historical figures who accomplished something benefiting others, often through their suffering. They may be leaders who are recognized as having special authority in giving religious and moral directions for life. In the modern secularized world, the special people may simply be celebrities, politicians, or intellectuals who seem to have special gifts or scientists who have made great discoveries that helped to explain the natural world. Even though idols, mythic figures, avatars, heroes, celebrities, religious leaders, politicians, and intellectuals crowd human history, there are certain figures who have won special attention beyond all others in fulfilling the human longing for incarnation. Furthermore, the longing for atonement is seen in the felt need for compassion that often comes through the sacrifice of the special person that benefits large numbers of people.

In this chapter we have considered the general preparation to receive Jesus Christ that is built into human beings in general in their capacities and desires. However, this general preparation was not sufficient because God undertook work among a special people—the people of Israel—so that people everywhere would understand why Christ came and did his work. In fact, both of the names the Human One (the Son of Man) and Messiah (Christ or the Anointed One) come from the faith of Israel. Like Christians since Christ, the people of Israel did not live up to their mission to be a "light to the Gentiles," but the need and the basis for the incarnation and atonement was clearly shown in the story of faith and faithlessness that preceded Christ's coming and is still going on among Christians.

Chapter 4

Longing for Incarnation and Atonement in Three Religions[1]

A THEORY OF THE DRAWING POWER OF BUDDHA, JESUS, AND MUHAMMAD

IN THE PRESENT CHAPTER I turn more specifically to a theory of why Buddha, Jesus, and Muhammad have exercised such preeminent drawing power for people. The previous chapter sets the general background of why people long for incarnation and atonement. This theory leads to what I call a general theory of special persons, but in this chapter I will apply this theory directly to the three founders of Buddhism, Christianity, and Islam—the three religions that have spread more widely than other religions. This is not to deny that these three religions have a number of versions, some of which have conflicted strongly with each other as well as with other religions. However, all of the versions make the founders central to their faith. Although all religions have deep roots in human prehistory, Buddhism, Christianity, and Islam are dated from the appearance of the three founders: Buddha, Jesus, and Muhammad. This leads to the question: what is the basis for the drawing power of Buddha, Jesus, and Muhammad, who have millions of followers from a wide variety of social and cultural groupings? To get at the answer, I will use a method (from sociology of history) that simulates the experimental method. I will first describe each of the key factors in the drawing power of the founders and then in a second step compare the religions of their followers with their respective "mother" religions

1. This chapter, like the previous chapter, makes extensive use of material in Montgomery, "Special Persons and the Spread of Religions."

(Hinduism and Judaism). This gives a measure of control in viewing the drawing power of the three founders. In other words, by contrasting the three most widely spreading religions with the other religions with which they are most similar and out of which they came—Buddhism with Hinduism and Christianity, and Islam with Judaism—we will isolate the factor that made the three religions spread more widely than their mother religions. In addition, we will look briefly at other religions that did not spread widely in spite of having founders but having characteristics that did not involve relating people to the transcendent combined with universal compassion. I believe it can be shown that the ability to give access to the transcendent or God combined with universal compassion is the key factor for the wide spread of the three religions.

Buddha

The earliest of the three founders, Buddha, lived in an era beginning in the fifth century BC when there were movements of warriors (*ksatriyas*) and merchants or landowners (*vaisyas*) in reaction against the dominant Brahmanism. Mahavira, the "great man" of Jainism, which likewise was in reaction against Brahmanism, was likely a contemporary of Buddha. Buddha gathered disciples who continued to revere him and sought to follow his teachings after his death before or shortly after 400 BC. However, it was not until the reign of the Emperor Asoka (c. 270–235 BC) that Buddhism began to spread through the sending out of "teachers of the dharma."

Sri Lanka was one of the first societies in which Buddhism became the dominant religion. Buddha subsequently became a revered figure among the Mon people in Myanmar and then throughout Southeast Asia. In Southeast Asian Theravada Buddhism, Buddha was elevated, especially by ordinary people, to be alive and a savior. Even though monks considered him only a human being, he was regarded as "supremely enlightened, proficient in knowledge and conduct, one who fares well (to ultimate Deliverance), world-knower, peerless driver of men to be tamed, teacher of the gods and of men, enlightened, the Blessed One."[2] A dissident group, the *Mahasanghika*, was largely responsible for initiating Mahayana Buddhism, in which Buddha was elevated to a transcendent, omnipotent, and omnipresent position but manifests himself in earthly form to conform to the needs of human beings.[3] In its Mahayana form, Buddhism spread throughout East Asia and also to Vietnam.

2. Medford, *Buddhism and Society*, 33.
3. Ch'en, *Buddhism in China*, 12n.

In what I consider one of the most significant statements ever made about Buddhism, John Noss noted that in its original form Buddhism did not find a response among the masses, but then he adds:

> But the masses became interested—secondarily in the teaching, primarily in *the man* [italics his]. Original Buddhism would not have had so great an effect on the history of religion in the Orient, if the coolly rational philosophy of the sage of the Sakyas had not been mediated through a warm and friendly personality that could be adored. Fortunately for the future of Buddhism, its founder balanced the arahat [saint] ideal of self-salvation with the ideal of compassionate goodwill toward all living beings, and practiced that compassion himself. Thus there grew up after him a cult that took refuge in *him* [italics his], the compassionate as well as enlightened one, even more than it did in his teaching, so difficult to understand and practice.[4]

Buddha was clearly a special person, but he became more than simply a special person like other special persons. Although a human being, Buddha became to his followers a transcendent person who could give people access to the transcendent and a special enlightenment. In addition to being a tangible figure that could be envisioned (many images of him have been created to aid envisioning), he exhibited the great compassion so desired by human beings, especially those living in the misery of traditional societies. Buddha's calmness through meditation and living in the moment through "mindfulness," together with his ability to "take what comes," have had and continue to have great appeal in the West. Thus Buddha has attracted both the suffering masses of ancient societies and those in modern societies with psychic sufferings.

Jesus Christ

Jesus Christ or Jesus the Messiah (Christ meaning Messiah in Greek), as he is known to his followers and many others, is clearly a very special person who has drawn the love and loyalty of billions of people worldwide. However, Jesus Christ is not simply a special person who is a leader, a hero, or a wonderful teacher, although he is considered all of these things; Jesus is considered a divine Savior who gives access to God the Father through his death and resurrection. People pray through him to God the Father and also to him. Furthermore, almost always associated with the Savior is his

4. Noss, *Man's Religions*, 172.

compassion for all people—especially for the poor, the oppressed, the hungry, and the homeless in the view of many people. This compassion was expressed explicitly and clearly in the death of Christ for the sins of the world. In this sense, all people are placed on the same level: as needing redemption, in other words, being spiritually "wretched, pitiable, poor, blind, and naked," which was said of church members (Rev 3:17) whether they realized it or not. No greater love can be expressed toward the Human One than in the words, "He died for me" (Gal 2:20).

The spread of Christianity has exceeded the spread of all other religions until today. Approximately one third of the population of the world express faith in Jesus Christ. Most important in that spread is that Christianity crossed all the sociocultural lines that divide human beings, even exceeding the lines crossed by Buddhism and Islam. Without the person of Jesus Christ at the center of the Christian message, this could never have happened. He continues to be at the center of Christian devotion.

Muhammad

Islam and Christianity share a common root that extends back to Abraham in the Hebrew Scriptures. In fact, Islam honors Jews and Christians by referring to them as "the peoples of the book." The special person central to Islam is Muhammad, who lived and died in Arabia and who initiated a revitalization movement among the Arab people that spread to many other peoples. This movement led initially to the conquest of a large territory that extended westward to the Atlantic and eastward to Central Asia and India. Beyond this conquest and continuing after the decline of Arab power beginning only about 150 years after Muhammad, the religion of Islam spread widely around the Mediterranean, southward in Africa, and eastward to much of Central, East, and Southeast Asia. It is important to remember, as many do not, that much of the spread of Islam was not associated with conquest. The Turks and Mongols conquered Muslims after which they accepted Islam. Furthermore, Islam did not spread to a great extent to many lands ruled by Muslims for a number of centuries: Iberia, Sicily, the Balkans, Greece, Africa south of the Sahara, and India.

Although clearly not recognized as divine, Islam gives Muhammad a very special place in the first of the five pillars of Islamic faith, which is the confession (the *Shahadah*), "There is no god but Allah; Muhammad is the Messenger of Allah." This confession or testimony is repeated in the five daily prayers, the second pillar. Thus, "the name of the Prophet is joined to that of God, and Muhammad becomes the gateway to obtaining God's approval.

Muslims might forgive anyone for taking the name of God lightly, but not so the name of Muhammad."[5] Regarding the Sufis, the most effective missionaries for Islam, Carl Ernst states that "Sufis came to view Muhammad as the being in light whose creation preceded the creation of the universe. His mission was universal, and in his *compassion* [italics mine] he alone of all prophets would intercede on behalf of humanity."[6]

It is very important to mention here the Qur'an (Koran). Although Buddhism and Christianity both have holy scriptures, these scriptures are not on the level of the Qur'an, in that the Qur'an is so closely associated with Muhammad as to be considered dictated to him by God. This compensates for the fact that Muhammad is not considered divine, as both Buddha and Jesus are considered divine. As noted by John Esposito, "In his lifetime, throughout Muslim history, and today, the Prophet Muhammad is seen as the 'living Qur'an,' the embodiment of God's will in his behavior and words."[7] Salman Sayyid makes it especially clear that the Qur'an is a Divine representation and a means of connection to God and the transcendent for the followers of Muhammad:

> The Qur'an at its most powerful offers its readers a challenge: it makes them think about the manner and direction of their lives and how they can aspire towards being rightly guided. At this level the glory of the entire Qur'an comes into play; all its verses produce the effect upon the Believer that cannot be reduced simply to the linearity of its writings, the content of its stories or to the majesty of its injunctions,for beyond these moments the Qur'an provides means of *accessing the transcendental* [emphasis added].[8]

Thus it is true that the Qur'an, considered as "descended" from God, may be linked to Muhammad so that they are jointly representative of God and the means of access to God. There is much more that can be said about the elevation of Muhammad, but it is clear that he along with the Qur'an is seen as providing the way to gain access and acceptance by God. Although not emphasized to the same extent, but parallel to the emphasis found in Buddhism and Christianity, the compassion of God for all humanity is central to the message of Islam. Every *surah* (chapter) of the Qur'an begins with, "In the name of Allah, the Beneficent, the Merciful."

5. Sanneh, *Piety and Power*, 45.

6. Ernst, *Following Muhammad*, 167.

7. Esposito, *Future of Islam*, 43.

8. Sayyid, *Recalling the Caliphate*, 163.

THE MOTHER RELIGIONS

The demonstration of the theory of the drawing power of Buddha, Jesus Christ, and Muhammad requires controlling as much as possible the data regarding special persons. This is done by comparing the founders of the three most widely spreading religions with the two other major world religions that formed the context out of which they came and with which the religions they founded have similarities. In this way, the special position of the three founders can be most clearly seen. Below I compare Hinduism as the context from which Buddha came and Judaism as the context from which Jesus Christ and Muhammad came. In the case of Muhammad, Christianity was also a part of the context from which he came.

Hinduism

Hinduism could be considered a conglomeration of religions, rather than a single religion, that developed primarily in the last millennia before the Common Era, which is marked by the birth of Jesus Christ. Although containing sophisticated philosophical thought, including belief in a high God know as Brahman together with a devotional tradition (*bhakti*), Hinduism usually places emphasis on worship of the numerous lesser divinities more immediately available to worshippers. Hinduism is distinguished from other major religions, especially Buddhism, by having no clear single founder.

At the time of Buddha, Hinduism existed primarily as a religion led by the high caste of Brahmans against which the rising castes of *ksatriyas* (warriors) and *vaisyas* (landowners and merchants) were reacting. The mythological and philosophical thought, along with the practices of worshipping numerous gods, in Hinduism eventually spread throughout South Asia, which is where over 90 percent of the followers of some version of Hinduism now live. Hindu thought and practices also spread to the courts and peoples of kingdoms in Southeast Asia, including in what is now Indonesia, the island of Bali being the major remaining place of Hindu influence. However, Buddhism and later Islam replaced Hinduism in most places in Southeast Asia (except for Bali), leaving the vast majority of Hindus in South Asia (India and Nepal). When Hinduism has spread to the West it has usually been through a particular *guru*, or "religious specialist," recognized as possessing special wisdom and powers. This is consistent with the theory of special persons that the central reason religions spread is because of the special persons associated with them. However, according to the argument of this book, Hinduism has not spread as widely as its daughter religion, Buddhism, because it did not have a single special person as a founder.

At this point it is important to note that religions are an important part of culture, so much so that in ancient societies there was no separate word for religion. It was simply part of life. Religions may spread in association with the spread of a particular culture. This was particularly true for Hinduism but also for Confucianism, which in many ways is more a culture than a religion. Buddhism, Christianity, and Islam also spread in some ways and to some places as dominant parts of cultures. Nevertheless, the success of these three religions beyond the success of any other religions is due to the special character of their founders.

Furthermore, peoples receptive to these three religions have been able to retain their distinctive cultures. This is especially true of Christianity because of its affirmation of the inherent worth of all peoples and the translation of the Bible into numerous languages. Christianity has been adapted to and expressed through a wide variety of cultures, leading to the development of nationalism in many parts of the world. It must be noted, too, that where Christianity has been associated with domination, it has stimulated nationalistic opposition. One example of such opposition would be among Hindus and followers of other religions in traditional societies, such as China, Japan, and nations in Southeast Asia. When not associated with domination, Christianity has stimulated the assertion of ethnic and national distinctiveness, for example among numerous indigenous minority groups.

Judaism

Turning to the important religion that provided the religious context for the origin of Christianity and that, together with Christianity, provided the religious context for the origin of Islam, the closest person to be considered the founder of Judaism is the figure of Moses. Moses is the figure most associated with the deliverance of the people of Israel from Egypt and the giving of the Law or the Torah, so basic in Judaism. However, Moses was preceded by other important figures, including the three patriarchs Abraham, Isaac, and Jacob, from whom the twelve tribes of Israel are descended, at least symbolically. In addition to these figures, there were the prophets and kings of Israel, whose stories and messages recorded in the Hebrew Scriptures enabled the faith of Israel to survive terrible experiences. This is primarily because the prophets explained to the people that their destruction was due to their faithlessness to God's covenant with them. The nation of Israel proved to be a failure. First, there was the failure of their first king, Saul. After brief successes under David and Solomon, the nation divided between the Northern Kingdom and Southern Kingdom. This was followed with the destruction by first Assyria and then Babylon. A remnant of the Hebrews taken into captivity returned under Persia's Cyrus the Great, but many Jews became part of a permanent Diaspora. The Jewish kingdom under the Hasmoneans, who had successfully revolted against Antiochus IV Epiphanes, came and went and was followed by the domination of Rome. Finally, the magnificent temple of Herod was destroyed by Rome and the Jews were driven from the land after at least two unsuccessful revolts. So ended the nation project, but the wonderful Hebrew Scriptures were produced and survived with the scattered people, preserving their faith in a faithful and just God.

Important scholarship, already noted, has brought out the struggle of Jewish people to see their God as coming to them in a person, a person who was both divine and human. Boyarin shows how Jewish thought, at least some of it both before and after Jesus, saw the Son of Man as a divine Redeemer.[9] He shows how crucial passages in both Daniel 7 and in the Jewish books *First Enoch* and *Fourth Ezra* portray such a figure. Peter Schäfer attacks Boyarin's analysis but, along with other Jewish scholars, recognizes the mutual influence of Jewish and Christian thinking.[10] Certainly many Jews had no problem seeing Jesus as the divine-human Messiah or Christ, even as a suffering Messiah. Many of these became the early Jewish Christians. It was only later, it may be argued, that Christian pressures caused Judaism to retreat to a kind of rigid monotheism. The binitarian thought among Jews, in contrast to Christian trinitarian thought, together with the longing for a Messiah that was expressed in the prophetic writings and that existed widely among the Jewish people, shows the built-in tendency to seek a tangible and personal Savior. The expectation of the coming of a Messiah was especially strong at the time of Jesus. At any rate, according to the theory of the drawing power of the three founders, although Judaism was highly attractive to many non-Jews (some of whom became the proselytes or "God fearers" in the Roman Empire), ultimately Judaism failed to become a missionary religion and to spread widely other than by migration. This is because it did not recognize a Savior who could be envisioned, loved, and followed based particularly on the compassion of the Savior for all people. Judaism remained primarily an ethnic religion, unlike the followers of Buddha, Jesus Christ, and Muhammad, who carried their faith across numerous ethnic, national, and geographical borders.

9. Boyarin, *Jewish Gospels*, 56–59.

10. Schäfer, *Jewish Jesus*, 70–85.

OTHER MAJOR RELIGIONS WITH FOUNDERS

So far we have briefly described the three founders of the three most widely spreading religions and compared them to the two religions out of which they came, Hinduism and Judaism, in this way controlling for religious similarity. We have seen that, unlike their mother religions, Buddhism, Christianity, and Islam elevate a single special person who shows great compassion and offers to all peoples a means of access to God and salvation. However, I will control for another similarity by considering other religions that had single founders or central figures more clearly than Judaism and especially Hinduism. Other religions, particularly Confucianism, Taoism, Zoroastrianism, Manichaeism, and Jainism, all have single founders. Although each case is different, in none of these religions is the founder given the transcendent savior status of Buddha, Jesus, or Muhammad; or if they were granted such a status, they were soon surrounded by numerous additional divine figures. This latter tendency is also seen in Buddhism and Christianity, but it never overcame the centrality of Buddha or Jesus.

Confucius was a sage and teacher, not a prophet and certainly not a mediator to the Divine or a bringer of salvation. His teachings did become important, not only in China, but also in Korea, Japan, and Vietnam, helping to form the "cultural area" of the Far East, but that was the extent of the spread of Confucianism. To this day, it is a matter of debate whether Confucianism is even a religion.

Lao Zi, the probable founder of Taoism, is classified by Weber as manifesting "exemplary" prophecy along with Buddha, in contrast to "ethical" prophecy expressed primarily in the Middle East.[11] The exemplary prophets did not bring a message from a transcendent personal God who required obedience as the ethical prophets did, but rather gave teachings about ultimate reality to give people wisdom for living. Lao Zi was regarded primarily as a sage philosopher who taught about the impersonal Tao. When Buddhism came to China it rivaled Taoism, but at the same time there were attempts to combine them and they were sometimes confused in the perceptions of people. When the followers of Taoist philosophy saw the way in which Buddhism spread, they followed the Buddhist example and elevated Lao Zi and gave him heavenly associates. This could also be seen as a general propensity in popular religion, including popular Buddhism and Christianity. Furthermore, there were numerous other gods already present in Taoism. Although Lao Zi was (is) worshipped, he never gained the

11. Weber, *Sociology of Religion*, 55.

significance of Buddha as providing a means of salvation or as extending compassion to all people.

Jainism is thought to have been founded by Nataputta Vardhamana, who was given the title Mahavira, meaning great man or hero.[12] Jainism and Buddhism developed in the same time period beginning in the fifth century BC as sectarian movements in a period when non-Brahmans (warriors, merchants, and landowners) were reacting against the dominant Brahmanism. Comparing Jainism and Buddhism to Confucianism, Weber states:

> Confucianism, the ethic of a powerful officialdom, rejected all doctrines of salvation. On the other hand, Jainism and Buddhism, which provide radical antitheses to Confucianist accommodation to the world, were tangible expressions of an intellectualist attitude that was utterly antipolitical, pacifistic, and world-rejecting.[13]

Mahavira and Buddha both represent exemplary prophecy. While Mahavira, founder of Jainism, was believed to be a savior who descended from heaven to enter the womb of a woman and was sinless and omniscient, as time passed his status was reduced or at least obscured by veneration of the savior beings (*Tirthankaras*) who had preceded him.[14] Jainism, with its emphasis on asceticism or world renunciation and its philosophy of fallible human thought, has had a great influence on Indian culture, including on Mahatma Gandhi. According to my theory of the elevated human savior as influencing the spread of religions, Jainism could possibly have spread like Buddhism. However, over the period of time that Buddha was elevated to be a savior, Mahavira was not. The major difference seems to be that the salvation offered through Jainism was restricted to those who could follow *ahimsa* by breaking off every attachment to the world and its objects. Although also world-renouncing, Buddhism's "middle way" made it possible for followers to be less ascetic and also to achieve salvation.

Staying within India, but coming many centuries forward to the fifteenth century, we come to the religion of Sikhism, whose founder, Nanak, followed a tradition of teachers who stayed within Hinduism. However, responding and reacting to Islam, he emphasized the basic truth of monotheism, but not through acceptance of Muhammad the Prophet. The guru Nanak died in 1538 but appointed a successor. Even though it is said that Nanak's body disappeared after his death, he was not elevated to a position of becoming the single central figure of Sikhism. While followers increased

12. Noss, *Man's Religions*, 131.

13. Weber, *Sociology of Religion*, 122.

14. Noss, *Man's Religions*, 459.

and became increasingly militant, nine gurus followed Nanak, leading to the tenth guru, Govind Singh or Govind the Lion. He directed that there should be no more gurus, but the *Granth* (the writings of the gurus) should become their guru. The *Granth* is worshipped as a divinity in *Amritsar*, the Golden Temple of the Sikhs. Although Sikhism appears at first also to have the potential to become a religion that spreads widely, it clearly does not fit the criteria of having a *single* figure as a means of access to God and salvation.

Continuing to examine various world religions, but returning to an earlier period, we come to Persia, where Zoroaster, the founder of Zoroastrianism, probably lived in the seventh century BC. Zoroastrianism had the same source as the religion of the Vedic Aryans, from which Hinduism also developed. Zoroastrianism probably influenced Mahayana Buddhism during the latter's spread to Central Asia and China. However, as Weber notes, Zoroaster, along with Muhammad, belonged to the Near Eastern ethical prophets, who looked to a "personal, transcendental and ethical god," unlike the Asian exemplary prophets, who looked to "super-divine, impersonal forces."[15] Like Muhammad, Zoroaster strongly opposed the popular religion of his day in the name of the one god Ahura Mazda, the high god already known. The sacred book of Zoroastrianism, called the *Avesta*, has numerous portions. The most important of the portions is the *Yasna*, containing the *Gathas*, because it clearly is the most ancient source of information on Zoroaster's life and thought. Zoroastrianism became the religion of the Achaemenid rulers, beginning with Cyrus the Great of biblical fame.

Regarding the high position originally accorded Zoroaster, Noss writes:

> A highly worshipful attitude came to be taken toward Zoroaster himself. To the adoring eyes of his later followers, that very human man, "the shepherd of the poor" who appears in the Gathas, became a godlike personage whose existence was attended by supernatural manifestations. Heaven and Hell were thrown into commotion by him. His coming was known and foretold three thousand years before by the mythical bull; and King Yima, in the golden age, gave the demons warning that their defeat was impending.[16]

Miracles were said to attend the birth and the adult life of Zoroaster. He was venerated widely, including by the Greeks and the Romans. All of this bode well for the spread of Zoroastrianism according to our theory.

---

15. Weber, *Sociology of Religion*, 55–56.

16. Noss, *Man's Religions*, 459.

The problem at this point, then, is to consider why Zoroastrianism, with its single prophet, did not spread as widely as Christianity or Islam or even Buddhism. According to our theory of the importance of a single human being serving as means of access to God, Zoroastrianism demonstrated that it had a high potential to spread widely, but in the end it failed because of a rising tide of popular religion that reduced the importance of Zoroaster. The old Aryan nature worship came back into the religion. Even more important for reducing the focus on Zoroaster were the many angels (*Yazatas*) in popular religion. Furthermore, the divinity Mithra, the god of light, came back in popular religion, along with Haoma, the god of sacred intoxication, and other foreign gods and goddesses.

Zoroaster in his lifetime rejected all these divinities. After this revival of popular religion during the period of religious pluralism from the time of Alexander the Great, especially under the Parthians, Zoroastrianism was established as a rigid state religion by the Sassanid dynasty that began in AD 226. The latter-day polytheism and ceremonialism that followed Zoroaster were formalized into orthodoxy.

One of the so-called heresies of Zoroastrianism, Manichaeism, spread much more widely than its mother religion. This phenomenon is seen in the cases of Buddhism and also Christianity, and Islam, which spread more widely than their mother religions of Hinduism and Judaism, respectively. Manichaeism had the founding figure of the martyred Mani, who died in prison or, as in one version, whose body was crucified, stuffed, and hung on the gates of Seleucia-Ctesiphon in Iran between AD 273 and 276.[17] Manichaeism spread both eastward and westward from Iran. Understandably, it often became confused with Christianity, especially in Central Asia. However, Mani himself faded in significance. Manichaean theology, not any loyalty to its founder, found its way into movements that sought to purify or bring greater spirituality to established Christianity by professing a dualistic view of the material and spiritual. Forms of Catharism, such as Bogomilism in the Balkans and Albigensianism in France, trace their theological roots in part to Manichaeism.

To summarize, there is a vast literature describing these and the other religions of humanity, including the various religions of preliterate people often designated as Animism or simply primal religion, which underlie most religions, particularly their practices. It is obvious that these other religions did not spread as widely as Buddhism, Christianity, and Islam. Although several of the other major religions had designated founders— and almost all had heroes and various model figures, some of whom were

---

17. Moffett, *History of Christianity in Asia*, 110.

(are) considered divine or semi-divine—they did not have single human founders who provided access to God and salvation as did Buddha, Jesus, and Muhammad, the last with the divinely dictated Qur'an. Their founders were more likely to be regarded as sages than saviors, except for the prophet Zoroaster. In almost all religions, the single figure of the founder has had additional helpers or interceders. Of the three most widely spreading religions, this has been most notable in Buddhism, but it is also a characteristic of some forms of Christianity. It could be (and is) argued that this has negatively affected the spread of Christianity beyond a particular ethnic group. In other religions, however, the additional helpers have practically overwhelmed the importance of the founder. In addition to the central importance of the founder, although the concept of compassion is present in most religions as a laudable virtue, in Buddhism, Christianity, and Islam compassion receives a special emphasis and is modeled in the founders.

CONCLUSION

The drawing power of special persons is so obvious as to be a taken-for-granted feature of human life. In other words, paradoxically, most people do not think of this drawing power as a special phenomenon needing explanation. Like religion in early societies, it is an accepted aspect of culture. Every society contains such persons and some of these persons gain international following. The pope is a clear example of a person with international drawing power, but in addition there are numerous other figures in every society that draw admirers, if not devoted fans and followers. Impressive evidence of the drawing power of special persons is seen in the excitement and the rap expressions on the faces of the devoted fans and followers of special persons. Just to be in the presence of famous special persons is often felt to be an "unreal experience," perhaps a spiritual or religious experience. The drawing power of special persons is certainly a contributing factor to the drawing power of Buddha, Jesus, and Muhammad, but their drawing power has exceeded all others and been based on the special characteristic of providing access to God or the transcendent.

This book on the incarnation and atonement of Jesus Christ has come to this subject from the broadest possible perspective. The second chapter looked at total reality, which included the twofold aspect of creation and humanity: supernatural and natural. The third chapter considered the evidence that human beings have an inner longing for incarnation and atonement, especially as this is expressed through the desire for direct contact with God and for compassion. It noted that popular religion is characterized by the desire for contact with the Divine through immanent, accessible, and tangible objects, but this contact is especially important for obtaining compassionate help in the difficult circumstances of life. Special persons have special drawing power because they are tangible and meet human needs for authoritative moral direction. This fourth chapter extends theoretical perspectives to explain why the founders of the three most widely spreading religions have been able to attract so many followers. These three religions are in fact distinguished by their offer to all people of a single human founder who is able to give access to the Divine and salvation extended through compassion for every individual. The founders are made immanent, accessible, and tangible in biographies and in teachings, and the stories of their compassion are treasured. Buddha, Jesus Christ, and Muhammad are each perceived differently, but each provides a unique means of access to God and salvation and offers compassion.

Because of the human tendency to seek contact with God, particularly to gain divine compassion and aid for the many problems faced by human beings, people have at various times and places sought to augment the three figures of Buddha, Jesus Christ, and Muhammad with secondary intermediaries. This was (is) especially the case for Buddha and Jesus Christ, who were elevated to the transcendent level and subsequently seen by large numbers of people to be somewhat separated from human need. This made the creation of intermediaries all the more likely. Nevertheless, the fact is that the singular figures of Buddha, Jesus Christ, and Muhammad have made it possible for the three religions that focus upon them to spread to a greater extent than any other religions.

The cursory view of the three founders, as well as other religious founders, in this chapter does not deny that there are other important aspects of the religions they founded that have been influential in how religions spread or did not spread. For example, moral guidance and energy together with the ability to gather and organize people are important elements in religions affecting their spread. The ability to gather dispirited and disorganized peoples together was especially important in the early days of Islam in gathering the various Arab tribes after the defeat of the two empires of Byzantium and Persia left a vacuum in the Middle East that needed to be filled. Whether the revisionist history of Islam is true of not, it is clear that the early Ommayad rulers, Mu'awiyah and Abd al-Malik, needed to unite the Arab people, including the various disputatious Christian groups under them. Islam provided the universal religion that could accomplish this.[18] In addition to the religious factors, social conditions in receiving countries

---

18. Wade, *Faith Instinct*, 190.

facilitated or blocked the spread of these religions. These are important to understand, and I have studied and written about these factors.[19] However, in this book I have focused on the most crucial factor in the content of the three religions that attracts human beings.

Before proceeding to the remaining part of the book, which focuses on Jesus Christ, there remains an important consideration affecting the acceptance and human expression of the incarnation and atonement of Jesus Christ. This factor has already been mentioned in Christian Smith's discussion of personhood: the brokenness of human beings.[20] The longings of human beings for incarnation and atonement have been discussed, but it is important to recognize that human beings also resist God, who has come to the earth for them and has expressed great compassion for them.

19. Montgomery, "Spread of Religions and Macrosocial Relations"; *Diffusion of Religions*; *Lopsided Spread of Christianity*; *Why Religions Spread*; "Conversion and the Historic Spread of Religions."

20. Smith in *What is a Person?* discusses brokenness in a number of places, but especially in pages 75–78.

Chapter 5

Longing for God Mixed with Resistance—Part I

HUMAN DUAL TENDENCIES

WHEN PREACHING TO THE Athenians, Paul testified to the human "search for God." He said God made human beings "so that they would search for God and perhaps grope for him and find him—though indeed he is not far from each one of us" (Acts 17:27). A major point of the first part of this book has been to provide evidence that this search, or better, groping, is seen throughout human history. But because human beings long for a tangible and visible expression of transcendent power and also for compassion from such power does not mean that they openly and willingly receive what they long for. Human beings are ambivalent about what is offered by God and historically have resisted the overtures of God. While human beings were made so that their humanity finds fulfillment in communion with God and other human beings, they resist and avoid God, as Adam and Eve disobeyed and then hid from God even though God came searching for them (Gen 3:1–8). This was followed in the Bible story by broken human relationships: Cain and Able, pre- and post-flood people, and the Tower of Bable (Gen 4–11). The Bible and Christian theology have an explanation for the tendency to resist God and loving relationships even while there is longing for both. The short word for it is "sin."

While the yearning for God is based on the image of God placed in human beings, which gives them the capacity and need for communion with God and fellowship with others, the tendency for human beings to resist God and seek to escape from fellowship with and responsibility to God and for others is a result of human beings turning inward on themselves and away from God. This is represented in the story of Eve and Adam in Genesis 3, just cited, a story in primitive language but with deep theological meaning. They desired and took the fruit based on its value to themselves apart from God. They chose to trust their own judgment rather than to trust God. The choice to eat of the fruit of "the tree of the knowledge of good an evil" was an act based on the human desire for autonomy apart from God rather than for a trusting and loving relationship with God. It was also based on the desire to know only what God knows fully, becoming experts in knowing the difference between good and evil, thus becoming divine on their own terms. This kind of presumed knowledge feeds human judgment of and alienation from others. (Something that is rife in the Christian community itself). The story shows that the root of sin is the broken relationship of trust in God. At its base, then, sin is theological, not behavioral. Bad behavior follows the broken relationship.

With a realization that I am treading on dangerous ground, I am writing in this and the next chapter about various overlapping types of resistance to God, which are really aspects of resistance that often work simultaneously. I call it "dangerous ground" because it is clear in the story of the fall in Genesis 3 that one of the main characteristics of sin is its subtly and power to deceive. Others will be able to modify, elaborate, or disagree with my selection of types of resistance. Some may see a "liberal bent" in my selections. Nevertheless, I believe that Christians are called to identify (with the help of the Holy Spirit) as carefully and humbly as possible our human and especially our Christian resistance to God's work in the world. It is not our calling to judge and condemn one another as Christians have often done, but at the same time we are called to seek to improve and make clearer our witness to Jesus Christ, beginning with ourselves. Perhaps God has brought the church in the United States and even the whole world to become highly diverse but, unlike in previous times, to be in close approximation so that Christians can, if they are willing, learn from each other and change according to what is learned from others, including from other religions.

To a great extent, the history of human resistance to the "Word made flesh" or the incarnation, and to God's way of redemption represented in the atonement, can be seen in the story of the whole Bible, but it has continued in Christian history up to the present. Christianity has repeated the story of resistance to God found throughout the Hebrew Scriptures or Old Testament. The longing for God can be observed in all human beings, especially in their religions, as we have seen in the previous two chapters, but resistance to God can also be seen in the same sources. However, in the Bible, because of its honesty, both the longing for God and the resistance to God is made clearer *among the people of God* than is seen in human life generally. In short, the revelation in the Bible shows clearly what can only be known partially by studying human beings in general and their religions. It is important, however, not to see sin or resistance to God, as many do, only in individual terms. One of the great lessons of the Bible and human history is that good people can do bad things and support bad causes and bad people (or unbelieving people) can do good things and support good causes, particularly at the societal level. Living in the days of racial segregation, I knew people who were racist in personal attitudes who otherwise were good people. And white people today living unconsciously in white privilege or a racist system (I include myself) may be personally good people or not personally bad people. Even more mysterious is how God brings about good through evil actions, such as the destruction of Jerusalem by Babylon and the destruction of Western colonialism in World War II.[1]

Human religions are social bodies because people live in social groups and are socialized into them. In other words, resistance to God, like longing for God, is made part of human social relations and institutional structures so that numerous people are socialized into resistant patterns or ways of thought and life, just as they are socialized into ways of thought and life that are open to God. As sociocultural forces, resistance is found in the "principalities and powers" against which Christians are called to struggle (Eph 6:12, KJV).[2] The power of the various forms of resistance discussed below is that they become sociocultural forces into which people are socialized and that come to dominate groups of people through what they take for granted.

It is important to remember that because sin is universal, as the Bible makes clear, so too resistance to God exists in all people as individuals and groups. A Christian task is to try to recognize the temptation to resist God (even though that recognition will never be complete) and obtain God's help to overcome the temptation. It is important to remember that we are promised help to become free from domination by the forces opposed to God. In the following sections of this chapter and the next chapter, we will look at various forms of resistance to God, in particular how Christians are drawn into resistance. The reason for this focus is that resistance to God among Christians is the major hindrance to the *missio Dei* (the mission of God) to bring salvation to humanity.

I must comment on whether Christians face the influence of Satan or a personal evil force. I have no trouble believing in a personal evil force, as the statement in the Lord's Prayer can be translated, "Deliver us from the

---

1. I deal with this in greater detail in Montgomery, *Real New Age and the Opposition*, 120–21.

2. I discuss the "principalities and powers" as sociocultural forces in ibid., 70–88.

Evil One." The problem with thinking of Satan and devils is that this kind of thinking can become a distraction. What is most dangerous is to try to identify some influence or force with a personal devil; evil is too subtle to be easily identified. If evil is thought of as personal in the form of Satan, then it is best to think of Satan as bound and the believer as protected by Jesus. Although we do not need to fear the Evil One, we should be prepared for evil to reappear or be "unbound" from time to time. The appearance of Hitler after a period of blessings through Christian contributions (translation of the Bible, beautiful churches, advancement of philosophy, music, literature, and science) is a good example of an "unbinding" of the Evil One. Of course, mixed with the wheat are always the weeds and so even in the good things we can see roots of later evil. Nevertheless, we should not try to pull up the weeds ahead of time (Matt 13:24–30).

Perhaps most important about what I am saying in these two chapters is the point, already noted, that the most dangerous form of resistance to God is found among God's people. In fact, the whole Bible is a story of God working with the people of God so that they can represent God to the people of the world. In other words, the Bible itself is about what God did and continues to do to show what God is like. Jesus Christ came to God's people, a people who had a history of experience of salvation from slavery, revelation of God's will in the law, and many messages from the prophets. Then Jesus was opposed, not by prostitutes and clearly bad people, but by "good people" who were religious leaders. To this day, the greatest hindrance to the spread of the gospel is by professed Christians. It is for this reason that I concentrate on resistance to God from Christians.

RESISTANCE THROUGH IDOLATRY

An early human way of resisting God was by focusing on and desiring God's creation for its value to the self and to use for the self. Worshipping a tangible representation of God facilitates avoiding God and using creation for the self. When there are literal objects or figures that are overtly worshipped it is commonly known as idolatry. However, the human love for and grasping after God's creation rather than God—namely, what is basically idolatry—has continued and even expanded in the modern world. Every one of the forms of resistance in the sections below may be seen as a form of idolatry. In idolatry, human beings take whatever God gives but then put it in the place of God in their devotion. Primitive idolatry involves the worship of images, but the more sophisticated and dangerous forms of idolatry are when even elements of God's self-revelation are made into idols. These forms of idolatry that gain influence over believers in God will be discussed below. The human tendency toward idolatry is dealt with extensively by Paul in the first chapter of his Letter to the Romans, where he wrote, "they exchanged the truth about God for a lie and worshiped and served the creature rather than the Creator, who is blessed forever!" (1:25). Paul's dealing with idolatry, first in his discussion of human resistance to God, shows its basic presence in all resistance, but notice that Paul deals most extensively with the resistance of God's people (2:12—3:31), showing that all are under just condemnation in order for God to show mercy to all.

Returning to resistance to God through tangible images, as already noted in chapter 3, pre-literate human beings tended to locate God and the powers of the supernatural in natural objects or areas, such as mountains, groves, stones, and trees. They also carried objects or fetishes meant to ward off evil. At the same time, many retained a concept of a high God and of superhuman spiritual powers. Sadly, they, like many modern people, tended to lose touch with a God who seemed distant. As civilizations developed with permanent structures and artistic works, human beings created images of various divinities, placed them in temples, and carried out worship ceremonies before them. Images of divinities were (are) carried around in festival ceremonies. A careful reading of the Hebrew Scriptures shows that actually the prophets of God in Israel had to attack idol worship specifically because it was practiced by so many of the Israelites. In Isaiah 46:5–7 we read:

> To whom will you liken me and make me equal, and compare me, as though we were alike? Those who lavish gold from the purse, and weigh out silver in the scales—they hire a goldsmith, who makes it into a god; then they fall down and worship! They lift it to their shoulders, they carry it, they set it in its place, and it stands there; it cannot move from its place. If one cries out to it, it does not answer or save anyone from trouble.

In Psalm 135:15–18 we read: "The idols of the nations are silver and gold, the work of human hands. They have mouths, but they do not speak; they have eyes, but they do not see; they have ears, but they do not hear, and there is no breath in their mouths. Those who make them and all who trust them shall become like them."

As I pointed out in chapter 1, the creation of idols demonstrates the desire of human beings to worship—and not only to worship, but to envision—God and have some sense of nearness to God, who seems distant. Nevertheless, idols are movable and can even be carried about. The great appeal of worshipping images is that people can make divinities that accord with how human beings think and behave. Though the images may appear fearful, they are not very demanding; they can actually be manipulated. Furthermore, they do not require any change in human moral behavior, even though people with authority (rulers and parents) may use them in seeking to coerce compliant obedience. In the end, the worship of physical idols is rather childish so that people have given up such practices as societies have modernized. However, as noted above, the temptation to resist God is much more subtle than found in the creation of idols or tangible figures and seeking to worship through them. Any object that takes the place of God in human devotion is an idol. Paul speaks of greed as idolatry (Col 3:5). This is probably the major form of modern idolatry, which permeates commercialized societies. People who disdain the superstition related to worshipping idols may be resisting God even more strongly through their love of money, fame, and power. Such idolatry is even more dangerous than worshipping literal idols because it is usually less obvious than bowing before a statue. It should not be thought, however, that only affluent modern societies are permeated by the love of money; the love of money permeates all societies, including those who worship statues.

It should be noted that, given human frailty, idolatry is easily mixed with faith and certainly with expressions of faith. This is demonstrated in the Bible with the worship of the golden calf by the people of God in the wilderness (Exod 32). It is also demonstrated by the continuing imitation by the Israelites in Canaan of the idolatrous religious practices of their neighbors, especially up to the destruction of Jerusalem and the temple in 587 BC. The most dangerous forms of idolatry, which is idolatry by religious people, will be explored below.

RESISTANCE THROUGH WORSHIP

The most dangerous forms of resistance to God are found within religion, because these forms of resistance to God are easily hidden and at the same time distort the knowledge of God. Most serious of all, they hinder the *missio Dei*. The most important part of religion is worship, but worship itself can be used as a form of resistance. This is because worship—even when private, but especially when public—usually requires some form outward expression and ceremony. As already pointed out, a serious failure in worship is the separation of worship from morality or right behavior. This separation takes place in any temple or church worship, which usually requires a special building. The building created for worship and the ceremonies conducted within it are usually closely related, so I am treating them together as a means of resistance to God; but they can also each become means of resistance. Simply appearing in the worship building or carrying out the ceremony can be considered "sufficient" to gain God's approval.

The prophet Jeremiah told the people, "Do not trust in these deceptive words: 'This is the temple of the Lord, the temple of the Lord, the temple of the Lord'" (Jer 7:4). He castigated the people for paying more attention to their worship ceremonies in the temple than to both maintaining loyalty to God alone and maintaining right human relationships (Jer 7 and 26). All of the Hebrew prophets were particularly strong in their condemnation of those who worshipped Yahweh while treating others unjustly. As important as worship with sacrifices were, the Hebrew Scriptures make clear that God is looking at the heart and at right behavior (Ps 51:15–17; Amos 5:18–24; Isa 1:12–17; 58:1–14; Mic 6:6–8).

The fall of Jerusalem in 587 BC marked a major change in the religion of the Israelites in which idol worship virtually disappeared among them. Before the destruction of the Temple, it is clear that the use of images in worship was mixed with religious ceremonies honoring Yahweh. They had learned their lesson regarding the worship of images through the destruction of the Temple combined with the message of the prophets! However, after the people were restored to the land and to temple worship as the prophets had promised, they continued to let worship itself come between them and God.

Furthermore, by the time of Christ, a magnificent new temple was constructed. It was much larger than the temple built after the Restoration, though it was built by a not-fully Jewish king, Herod, to gain political points from the people. Jesus predicted this temple, greatly admired by the people, including his disciples, and honored by him, would be destroyed (Matt 24:2). It was destroyed in AD 70, with no new substantial Jewish temple ever again constructed in Jerusalem. It is worth noting that the destruction of the temple in AD 70 and the final dispersion of the Jews after the Bar Kokhba revolt (AD 132–135) resulted from their revolting against Rome based very largely on their apocalyptic beliefs, a classic misuse of messianic and apocalyptic thought. Without these revolts Jews might have been able to stay in the land perhaps until the present. Nevertheless, the destructions of the temple before and after Christ illustrates that the place and the ceremonies of worship in any location can be a subtle means of avoiding responsibility to God. This form of idolatry has also influenced Christians to the present time. Magnificent cathedrals and other church buildings today may have very few worshippers, and there may be more picture taking than prayers within them. Megachurches with giant auditoriums may be packed with people, but "attendance" can still take the place of "doing justice, loving kindness, and walking humbly with God" (Mic 6:8).

It is almost impossible to conceive of a religion that does not include liturgy and ceremonies, including Christianity. Even churches that are non-liturgical develop patterns for worship in which similar words and acts are used repeatedly. Attending worship itself is a ceremonial act. I mention this because, as just stated, it is possible for people to use their practice of attending church as a means of resisting a serious encounter with God and his call for faithfulness in all of life. Church religion can become a kind of cultural substitute for "wrestling with the spiritual forces of evil" (Eph 6:10–12) that are against God's will or service to those in need. In short, through churches and worship people can become comfortable with sociocultural forces that are opposed to God.

As Christianity grew, it broke out of its original house churches and at the same time developed routine worship ceremonies. As we know, church buildings became magnificent cathedrals and worship services elaborately beautiful, especially with inspiring music. However, none of this prevented some of the terrible failings of Christianity in history, as in the Byzantine Empire and the cruel wars among the Western Christian nations and against non-Christian nations.[3] Worshipping Christians were among those who supported slavery, segregation, suppression of women, suppression of those having sexual orientation different from the majority, wars of destruction and ethnic cleansing, oppressive governments, and a host of other distortions of the witness to the gospel of Jesus Christ. All the resistances to God, particularly those that are overtly religious, are related to each other. Resistance through worship is very close to resistance through what people know as moral behavior.

RESISTANCE THROUGH MORAL LAWS

Like all of creation, the moral law revealed to the people of Israel is a gift from God, showing us God's nature and God's will for human beings—what God is like and what God wants human beings to be like. In response to the gift of salvation, the one true God demands moral behavior that is according to God's revealed will and that is a great blessing to human life. Surprisingly, even moral behavior can become a barrier between human beings and God. This is when moral behavior is seen as a means of gaining God's favor, not expressing gratitude to God. The fact that moral behavior is a response to salvation and not a criterion for salvation is stated plainly in the introduction to the Ten Commandments in Exodus 20:1 and Deuteronomy 5:6: "I am the Lord your God, who brought you out of the land of

3. Jenkins, *Jesus Wars*, 229–78.

Egypt, out of the house of slavery; you shall have no other gods before me."
As a matter of fact, the deliverance from slavery in Egypt became the basis
of the understanding of justice in Israel as deliverance of those least able to
care for themselves, namely, treating others as God had treated them when
they could not deliver themselves. The exodus also accounts for the history
of Jews in the struggle for justice.

Although it is made clear that obedience to the moral law is to be in
thanksgiving to God, in post-exilic Israel following the destruction of the
ceremonial center of Israel (the Jerusalem temple) obedience to the law was
clearly made a criterion for, rather than a product of, salvation. This elevation (really lowering) of the law is seen particularly in the Book of Ezra.
In the centuries following the restoration to Jerusalem and Judea, legalism
(along with ceremonialism, discussed above) became a means for escaping
responsibility to God. When morality itself is made into an idol, it takes the
form of a set of rules that human beings feel that they can manage. Typically,
people who make or pronounce the rules place them beyond what ordinary
people can do, in order to keep people subservient and themselves in positions above the rest of the people. As one who lived in China for many years,
I observed that public laws seemed often to be made on the basis of goals for
behavior rather than on the basis of what people can practically observe. In
contrast, in the concept of common law that developed in England and has
tribal roots rather than imperial roots, laws should arise from the common
moral standards of the people. I am moving from moral to civil laws, but
they are parallel here to some extent and both can become a means of social
control by a few.

Legalism is a particularly subtle means of hiding from God, because
particular religious and moral rules appear to be so demanding and obedience to such legal requirements (carefully selected) appears to be an expression of great piety and devotion. Jesus, following the prophetic tradition,
spoke directly to the tendency of the religious leaders to emphasize following outward rules while neglecting "the weightier matters of the law: justice
and mercy and faith" (Matt 23:23). Followers of the rules for keeping the
Sabbath often tried to interfere with Jesus carrying out deeds of mercy or
simply meeting ordinary human needs on the Sabbath (Matt 12:1–8).

The subtlety of "keeping the rules" is that it creates a feeling of piety
and spiritual pride. Paul speaks of the sense of religiousness that comes
from obeying religious regulations:

> Why do you submit to regulations, "Do not handle, Do not taste,
> Do not touch"? All these regulations refer to things that per-
> ish with use; they are simply human commands and teachings.

> These have indeed an *appearance* of wisdom in promoting self-imposed piety, humility, and severe treatment of the body, but they are of no value in checking self-indulgence. (Col 2:20–23)

Even when the law is seen only or primarily in terms of right behavior toward others and not simply ceremonial rules, it is still possible for it to become a means of escape from God. This is an even more subtle temptation than the one offered by ceremonial rules. The struggle of Paul to make plain both the value of the moral law and its danger as a hindrance to true faith and obedience to God is very evident in his Letter to the Romans. He recognized that by emphasizing strongly that salvation was by God's grace only and not by obedience to the law, he was in danger of being misunderstood as being opposed to the moral law. He echoed his critics when he asked, "What then are we to say? Should we continue in sin in order that grace may abound? By no means! How can we who died to sin go on living in it?" (Rom 6:1–2). And yet Paul was ultimately mobbed, arrested, and imprisoned because it was believed that he was attacking the law of God. The same was true earlier of Stephen—accused of speaking "blasphemous words against Moses and God" (Acts 6:11)—whose death Paul (Saul) had approved.

The method of avoiding responsibility to God through obedience to always *selected* requirements of God's law, whether moral or ritual, is a universal practice in all religions, including the Abrahamic religions of Judaism, Christianity, and Islam. The carrying out of certain practices takes the place of having a genuine encounter with God through God's incarnation and atonement in Jesus Christ and then following Christ, the Human One. Behavior deemed to be required by God becomes the criteria for acceptance by God, rather than the grace of God, extended most clearly, as believed by Christians, through the death and resurrection of Christ. It is not too much to say that the law as understood and interpreted by human beings can be idolized or made into a substitute for God. Thus the revelation of God's nature in the written moral law actually becomes a barrier between human beings and God! This is why God, above all, is revealed through a Person, the living Word, Jesus the Christ. Sometimes even Christ is turned into a moral law. This is when Christ is considered as a teacher and an example only, rather than a Savior, who gave his life for all. Even the gospel itself can be turned into law, as we shall see, when people make it into a burden, a required formula to be repeated for salvation, rather than a means to a new life of freedom under God. There is nothing sacred that is beyond being misused and turned into a barrier to God.

I will note here that there is a danger of moral relativism when people have no moral authority. This will be dealt with especially in chapter 11 on the authority of the Human One. The Bible and the moral laws within it do have authority to the believer, but their authority is derivative or understood through Jesus Christ. It is to him that "all authority in heaven and on earth was given" (Matt 28:18). It is unfortunate, but understandable given human nature, that people want more explicit moral directives than they hear from Jesus, although loving God and your neighbor at all times is more difficult than any explicit command. This is what "following Jesus" means.

RESISTANCE THROUGH THE CHURCH

The resistances discussed since "Resistance through Idolatry" are resistances that are primarily through religions, but especially by the people of God in the Hebrew Scriptures and to the present day. The body of believers or the church is highly important for Christians, but it may also become a means of resistance to God as many other aspects of the Christian life.

The church in its first three hundred years maintained both movement and institution characteristics, but in the fourth century the institution characteristics came to dominate because of the establishment of the state church. To the great detriment of the church, in the fourth century Christianity was made the official religion of the Roman Empire and also in the following Byzantine Empire. The state church pattern was continued as Christianity spread northward among the European tribes and has continued up to the present. The institution of the church that found expression among the many ethnic and national groups by its physicality and organizational power provided a particular opportunity for resistance to God through making it an idol. The leaders of the churches and the nations came to stress conformity to its rules and rituals as the only means for maintaining a relationship with God, as well as expressing loyalty to the nation or ethnic group. Baptism and Holy Communion and a number of additional ceremonies became formalized as the visible and tangible means of maintaining a relationship to God.

A large portion of the Christian public came to emphasize assent to church teachings as opposed to trust and commitment as the meaning of faith, membership in the institutional church as opposed to service, and following church leaders as opposed to following Jesus Christ. The church became in effect an "earthly kingdom" or "of this world" (not simply in the world) increasingly comfortable with exercising earthly power. Accompanying the elevation of church leaders in power, Christ was viewed as Divine Ruler and Judge (*Pantocrator*). The local or regional Christian church became identified or closely allied with local and regional governmental authorities. Christianity tended to follow ethnic and national lines, and therefore Christians based their identities in ethnicity and nationality instead of in their relationship to the living Christ. From the earliest days, resistance to the church that seemed more "of the world" than representing God in the world took place repeatedly. The reaction against the powerful and dominating visible church took many forms, including the whole modern movement against religion as such. A major reaction gained ground in the sixteenth century in the form of the Protestant churches. However, these churches continued the state church pattern and were supported by nationalistic movements in various countries. Their major religious means of resisting the dominating Roman Catholic Church was through the use of the Bible. This led to another form of religious resistance to God that continues a line of resistances found among Christians. This form of resistance and other forms became particularly associated with Protestant churches in the modern era. The modern secularization movement was an unintended effect of the Protestant Reformation. It has been a movement with strong anti-Christian aspects mixed with religious opposition to state and church, but at the same time another unintended effect, becoming ever clearer, has been a certain clarification of the call to faith (the "faith option"). This will be discussed in chapter 9.

Chapter 6

Longing for God Mixed with Resistance—Part II

RESISTANCE THROUGH THE WRITTEN WORD

CHRISTIAN LIFE, PARTICULARLY AMONG Protestants, relates closely to the written Word, the Bible, the revelation of God that includes directions for the faith and behavior of believers. According to the Bible, the self-revelation or self-extension of God for the salvation of human beings was through the Word and the Spirit. But what is that Word? It is primarily the living Word who is described in the written Word. The written Word points to the living Word, Jesus Christ, who is the image of God (Col 1:15) and the full revelation of what God is like and what God intends human beings to become as new creations in Christ. The written Word for Christians consists of the Hebrew Scriptures, or the Old Testament, together with the New Testament.

It took several hundred years after Christ before the Old and New Testaments were recognized in what is now called the Bible. The process in which this took place and the work to make the Bible available in many languages is not important to describe here. What is sad is that the Bible—what is recognized by Christians as the written Word—although a gift from God, can actually become for many Christians a means of resisting God.

By focusing on the "inerrant words of the Bible," Christians can make an idol of the Bible and thereby avoid encountering the living Word presented in the Bible, Jesus Christ. This is "bibliolatry," or biblicism. Christian Smith, a Christian and a sociologist of religion, has written very effectively of how biblicism is not a truly evangelical understanding of Scripture.[1] In

---

1. Smith, *Bible Made Impossible*, 3–26.

fact, as he points out, to claim that the Bible is without error and to apply that concept to all the knowledge and details in the Bible so that the Bible is made into a kind of "manual for all of life" is actually made impossible by the very diversity of interpretations of the Bible. The most serious problem for those who focus on the literal words of the Bible or simply lift texts out of the Bible is the tendency to ignore the context of biblical passages and the larger or basic message of the Bible, particularly as it is found in Jesus Christ. For example, the Bible gives no direct instructions against the practice of slavery, yet today very few Christians would agree that slavery should be condoned. This view took some nineteen centuries to be clarified and established among almost all Christians. There are many other practices based on principles from the Bible gained from careful interpretation that have taken centuries to be recognized: human rights, democracy, science, modern medicine, mass education, elevation of the status of women, and advance of gay and transgendered people's rights. All of these could be called "Exoduses" from types of slavery and oppression. Sadly, Christians have been among those opposing many advances in the quality of human life, including all the advances just listed, and so the struggle continues. In regard to the current struggle to give equal rights in church and society to those whose sexuality is different from the majority, important studies of the Bible, as well as science and legal history, are helping to change traditional understandings.[2] In addition and primarily, simple contact with homosexuals and transgendered people who are friends or members of families and churches, with the discovery that they are very much like other people, has helped to change many people's views.

The legalism of clinging to selected written words of the Bible and narrow interpretations, evident especially among Protestant Christians, is like all idolatries: an attempt to find a security apart from the living God. It is placing the derivative authority of the Bible above the absolute authority of Jesus Christ. It could also be seen as an inability (unwillingness) to follow Jesus Christ and the Holy Spirit, who are always moving into the future. It has a similar use as all idolatries and legalisms, including the idolatry of the church: control and elevation of the self or the self's group over others. It is a type of authoritarianism through which Christians who claim to know "the inerrant words of God" or simply "what the Bible says" can then impose their will on others. Of course, individuals may be genuinely sincere or simply following their group or institution, as has been true of opposition to other advances in understandings in the past, as in the case of

---

2. Two important studies among others are Rogers, *Jesus, the Bible, and Homosexuality*; and Johnson, *Time to Embrace*.

the emancipation of slaves or the knowledge of evolution. People forget how these oppositions have failed in the past. They will eventually fail as greater justice is established and the realities of nature are clarified through science, which should be seen as a gift from God to benefit humanity. For many the infallible pope is replaced with the "inerrant" written Word, with both being supported by institutional and social authorities. Interpreters of the written Word confuse their interpretations of the Bible with the will of God. The Bible, of course, can only be known through interpretations, which, being human, are always partial. Direct quotations of the Bible, as important as they are, are always selected and thereby become part of an interpretation of the Bible. Perhaps most important, the Bible should be interpreted by the whole church over time, not simply by individuals.

Believers who are not able to impose their will—which they see as God's will—on others, may then judge others as wrong and sinful and often create schisms in churches. The needed graceful and forgiving attitude is replaced by a judgmental attitude. It is also true that those being judged often return judgment even more strongly. Just as there are important standards of behavior (morality), there are important statements of faith (verbally stated truths); but it is important to let both of them follow and rest upon a prior relationship to God based on God's grace through the incarnate Word, Jesus Christ, and the Holy Spirit. It is also wise to allow time for true interpretations of the Bible to be established, many times by the fruits of believers (Matt 7:20).

Christians have literally fought over what they believed were the correct statements of truth (creeds and confessions) and created numerous schisms among believers. With the loss of the authority of the pope, Protestants came to recognize a special authority in the written words of the Bible. The written words of the Bible provided a tangible source of authority. In this way the longing for a tangible contact with God found expression. However, the subtle danger of this worship of written words is that even more tangible sources of authority become recognized in the authoritarian charismatic church leaders and spokespersons considered as authoritative interpreters of the Word. The single authority of the pope is thereby replaced by numerous local authoritarian preachers in independent churches apart from the larger community of believers. The emphasis on both the written and orally stated words has led Christians to resist and escape the authority of the living Word, Jesus Christ, witnessed to in the Bible and by the Holy Spirit in the community of faithful followers over time.

By the first part of the twentieth century, many conservative Christians perceived the established Protestant church leaders as not showing proper respect for the Bible, in particular by adopting critical methods of studying the Bible, many learned from Germany. Unfortunately, some biblical scholars went (go) too far in applying a "scientific" approach in their historical and literary criticism, unnecessarily questioning faith perspectives in the Bible, and thereby drove many Christians away from the useful insights of a proper critical study of the Bible. This encouraged many who wanted to break with what they considered the "apostate" churches where proper critical methods of study were used. How to handle the Bible remains a major struggle in Protestant churches, dividing the mainline churches from the evangelical churches.

Bibliolatry has led to many distortions in interpreting the Bible based on selected and often literal interpretations, especially of the Old Testament and apocalyptic literature. This has caused an unusual emphasis on two covenants in dispensationalism, one with Israel and one with the church. Jesus Christ, who showed no interest in a territorial kingdom, is believed to be returning to set up a kingdom in Jerusalem. This interpretation is based on a misunderstanding of apocalyptic literature in the Bible. In the meantime, Christians are to do nothing about improving conditions for those who suffer in the world, which in any case is soon to be destroyed. While the church in the world is perceived as essentially a "spiritual fellowship," the state of Israel is seen as a precursor and sign of the coming kingdom. This viewpoint does not recognize that all the promises of the Old Testament regarding restoration to a place in the world or "ownership of the world" are fulfilled in Jesus Christ, not in a territorial kingdom. The promises have not been taken away but expanded to include the whole world ("the meek shall inherit the earth"; Ps 37:22; Matt 5:5) and in fact all things (1 Cor 3:21–22). One of the major problems with this "apocalypticism" is that it tends to make some people warlike as they look forward to a final battle (Armageddon) when Christ will return to earth and rescue the church. (Before Christianity, apocalypticism made the Jews the most rebellious of the peoples conquered by Rome.) They may even initiate a war to inaugurate God's rule of the world. At the same time, many people have been attracted to the dispensational movement, which has found a home in fundamentalism by its zeal for evangelism and missions and for reviving congregational life with an emphasis on witnessing to a personal relationship to Christ. Sadly, more sophisticated or educated Christians may fall into the temptation of looking down on the whole dispensational movement, not recognizing the sincere faith and love that is within it, particularly in those who are simply following other Christians or were raised within it.

One of the effects of resistance to the living non-violent and grace-filled incarnate Christ has been a kind of dehumanization of the Bible and of creeds in which the human element in them is not recognized. Even the human aspect of Jesus Christ is underemphasized. True, the Bible is author-itative for Christians, but it is an authority derived from the one who said, "All authority in heaven and on earth has been given to me" (Matt 28:18). This is never said of the Bible. For some, the Bible and church creeds become standards abstracted from human life, unlike the living Word, who was a vibrant participant in human life. The words of the Bible and the creeds of the church are important guides for Christians but, again, their authority is derivative. It is thus possible for Christians to make idols of them that crowd out the living and loving Holy Spirit given to the community of followers of the living and loving incarnate Word.

The tendency to not recognize the human element in the Bible and even in Jesus Christ may be identified as a docetic tendency. Docetism in the early church was the belief that Jesus Christ was only God masquerad-ing as a human. This is roundly condemned in 1 John 4:2–3. No Christian would probably admit to belief in Docetism, which would mean denying belief in the incarnation, but the tendency not to recognize the human as-pect of Christ or of the Bible has continued to the present. Again, it is based on the same sin that accounts for idolatry: the desire for security and power. If Jesus Christ is primarily seen as only divine, then one can put a strong emphasis on obedience rather than following. In other words, it takes away from having to think and requires only looking for literal words to obey. The docetic tendency is thus especially seen in turning the Bible into a manual or handbook of instructions instead of a living guidebook for life full of stories and directions for travel. The supposed clarity of seeing detailed rules adds to the authoritarianism of those who claim to explain them. The docetic tendency can be seen very clearly in the claim that the Qur'an was dictated by God, a view that some Christians have applied to the Bible. Of course, not recognizing the human element in the institution of the church is another example of the docetic tendency. There seems to be a human desire to control the divine and, through that control, to control others.

RESISTANCE THROUGH SPIRITUALITY

Another method of resisting God and creating idols is through how Chris-tians have responded to the gift of the Spirit. This may seem to be the most unlikely form of idolatry since the emphasis is on the Spirit and the spiritual life rather than the tangible and visible church. This makes this form of re-sistance extremely subtle and difficult to recognize.

The kingdom introduced by Jesus Christ was not an earthly kingdom or a kingdom "of this world," as Jesus told Pilate. However, the kingdom was clearly brought *into the world* by Jesus Christ. The twofold nature of Christ's kingdom—in the world, but not of the world—has been a major source for Christians to find a means of avoiding responsibility to God by emphasizing the not-of-this-world aspect of the kingdom. It is true that the not-of-the-world nature of the kingdom of Christ has given Christians the opportunity to live a spiritual life under the Holy Spirit, who brings rich fruit into the lives of believers: "love, joy, peace, patience, kindness, generosity, faithfulness, gentleness, and self-control" (Gal 5:22–23). It is a natural result, therefore, that Christians would be tempted to interpret Christ and the life under him as only an inner spiritual experience unrelated to what is going on around them. Some Christians go so far as to deemphasize the physicality or human nature of Jesus Christ, as noted above. What became primarily important was experiencing a spiritual life with Jesus while disregarding the organized church as being "of the flesh."

Thus, throughout church history Christians have vacillated between the physicality and the spirituality of the church and of their lives. Because of the many failings of the organized or physical church, some Christians are tempted to treat it with contempt and condemn it as apostate. In case any Christians (particularly Protestants) should not think that only the invisible or spiritual church is important, they should note John Calvin's words:

> But as our present design is to treat of the *visible* [italics his] Church, we may learn even from the title of *mother* [italics his], how useful and even necessary it is for us to know her; since there is no other way of entrance into life, unless we are conceived by her, born of her, nourished at her breast, and continually preserved under her care and government till we are divested of this mortal flesh and "become like the angels."[3]

Nevertheless, we see that from the earliest times Christians have often with justification periodically sought to purify the church by placing a greater emphasis on spiritual life. In other words, believers periodically felt that the church's life had become cold and merely routine. We see the problems of the church already in Revelation 2–3. Over the centuries, believers sought a more pure and intense spiritual life, but at a cost that could be harmful. The Montanists of the late second century emphasized the Holy Spirit and had characteristics similar to the modern-day Pentecostal and Charismatic movements. In the tenth century, Bogomils, originating in Bulgaria and showing influences from the dualism of Manichaeism, sought a more spiritual church and rejected ecclesiastical hierarchy, seen as "of the flesh." Their influence extended to the even larger movement of the

3. Calvin, *Institutes*, book 4, chapter 1, paragraph 4.

Cathars in medieval southern France. These movements saw the material world, including human sexual life, as originating out of evil sources. In contrast, other movements, such as the Waldensian, Lollard, and Hussite, leading up to the sixteenth-century Reformation, were basically orthodox but nevertheless sought greater purity and spirituality in the church. They primarily wanted to replace the authority of the church hierarchy with that of the Bible and thereby return to early Christianity, which they felt was not reflected in the contemporary church.

The temptation to make an idol of the Bible, as already noted, took the place of the temptation to make an idol of the church. Over the centuries and up to the present, Christians have tended to be divided between those making an idol of the visible church (Orthodox, Roman Catholic, conciliar Protestants, and others with successful church organizations) and those making an idol of the Bible (Protestant churches, particularly independent Protestant churches and organizations often influenced by dispensational-ists and identified as "evangelical"). For "Bible believers" and dispensation-alists, the organized church has been considered apostate.

A third group of Christians, cutting across both of the others (Charis-matic or Pentecostal), has been represented by those strongly emphasizing the work of the Holy Spirit. Their idol has been having an emotional spiri-tual experience. This has also been true for evangelicals emphasizing having a "born again" experience. Of course, there is a proper place in theology and in the Christian life for the visible church, the written Word, and the work of the Spirit; but some Christians have selected one of these aspects of the Christian life to elevate its importance so much that it actually be-comes a barrier between them and God. This is the definition of idolatry. The selected aspect is emphasized against other aspects at different times, creating divisions among the people of God and damaging the witness to the Incarnate One, Jesus Christ, present through the Holy Spirit.

In the nineteenth and twentieth centuries, in the evil condition brought on by slavery and racial segregation, an emphasis on the "spirituality" of the church, especially in American Southern churches, helped to provide Chris-tians with an ideology to avoid responsibility for social justice. This empha-sis affected many in American mainline Protestant churches, particularly during the struggle over slavery and later in the Civil Rights Movement, but has been carried forward particularly by evangelical independent churches. At the same time, beginning toward the end of the nineteenth century, as noted, dispensational thought emphasized the apostasy of the visible church and that the present age was the "dispensation of the Spirit." The sense that the organized church had become corrupt created openness to an ideology of spirituality supporting schism in the church and the founding of many independent churches or "spiritual fellowships." The American sociocultural emphasis on individual initiative and independency also provided a favorable context for initiating many independent churches, institutions, and agencies. Being a spiritual individual and part of a spiritual fellowship justified numerous separations among Christians. Denominations, many quite small but others with megachurches, were greatly multiplied.

Accompanying the emphasis on the spirituality of the Christian life and church, a literal interpretation of promises regarding the "possession of the land" was seen as having been fulfilled in the state of Israel. As already mentioned, this emphasis on the materiality of the promises to Israel has led to making the establishment of the state of Israel a special sign for the imminent return of Christ. The focus on apocalyptic literature in the Bible fostered a warlike spirit and a lack of interest in any improvement in world conditions. Resistance to the incarnate Christ through an emphasis on spirituality has proven to be an extremely subtle temptation for Christians to turn from fellow Christians and to neglect responsibilities for justice in the world. This resistance through spirituality has great appeal in the modern individualistic and localistic American culture. It is also appealing to the anti-authoritarian and anti-hierarchical (anti-bureaucratic) spirit that is especially strong in the United States, a continuation of the reaction against the authoritarian governments and churches of Europe. It also accords well with the American entrepreneurial spirit. Obviously, Christian resistance to the gospel of Christ may be mixed with some aspects of the Christian life that are not bad or evil. Furthermore, good people may be caught up in certain movements or the cultures of groups to which they belong. Best of all, God is able to "work things together for good" (Rom 8:28) in spite of the harm that may be done. Independent churches have made some important contributions in evangelism and education. I particularly appreciate their use of the social sciences of anthropology and linguistics, which mainline churches have tended to neglect. These paradoxes of good and bad are seen in other forms of resistance, which is one of the main reasons that Christianity has had diverse expressions from the beginning and will continue to have diverse expressions. God works through this diversity the best when Christians respect and learn from each other.

RESISTANCE THROUGH THE GOSPEL

Perhaps the most subtle of the temptations to resist Jesus Christ is the one found in an emphasis on the gospel of Jesus Christ itself, but particularly the words of the gospel itself used in a formulaic fashion. It is possible for

Christians to use the words expressing the best gift of God, the gift of God's self in the incarnation and atonement, in an idolatrous fashion. Although this is made difficult by the nature of God's revelation in Jesus Christ, namely, by the person of Jesus Christ himself, it is still possible for followers of Jesus to focus on the literal words of the gospel instead of on Jesus himself and his spirit of gentleness and love. The problem then develops in using the verbal gospel in a very aggressive way. The literal words become idols and are used as though they were magic apart from their meaning which is beyond words. This failure of Christians has driven people away from Christ. The misuse of the gospel of Jesus Christ itself is a very serious failing of God's people because it is a failure to witness to the whole person of Jesus Christ, which is the final command of the Lord: "You are my witnesses."

The resistance to God through the gospel is often combined with various other forms of resistance already mentioned. However, especially prominent is the resistance that places extreme emphasis on the verbal statement of the gospel and the importance of certain behaviors in the lives of believers while at the same time neglecting physical needs among people at large or of whole communities. The humanness of Jesus Christ is virtually forgotten while major emphasis is placed on his divine nature. Religious revivals are famous (or infamous) for placing a major emphasis on "getting right with God" while neglecting the weighty matters of establishing just relations between people and ministering to the suffering.

Accompanying this form of resistance is the tendency to impose particular interpretations of the Bible on others. Miroslav Volf speaks of the malfunction of faith when it is made coercive.[4] It involves a kind of hyperactivity in which faith is imposed on the unwilling. This is in contrast to the malfunction of idleness (to be considered next). All religions have shown a propensity to be drawn to political power, just as governments have sought to use religious authority to obtain legitimacy, God being the highest legitimating power. The insecurity of religious people in their beliefs and values cause them, including Christian leaders and groups, to seek political authority to make them official, monopolistic, or at least with dominating influence. This helped to create the state churches of Western and Eastern Europe that followed the formation of the official church in Rome in the fourth century. This same insecurity has also caused Christian leaders and groups in the United States, where no religious body can be deemed official, to seek governmental influence to favor their church or promote their particular interpretation of the Bible, often self-designated "evangelical."

4. Volf, *Public Faith*, 17, 37–54.

"Evangelical" is based on the term "gospel" or "good news." The problem is that it has become a label that has accrued additional meanings particularly associated with the political and social right. This is not the first time that biblical and Christian terms have accrued meanings that were not really representative of a positive witness to Jesus Christ. At this point my thought is that Christians should seek to be aware of the associations, deserved or not, that people have of Christianity and all of its many related parts. More important, however, is to seek to be true to all that Jesus Christ called his disciple to be and do, in short, to follow Jesus Christ. This requires above all that diverse Christians love one another, which includes listening to and learning from one another.

One of the most significant facts about the accounts in Acts is that there are only two or two and a half accounts of messages to Gentile unbelievers referred to in the preface of this book: Peter to Cornelius (10:34–43), Paul to pagan worshipers at Lystra (the interrupted sermon, 14:8–17), and Paul to the intellectuals at the Areopagus (17:16–33). In all three accounts Peter and Paul were complementary to their hearers and avoided mentioning sin. After all, the understanding of sin or resistance to God is really a growing understanding for those with faith. The approach used was far from the imposition of the gospel.

RESISTANCE THROUGH APATHY

We now turn in the opposite direction to a form of resistance to God that is equally subtle to the one just discussed. It may be the most common form of resistance among us Christians, particularly mainline Christians and those from the Roman Catholic and Orthodox churches, namely, the older churches in which people tend to rest in their traditions. Apathy strengthens the resistance to the gospel of the "hyperactive" or "intense" believers discussed above, who then withdraw from other Christians to form more "spiritual" churches and at the same time seek to impose their faith and values on others. By "resistance through apathy" I mean something very similar to what Volf discusses as the malfunction of faith in idleness.[5] It is a kind of religious secularism in which faith is compartmentalized to the religious or church life while the various other aspects of life, such as work and recreation, are dealt with "on their own terms," without considering their implications for the life of faith. Nonreligious secularism is fairly easy to recognize because in it God is ignored, but religious secularism is more dangerous. In religious secularism people go through the motions of being religious, either as a member of a

5. Ibid., 23–36.

religious body or stating that they believe in God, but they live much of their lives as though God was irrelevant to them.

In my previous book already mentioned, *The Real New Age and the Opposition*, I presented the view that opposition to the kingdom of Jesus Christ very often takes the form of dominating sociocultural forces, which often have religious or even Christian support. These are forces that include the institutions and cultures into which human beings are socialized and which they come to take for granted. Wink in his trilogy on "the powers" did much to help us realize that the social sciences actually rediscovered the fact that human beings are highly influenced by forces, identified as sociocultural forces, that seem to be "above us."[6] In that sense they are similar to the teaching in Paul's writings concerning "principalities and powers." Nevertheless, Wink makes clear that these "principalities and powers" are not simply identical to sociocultural powers, but contain both spiritual and material aspects.[7] My own view is that social scientists do help us realize the inner power of sociocultural forces affecting our attitudes and motivations. Like sociocultural forces the "principalities and powers" can be good, neutral, or evil in their influence. In Ephesians 6:12 Christians are challenged to wrestle with these powers. My application of the resistance through apathy is when we Christians easily "go with the flow" and accept the sociocultural forces into which we were socialized with little question and often without any consciousness of their strong influence on our inner thoughts, including our spiritual life. Wrestling in this case means becoming conscious of the sociocultural influences on us and then resisting those opposed to Jesus Christ. Paul says, "Do not be conformed to this world, but be transformed by the renewing of your minds, so that you may discern what is the will of God—what is good and acceptable and perfect" (Rom 12:2). I believe this is a call for Christians to be countercultural in some selected ways—not necessarily all ways, since some cultural influences are good or benign. However, when Christians simply go with many of the modern powerful sociocultural forces they are practicing a form of covert polytheism alongside their overt monotheism. This is not unlike what was practiced in ancient Israel, as well as by those who recognized (recognize) a "high God" while following numerous local gods.

As a boy I lived in China, but I grew up from high school years in the era when racial segregation in the Southern United States was an inherited and accepted social institution. The views and values associated with it permeated the culture and dominated people's lives, including mine. There

---

6. Wink, *Naming the Powers; Unmasking the Powers; Engaging the Powers.*

7. Wink, *Naming the Powers*, 104–40.

were some beautiful things about so-called Southern culture that empha-sized kindness and graciousness, but at the same time it was corrupted by the evil system of racial segregation, where much that was mean and de-structive of lives took place. People could be kind and gracious and at the same time have terrible racist attitudes. Peter's exhortation on Pentecost to "save yourselves from this corrupt generation" (Acts 2:40) applied to those living in the South, but also to all those living in America, which has been and still is permeated by racism, especially in its systemic form of white privilege. In a similar way, in the nation of Germany, which experienced many blessings from the gospel and in which a rich culture flowered with education, music, literature, science, and philosophy, great evil came to the surface and brought cruel destruction to millions in the Holocaust and in very destructive wars. Was this not an example of the release of the "ancient serpent" (Rev 20:1–3)? If so, such releases can happen again unexpectedly. The United States is not immune from such evils, meaning that Christians must continue to wrestle with "the powers" to prevent the outbreak of evil and limit it when it does appear.

The major outcome of apathy as people uncritically accept a domi-nating influence on their views and values is the unthinking perpetuation of suffering and death upon others, much of it covered by the excuse of individuals, "I never hurt anyone." Apathy is really an expression of self-centeredness, which is at the heart of human sinful resistance to God. Christians will never agree on how not to be "conformed to this world" and which principality and power (sociocultural force) to resist, but as we listen to each other and act with others in love, "all things" will "work together for good" (Rom 8:28). We are called on, in the midst of all our resistances, to "work out your [our] own salvation with fear and trembling; for it is God who is at work in you [us], enabling you [us] both to will and to work for his good pleasure" (Phil 2:12–13). Providentially, there are some important conditions in the United States that enable Christians to listen to or at least observe one another and thereby learn from one another and begin a self-correction ("always reforming").

SOME CORRECTIVE FORCES

We know that some form of resistance to God is inevitable because we are sinful, but resistances are different in different human beings, including different followers of Jesus Christ as both individuals and as groups. This means that we human beings, especially Christians, need each other to learn about our resistances and ways of overcoming them. We see this important fact revealed by Jesus Christ in bringing together twelve apostles and other followers to form a community of believers from the beginning of his work. Their diversity, even conflict, was apparent from the beginning. We learn from the New Testament that the various strengths and weaknesses of the disciples offset each other in the church, representing the body of Christ. Individual Christians and Christian groups can learn from other individuals and groups. This is a major value of the denominational system, but it works best when the denominations establish ways of interaction and cooperation.

Even on the secular level (nothing is really secular since God works in all things), we see that diversity in society is a source of strength. The United States is blessed with many subgroups and subcultures, but nevertheless, as with all societies, some subgroups tend to be dominant. The diversity of subcultures provides healthy challenges to and criticisms of those who participate in dominant subgroups. Freedom of speech and the press are important safeguards for those who are critical of some of the dominating viewpoints as well as of the powerful economic and political interests of the various groups. An independent judiciary is an essential feature in a society in order to protect minority groups and their views. Probably one of the most unrecognized influences in forming democratic societies is the experience of people in local congregations and associations. In many undemocratic societies people do not have experience in local organizations where there can be debate and joint decisions. Instead, they tend to follow charismatic leaders. In addition to mass movements, cathedrals and megachurches are not good seedbeds of democracies.

In addition to free speech and press and an independent judiciary, the social sciences provide important tools for exposing and examining some of the pervasive and dominating forces in society and for self-criticism by individual Christians and churches. One of the most important parts of the American heritage is the recognition that people need protection from bad and mistaken religion or even simply the domination of one religious perspective in the form of a religious monopoly, as these existed in Europe with its state churches. While compartmentalization of faith from the rest of life is a great danger, there is a place for humility of faith that actually employs the secular or non-faith approach as a means of correction for mistaken religious views. Faith is still the inspiration for doing this, but there is recognition that one's faith is partial and needs criticism and correction from others. Thus a secular government is a method of government in which religion cannot or should not be used as a political justification for policy and action. Just actions do not need religious justification. The image of God in human beings enables them to recognize justice. That is why, as Martin Luther King said, "The arc of the moral universe is long but it bends toward justice." Of course, individual Christian political leaders and Christian individual and group activists should still be inspired by their Christian convictions, but they should let the justice of their actions speak for themselves. This should be a matter of yes being yes and no being no (Matt 5:33–37), what I consider a New Testament exhortation to avoid trying to drag the name of God into an argument or dress up a viewpoint with religious language. The statement in Matthew was spoken to those who like to embellish their words (oaths and vows) with religious references, just as some today try to strengthen their arguments for some public policy by a religious reference. A major lesson learned the hard way in history is that religion and governmental power are not good partners. Both are damaged by too close an association. This does not mean, however, that religious faith should not inspire politicians. Furthermore, faith is very directly related to the moral actions required of governments.

Political arguments should not use religious language beyond the statement from the Declaration of Independence that "all men are created equal and were endowed by their Creator with certain unalienable rights . . . " However, moral arguments are very much part of political arguments. Jonathan Haidt has written perceptively about the moral bases of the various arguments used in politics.[8] His research puts forth a Moral Foundations Theory that posits six foundations used in political viewpoints. Different viewpoints (liberal, Libertarian, conservative) use different moral foundations in their arguments. The value in Haidt's analysis is that it encourages people to listen to diverse views different from their own. For Christians, of course morality has a basis in faith, but we should know that all people have moral views and Christians may agree with non-Christians on some points more than with other Christians.

The other important place for a secular methodology is in science, including the social sciences. God is not mentioned as a causal force in science, but of course the belief in God is a causal force. Even if what people believe is not real or true, it is likely to have real consequences. But Christians also believe that God is working in all things, especially human history. A lesson that has been learned is that religion, including the Bible, is not a good source for knowledge about the natural world, but it is a good place to learn about the effect of the natural world in human thought and life. Notice that I am not advocating secularism or secular humanism as ideologies but rather the use of the secular as a methodology for gaining knowledge of the natural world, which includes important aspects of human life. Scientific studies, including social scientific, are a protection from the introduction of

8. Haidt, *Righteous Mind*, 274–313.

wrong religious ideas for government policies. Scientific studies are carried out by biased human beings but, unlike theology, there are formal controls for bias in the studies, which means there is constant elaboration of theories.

From what has already been said in the first chapter, we must look to the revelation of God in the Bible and primarily in Jesus Christ for our knowledge of God and his will for our lives, both private and public. However, we only know revelation through human interpretation, which should be guided (especially together) by the Holy Spirit but will inevitably be partial. This is why, as said at first in this section, we need the diversity of the whole church and most of all the love of Jesus Christ, as we are reminded by Paul in 1 Corinthians 13:12–13: "For now we see in a mirror, dimly, but then we will see face to face. Now I know only in part; then I will know fully, even as I have been fully known. And now faith, hope, and love abide, these three; and the greatest of these is love." The face we will see is that of the Human One, who is perfect love.

CONCLUSION

It may seem strange that up to now in chapters 5 and 6 I have emphasized primarily resistance to God by the people of God, especially Christians. I have not said much about resistance to God by non-believers or people of religions different from the religions of the Bible, particularly Judaism and Christianity. The reason for this focus on the resistance to God of followers of Christianity is that it is this resistance that hinders the spread of faith in the Human One, Jesus Christ, sent by God into the world. Of course, all human beings resist God in some way, but the resistance of Christians is the most harmful because of the distortion it gives to God's work of salvation, the *missio Dei*.

Resistance to God in some form of idolatry is unavoidable by human beings, including Christians. In this sense, we all struggle with polytheism, just as the ancient Hebrews, because to be devoted or committed to anything more than to God is to make a god of that object. The point for Christians is to recognize the subtle forms that this idolatrous resistance takes, especially when it comes in the form of a sociocultural force that includes religious views. The United States is filled with religious subcultures that easily become idolatrous to their members as they become more important than listening to God and following Jesus. These are the powers that we are to wrestle with and to which we are not to be conformed (Eph 6:12; Rom 12:2). It is even possible for Christians to act immorally as they follow sociocultural influences that are harmful to people, of which there are many examples in history. Wrestling with the powers certainly has the meaning of listening to one another as well as to the voices of other religions and of our secular critics in society. As Christians, we need to be humble in self-examination. This means cultivating the spirit of Gamaliel, who believed that God's truth would be revealed over time (Acts 5:34–39). Many churches and members of churches need the spirit of Gamaliel!

Christian doctrine is that God has not remained silent or inactive, but has reached out to fallen humanity, revealing the nature of God and the destiny of human beings. More than revealing only, God has made it possible through the death and resurrection of Jesus Christ for human beings to have free access to God and to receive the Spirit of God. This is a fulfillment of the longing of human beings for contact with God and new life in ongoing fellowship with God and one another.

Chapters 5 and 6 have pointed out that human beings have an inherent tendency to resist God and the life God offers in order to become beings in which the image of God is restored. This tendency means that every gift and act of God can be used in some way as an idol or a replacement for God, from creation itself to the words of the gospel of salvation through Christ. God has created human life so that human beings can live, even as religious and Christian persons, as though God was irrelevant to their lives or much of them. In the end, it is the human ego that sets itself against God and seeks autonomy from God. The ego seeks to please itself first, for example, expressing itself in greed, which Paul speaks of as idolatry (Col 3:5). It may also express itself in any kind of ambition, including those found in the church. In other words, the ultimate human idol is the self. The whole purpose of the saving activity of God in becoming incarnate in Jesus Christ— dying and rising, and then sending the Holy Spirit—is to replace the idol of the self with God, virtually turning the ego inside out. And, contrary to the human view that God at the center of life means confinement and loss of freedom for the self, it means exactly the opposite: freedom and new life with true freedom in Christ. That should be our Christian witness, but it has often not been clear in Christian history and individual Christian lives.

Taking a historical view of Christian resistance to God, the fourth century marked the Christian fall for the temptation that Jesus rejected in the wilderness. In that century, Christianity became allied with the coercive power of government as a means of advancing its own goal for earthly security and power. The outcome was the creation of massive apathy among nominal Christians as members of national or ethnic churches. This took place, along with compartmentalization of the faith to the religious section of life, while otherwise pursuing personal goals. Being religious was left to the specialists. My view is that the fourth-century fall helped to create Islam and eventually Communism, both of which resisted Christianity.

The fourth-century fall was carried forward for many centuries with the many European state churches. These forms of resistance were discussed above. The reduction of the power of the church, and particularly its formal separation from government since the seventeenth century, has given a new opportunity for large numbers of Christians, not just a few specialists or "set aside ones," to live daily faithful lives. However, as in previous ages, even the Christians seeking to live daily faithful lives have divided among themselves. There are numerous divisions, but the two large divisions among Protestants are between those generally known as evangelicals, many of whom stress orthodoxy of faith apart from the established or organized church, and those generally seen as mainline Christians, who stress the encompassing fellowship in the church along with involvement in social justice issues. Others, reacting against both groups, stress spirituality apart from organized religion altogether. I have not mentioned the two older churches, the Eastern Orthodox and Roman Catholic Churches, as well as a number other churches with historic roots. This is because I am writing from within the Protestant tradition, but I believe all of the resistances mentioned in chapters 5 and 6 apply to all Christians and Christian churches. At the same time, I believe that increasing freedom of religion is exposing more clearly than ever the various forms of resistance to God found in all peoples and religions and most importantly in all forms of Christianity. There are, of course, many other forms of resistance to God revealed in Jesus Christ. C. S. Lewis wrote very perceptively on how subtle forms of resistance to God can affect individuals in his *Screwtape Letters*. I have only tried to apply some insights that I have gained from the Bible that apply primarily to groups. However, my views are certainly partial and can be elaborated and changed. What is most important is that we Christians learn from each other "in the Lord." A hopeful effect of the secularization process in history, which contains strong anti-Christian elements, is the unexpected clarification of the "faith option," in other words, the option to choose to recognize God's choice of us.

Chapter 7

Christian Claims about Jesus Christ— His Person

TURNING TO JESUS CHRIST

AFTER CHAPTER 1, WHICH deals with Jesus' favorite name for himself, the book deals with my view of reality and human beings as a whole (chapter 2), human beings as they were created with built-in longings for contact with the Divine (chapter 3), and then with the three historic religious founders who have attracted more diverse peoples than any other persons (chapter 4). Chapters 3 and 4 present an overall social scientific theory based on the observation of human behavior of why people are attracted to Jesus Christ. Of course, as a Christian, I believe God created human beings to be attracted to special persons such as Buddha, Jesus, and Muhammad. But beyond being created the way we are to be attracted to and find fulfillment in Jesus Christ, we need the special action of God to enable us to actually find and follow Jesus. Chapters 5 and 6 set forth the major reason for the need for divine help because of the resistance of human beings to God. God acted to overcome this resistance through the incarnation and atonement of Jesus Christ. Even though resistance to God continues among God's people, they are nevertheless the central means by which God makes known to all people the meaning of what Jesus Christ has done. Through the work of the Holy Spirit in using the witness of the people of God and in moving in the hearts of the hearers of their witness, God brings reconciliation and redemption to the world. Since resistance to God continues to exist in God's people, they become a major focus for the work of God, seen throughout the Bible and especially in the sending of Jesus Christ. Subsequently God continued to work in order to clarify the gospel of Jesus Christ to the world. We took up some ways we humans resist God in chapters 5 and 6 to understand the difficult task facing God's people to become what we should be. Since Christians have caused the greatest damage to the spread of the gospel of Jesus Christ, we can understand why this is the major focus of Jesus Christ and the Bible as a whole. This is what one would expect since non-believers are not expected to represent the gospel of Jesus Christ. In addition, it should be expected that the forces opposed to God would be directed especially at damaging the witness of Christians to the revelation of God through Jesus Christ.

In order to understand the gospel of Jesus Christ more fully, in the next two chapters (7 and 8) we look specifically at Jesus Christ—the claims made about his person and his work. My approach, as in "classical Christianity," is based on what the early followers of Jesus believed about him as this is revealed in the names he was called and by how they described the significance of his work. Although there are different emphases in thought and beliefs by the early followers, there is remarkable unanimity in their claims about Jesus.

I recognize that the formation of the New Testament canon and classical doctrinal statements took place over some centuries. However, in spite of the arguments of some, I believe these developments emerged from within the Christian community more than they were imposed from without or even by the leaders of Christianity. From what I know of the extra-biblical writings, it is rather plain to me that the recognized New Testament writings are superior. Even if parts of the extra-biblical writings are acceptable, the New Testament writings are clearly sufficient to convey a clear witness to Jesus Christ and his gospel. Nevertheless, the fighting among Christians in doctrinal and ecclesiastical disputes, beginning especially in the fourth century and continuing to the present, are shameful and hindered the witness to Christ.[1] The persecution of Jews up to the present has been a special hindrance to the spread of the gospel. I believe that without the alliance with government coercion enforcing orthodoxy, the Christian denominational system seen clearly now in the United States would have emerged beginning in the early centuries, especially after the church was legitimized in the beginning of the fourth century. This would have enabled the various emphases within Christianity to have emerged naturally over the course of time. Some of the extreme oppositions to Christianity, such as the Cathars of the medieval period, who were cruelly crushed, would not have emerged. Also, the terrible religious wars following the Reformation would not have taken place. Non-alliance with government coercion might have even pre-

---

1. Jenkins, *Jesus Wars*, 229–65.

vented the rise of anti-Christian elements in the secularization movement. As imperfect as it is, I believe the denominational system is better than the national and ethnic state church systems that developed in the West and the East, with their authoritarianism and coercive powers. In the denominational system, at least there is an opportunity for Christians to discuss and work with one another peacefully without military conflict, as in the centuries after the fourth century leading up to the religious wars of the sixteenth and seventeenth centuries. But let us turn now to learn about Jesus Christ.

EXTRAORDINARY CLAIMS

The Bible as a whole contains numerous claims of believers about God, a principle one being that there is one true, though mysterious, God who created and loves the world and who has acted and is active to redeem the world. I believe that the Abrahamic religions (Judaism, Christianity, and Islam) agree on this basic view of God. However, the New Testament contains added extraordinary claims about Jesus Christ as God incarnate, through whom God has personally acted and relates to human beings. The incarnation and atonement are the central expressions of God's action in Jesus Christ, revealing God's great love and compassion for all human beings. These claims go far beyond the claims made for any other founders of a religion, including the claims made for the founders of the two other most widely spreading religions, Buddhism and Islam. I said in chapter 4 that Judaism, although it won converts in the Roman Empire, did not become a spreading religion through missionary activity primarily because it did not elevate a single, tangible human being who could draw people to God through compassion and the offer of salvation to each individual. Nevertheless, Judaism, without the terrible persecution of Christians that took place under the state church, might have sustained a "Jewish Christianity" that recognized Jesus as the Messiah. Nevertheless, Judaism has been a major influence for seeking justice for all human beings based on the revelation of God in the marvelous Hebrew Scriptures, the Christian Old Testament.

The claims regarding Jesus Christ are fairly familiar and are becoming ever more familiar in the world today. They are almost too numerous to be able to list. Nevertheless, because they are so extraordinary, I will list some of the major claims regarding Jesus Christ, primarily through the names he was given. Although I believe them, my purpose is not to argue for their truth, because it was not the way of Christ to argue about who he was. Rather, my purpose is to recognize the extraordinary nature of the claims regarding Jesus and to place acceptance of them at the center of what it means to be a follower of Jesus Christ. This acceptance is more than simply an intellectual acceptance, but rather at its center is a "heart acceptance" that includes a commitment to be a follower of Jesus Christ through trust and love. I believe it is the Holy Spirit of God that makes this act of faith with commitment possible, although I also believe that the Holy Spirit works through many different circumstances and conditions, including a Christian family and social conditions in which people are free to make religious choices. Even where there is not religious freedom, people may choose to follow Christ when they learn of him.

The claims are almost too familiar because most of us Christians believe we know their meaning, when they are really symbols of deeper realities than we can fully understand. The value of chapter 1 on the most important name that Jesus used for himself, the Son of Man or the Human One, is that it reminds us of the very ambiguous meaning of this name being a key to accepting the mystery of the person of Jesus. As noted at the end of that chapter, Wink reminds us very strongly of the mystery of who Jesus was.[2] Nevertheless, I believe the Christian acceptance of the name the Human One for Jesus means that a basic Christian belief is that Jesus is the *standard* for what is a true human being—the one through whom God shows what human beings are intended to be and will become through faith, as well as what God is like, namely, the image of God.

Paul declared to the Athenians, "While God has overlooked the times of human ignorance, now he commands all people everywhere to repent [turn], because he has fixed a day on which he will have the world judged in righteousness by *a man* [italics mine] whom he has appointed, and of this he has given assurance to all by raising him from the dead" (Acts 17:30–31). This judgment is not before a throne as we imagine thrones or in a court room. Rather, this judgment is the self-evident kind spoken of in John 3:17–21, which I believe is being revealed, slowly to us, in these "last days." John in this passage emphasizes that Jesus was not sent into the world to condemn the world, but to reveal God's light in contrast to darkness. The emphasis is also that sin or resistance to God is self-punishing. The problem is that Christians have not always made the light of Christ clear so that people could perceive following Jesus Christ for what it is, namely, self-rewarding and deeply fulfilling.

As to the future, 1 John 3:2 states to believers, "Beloved, we are God's children now; what we will be has not yet been revealed. What we do know is this: when he is revealed, we will be like him, for we will see him as he is." In other words, the destiny of the redeemed is to become human beings

2. Wink, *Human Being*, 257–60.

like Jesus, restored to be in the image of God according to God's intention for human beings. At the same time, the name the Human One (the Son of Man) connects Jesus to his eschatological message and the basic message of the New Testament: the last days have been initiated; the kingdom of God has been brought to earth and the change in human beings has begun, but very slowly (as we count time) and unclearly as yet. The major names of Jesus used by his followers are discussed below because they reveal what his followers believed and claimed about him.

MESSIAH (CHRIST)

The term *messiah* means simply "anointed one." *Messiah* was applied to the Persian emperor Cyrus the Great, who enabled the Jews to return to Jerusalem from exile (Isa 45:1). However, as is well known, the term came to mean primarily the expected heir to the Davidic throne, who would bring deliverance to God's people. This was certainly the expectation of the Jewish people by the time of Jesus and it was the term applied directly to Jesus by the Apostle Peter in answer to the question, "But who do you say that I am?" (Mark 8:29). It is very important to note that Jesus, although he did not deny his messiahship, did not want it said about him because he did not want to be considered the kind of Messiah that was expected, which was the founder of a triumphant earthly kingdom.

Even at his trial, when he was asked directly, "Are you the Messiah, the Son of the Blessed One?" (Mark 14:61), Jesus refused to accept what he knew was on the mind of the high priest when the title Messiah was used. Instead, Jesus used his often-preferred title, the Son of Man (the Human One), to express the kind of role in which he saw himself: a role fulfilling the eschatological message of Daniel 7. In spite of the problem in the ordinary contemporary conception of what the Messiah was to be like, the Greek term for the Messiah, *Christos*, became the normal title used for Jesus by the followers of Jesus. In other words, he was referred to constantly by Christians then and to this day as Jesus Christ or Jesus the Messiah. This means simply that Christians then and to this day see Jesus as the fulfillment of all the Old Testament promises regarding the Coming One. Jesus reinterpreted the meaning of the Messiah by his life, death, and resurrection. Christians claim that the Messiah of this new understanding has come and he is Jesus. This means that he is the bringer of the deliverance God intends for his people, not necessarily the kind of deliverance his people may desire.

As much as people might want a deliverance that brings earthly security and makes them the dominant center for all the peoples of the world (as appears to be offered in Isa 2:1–4), Jesus offers the central kind of deliverance that God offers to humankind. This deliverance or salvation is explained in numerous ways in the New Testament, but it is essentially a reconciled relationship with God as emphasized by Paul in 2 Corinthians 5:16—6:2. As a reconciled people of God living in the world, new relationships between people become real, which leads to changed conditions of life. These changed conditions have taken place over the centuries up to the present. They begin with reconciliation to God and to one another, but given human resistance to God discussed in the previous chapters, it is not surprising that deliverance from oppressive conditions has also taken place only over centuries. The history of Israel has been repeated in the history of Christianity, both in many deliverances and rebellions. This will be discussed in chapter 9 on history subsequent to Jesus Christ on earth. Nevertheless, Paul's affirmation is that "in him [Christ] every one of God's promises is a 'Yes'" (2 Cor 1:20)—this from one who originally thought that following Jesus was diametrically opposed to the will of God and probably that it would lead to the destruction of national Judaism. There is no waiting for another Messiah, since Jesus came and accomplished what all human beings need: to be related to God by faith and to others by love. But Jews and Christians both still wait for the Messiah—Jews for his First Advent and Christians for his Second Advent. In the meantime, Jesus has been coming to human beings in the needs of other human beings and various deliverances have been taking place.

I must add a word about the issue that troubles contemporary Christianity: what is the proper relationship between bringing deliverance through personal faith in Jesus Christ and through establishing justice in social conditions. I will deal with this again in chapter 9 on subsequent history. Here I will simply state that the exodus of the Israelite slaves from Egypt is central to the emphasis in the Bible on justice as bringing deliverance to those who cannot help themselves. This is constantly repeated in the Hebrew Scriptures (the Old Testament). Note that James 1:27 speaks of "religion that is pure and undefiled" as being "to care for orphans and widows [symbolical of all who are unable to help themselves] in their distress, and to keep oneself unstained by the world." Regarding the exodus, I point out that it involved not only deliverance from the social condition of being slaves but also growing as a people of the covenant in faithfulness to God. That is why the foundational Ten Commandments were given. That is why in the Bible the spiritual life of faithfulness and deliverance from unjust social conditions are not separated.

Christians need to show ethnic Jews that they are loved and highly respected for the contribution of their experience told in the Hebrew

Scriptures. Their love of nature for its basic goodness and of justice in human affairs is especially appreciated. I would like to believe that if more or perhaps a majority of Jews had accepted Jesus as the Messiah, and the state church had not been established with Jews suffering terrible persecutions, that a Jewish Christian denomination might have been established. That would have contributed greatly to Christian understanding of the Hebrew Scriptures and the Jewish character of Jesus, as well, of course, of the unity of evangelism and action for social justice.

SON OF GOD

Jesus is referred to throughout the New Testament as the Son of God. The title begins to be used from the time of Jesus' baptism, when a voice is heard from heaven saying, "You are my Son, the Beloved" (Mark 1:11). Matthew (3:17) adds, "with whom I am well pleased," and Luke (3:22) adds, "with you I am well pleased" or, according to some texts, "You are my Son, today I have begotten you." In John 1:34, John the Baptist states after the baptism of Jesus, "I myself have seen and have testified that this is the Son of God."

In John 5:19–29 there is an exchange of Jesus with people in which he refers to "the Father" and then to himself a number of times as "the Son." He makes the reference to himself again as "the Son" in John 8:36. Even though in these passages Jesus refers to God as his personal Father and to himself as the Son, he still also refers to "the Son" as "the Son of Man" (John 5:27; 8:28). The Son of Man remained his favorite title for himself, even though he did not hesitate to claim a special relationship to God the Father as "the Son." In John 5:27, "the Son of Man" is made the standard of judgment at the resurrection, just as Paul stated to the Athenians (Acts 17:31).

The title Son of God is also used by forces of evil. In the wilderness, the tempter says, "if you are the Son of God, command these stones to become bread," and again, "If you are the Son of God, throw yourself down" off of the temple (Matt 4:3, 6). Mark 3:11–12 reports, "Whenever the unclean spirits saw him, they fell down before him and shouted, 'You are the Son of God!'" But Jesus "sternly ordered them not to make him known." As with the term "Messiah," Jesus wanted to establish his own identity and not accept the identity conferred on him by others with the wrong connotations and in an inappropriate manner. Nevertheless, the term "Son" is applied again to Jesus, but here it is by God at the transfiguration: "This is my Son, the Beloved" (Mark 9:7). Matt (17:5) adds, "with whom I am well pleased." In Luke (9:35) it is, "This is my Son, the Chosen." These statements are a reaffirmation of the statements made at his baptism. In all cases at the transfiguration the disciples are told to "listen to him!"

In John's (1:18) prologue we read, "No one has ever seen God. It is God the only Son [alternatives are 'It is an only Son, God' or 'It is the only Son'], who is close to the Father's heart, who has made him known." John 3:16 also makes the famous statement, "For God so loved the world that he gave his only Son, so that everyone who believes in him may not perish but may have eternal life." John makes the most use of the title Son for Jesus. For example we read in 3:35–36, "The Father loves the Son and has placed all things in his hands. Whoever believes in the Son has eternal life; whoever disobeys the Son will not see life, but must endure God's wrath." It is worth noting here that "disobeys the Son" indicates that following Jesus does not mean simply making an affirmation, but means a life of "walking in the way." It is also worth noting that the "wrath of God" does not refer so much to an emotional state, as it might in human beings, but to a separation from God or living apart from communion with God that is basically self-imposed. "Wrath" conveys the sense of the terrible condition brought on the self by rejection of the salvation offered in Jesus. In John 10:34–38, in another dialogue when Jesus is accused of making himself God, Jesus asks:

> Is it not written in your law, "I said, you are gods"? If those to whom the word of God came were called "gods"—and the scripture cannot be annulled—can you say that the one whom the Father has sanctified and sent into the world is blaspheming because I said, "I am God's Son"? If I am not doing the works of my Father, then do not believe me. But if I do them, even though you do not believe me, believe the works, so that you may know and understand that the Father is in me and I am in the Father.

In this interesting dialogue, Jesus affirms his special relationship to the Father that is signified by the word "Son"; but at the same time he does not want his hearers to focus on names, but on what he is doing. His words also show that the way Jesus presents himself was not highly aggressive ("a bruised reed shall he not break"; Matt 12:20). We are reminded here that Son of God, like Son of Man, can be ambiguous, contrary to what many Christians may think. As Boyarin points out, "the son of God" is actually used as a primary reference to the human king of Israel.[3] Thus Jesus wants his hearers to know that they may be, or may become, sons of God. Here again Jesus is referring to the human destiny to become divine, but there clearly are levels of divinity.

---

3. Boyarin, *Jewish Gospels*, 26–31, 47.

Of course, the term "son of God" has nothing to do with biological descent, but refers to "having proceeded from" and "being intimately related to as a child to a parent." The concept of biological descent from God is a great problem for Muslims, but this does not occur to Christians in thinking of "the Son of God." The term can be applied to all people because all people proceeded from God, as Paul reminds the Athenians, quoting their poets: "for we too are God's offspring" (Acts 17:28). Jesus even wanted his hearers to know that they could be called gods, meaning they were closely related to God and have a supernatural nature. Human beings are not simply animals. Thus, it is clear in the New Testament that the sonship of Jesus Christ is comparable in *some respects* to the sonship of all people. In Mark 3:35 Jesus declares that all who do the will of God are his brother, his sister, and his mother. As already noted in chapter 1, he also places himself on the level of humanity with his name the Son of Man, or the Human One. Nevertheless, Christ's sonship is on a different level from that of all other people because of his special relationship to God the Father. John 3:16 speaks of Jesus as God's "only [*monogene*] Son." This can be understood as "unique in kind" or the "only example of its category." To refer to Jesus as God's Son is certainly a favorite designation throughout the New Testament in the various literary traditions and undoubtedly reflected a common designation given to Jesus among the Christians. Nevertheless, it is important to recognize that the name Son of God in itself is not necessarily a reference to divinity. The Israelite kings, for example, were spoken of as sons of God. At the same time, the title in the New Testament points toward divinity. It is important in interpreting the Bible to become accustomed to ambiguity and double or more meanings. At the same time, I would say that we should not put too much weight on mere words, as some Christians do, but rather on the reality that is behind them and to which they point, much of it beyond our understanding.

THE COSMIC CHRIST: IMAGE OF GOD AND WORD OF GOD

Probably the divinity of Jesus is emphasized more strongly by the term "image of God" and its associations than by the term "Son of God," but again the term points toward both humanity and divinity. Most people are familiar with the statement in Genesis 1:26 that human beings were made "in the image of God." This statement turns on its head the common use of the word "image," which refers to what human beings create from their concepts of supernatural beings. It is primarily the Pauline writings (the earliest Christian literature that we have) that use the term "image of God" to refer to Jesus Christ, but it is especially what God accomplishes through Christ in both creation and redemption that points to his divinity. In Colossians 1:15–20 Paul makes the most complete statement of the Cosmic Christ found in the New Testament:

> He [Christ] is the image of the invisible God, the firstborn of all creation; for in him all things in heaven and on earth were created, things visible and invisible, whether thrones or dominions or rulers or powers—all things have been created through him and for him. He himself is before all things, and in him all things hold together. He is the head of the body, the church; he is the beginning, the firstborn from the dead, so that he might come to have first place in everything. For in him all the fullness of God was pleased to dwell, and through him God was pleased to reconcile to himself all things, whether on earth or in heaven, by making peace through the blood of the cross.

Not only is Jesus Christ the image of God, but, as already seen above, God's purpose is to change believers into that image, namely, to make people to become like Christ; and that process is accomplished through Christ and the Holy Spirit. The process begins in this life for believers: "And all of us, with unveiled faces, seeing the glory of the Lord as though reflected in a mirror, are being transformed into the same image from one degree of glory to another, for this comes from the Lord, the Spirit" (2 Cor 3:18). It is the destiny of the redeemed: "Just as we have borne the image of the man of dust, we will also bear the image of the man of heaven" (1 Cor 15:49).

Another clear reference to Jesus as being like the image of God, without using the term "image," is made in Hebrews 1:3: "He is the reflection of God's glory and the exact imprint of God's very being, and he sustains all things by his powerful word." The Greek term *charackter* means impressed character, which is translated "express image" in the King James Version, "the very stamp of his nature" in the Revised Standard Version, and "exact imprint" in the New Revised Standard Version. The writer of the Letter to the Hebrews is using a term that refers to the impression, reproduction, or representation made on coins. What is more, classical Greek writers use this term to state that human beings were made in the form of God. Another term, *eikon*, is also used by Greek writers to refer both to representations on coins and to the creation of human beings in God's image.

The Johanine literature does not use the image term but another term to refer to the Cosmic Christ: the "Word" (*Logos*). In both cases, the connection of Jesus with creation as being the means of creation is made explicit. The famous opening of the Gospel of John (1:1–5) states:

> In the beginning was the Word, and the Word was with God, and the Word was God. He was in the beginning with God. All things came into being through him, and without him not one thing came into being. What has come into being in him was life, and the life was the light of all people. The light shines in the darkness, and the darkness did not overcome it.

In the Book of Revelation, the Rider on the White Horse in the triumphant vision in chapter 19 has the name "the Word of God" (Rev 19:13), and a little later we see on his robe and thigh the name "King of kings and Lord of lords" (19:16). As the Word of God, Jesus is clearly both coexistent with the Father and, as Paul had affirmed in Colossians, the means of God's creation of all things. There is a remarkable parallel in Proverbs 8:22–31 between the role of Wisdom and the Word, showing this early sensibility to the extension of God in the creation of all things. In the Gospel of John and Colossians this cosmic status is given to Jesus Christ. He is the means of both the creation and upholding of all things in nature and of the new creation that has begun in the redemptive action of God that will be completed at the end of history in a "new heaven and a new earth." This brings us to the terms used for Jesus Christ that relate him directly to the work of salvation.

SAVIOR

Joseph is told to name the son of Mary Jesus, "for he will save his people from their sins" (Matt 1:21). The name Jesus comes from Joshua, referring to salvation. The angels announce to the shepherds that there is born to them "in the city of David a Savior, who is the Messiah, the Lord" (Luke 2:11). The Samaritans, after having met and heard Jesus, tell the woman who had met Jesus at the well, "It is no longer because of what you have said that we believe, for we have heard for ourselves, and we know that this is truly the Savior of the world" (John 4:42).

When Peter and others are called before the priestly council, Peter states of Jesus, "God exalted him at his right hand as Leader and Savior that he might give repentance to Israel and forgiveness of sins" (Acts 5:31). In his sermon in the synagogue in Antioch in Pisidia, Paul declares, "Of this man's [David's] posterity God has brought to Israel a Savior, Jesus, as he promised" (Acts 13:23).

In the New Testament letters there are numerous references to Jesus as Savior, although God the Father is *also* referred to as Savior. For example, in the First Letter to Timothy 1:1, we read, "Paul, an apostle of Christ Jesus by the command of God our Savior and of Christ Jesus our hope." Later in the letter we read: "For to this end we toil and struggle, because we have our hope set on the living God, who is the Savior of all people, especially of those who believe" (4:10). However, in the Second Letter to Timothy 1:9–10 we read, "This grace was given to us in Christ Jesus before the ages began, but it has now been revealed through the appearing of our Savior Christ Jesus, who abolished death and brought life and immortality to light through the gospel." Thus, salvation comes through both God the Father and Jesus Christ, the Son. Notice that grace came through Christ Jesus before Jesus existed on earth. The language of God the Father and Jesus as Savior is also used in the Letter to Titus 1:3–4, where we read of "God our Savior" and "Christ Jesus our Savior." In First John 4:14 it is stated plainly, "And we have seen and do testify that the Father has sent his Son as the Savior of the world." If there is any confusion, it is clear that God acted to save the world by sending Jesus Christ, who carried out the work of salvation, so that both God the Father and God the Son may be spoken of as Savior.

If it is asked, "Savior from what?" there are numerous answers that are possible, because there are numerous words to describe the human condition. Perhaps the simplest answer was given to Joseph when he was told "he will save his people from their sins" (Matt 1:21). Once again there are many words to describe the human sinful condition. It is important that the whole Bible be taken into account, beginning with the fall in Genesis 3. It is especially important not to rely on conventional concepts of sin, such as the "seven deadly sins."

Conventional concepts of sin tend to be both individualistic and focused on the "sins of the flesh" while largely ignoring the unconscious sins of omission, such as "passing by on the other side" of human suffering. The basic condition of sin is theological as represented in Genesis 3, when human beings acted on the basis of what was good for themselves without reference to God's command and then hid from God. Salvation, then, is overcoming the separation between God and human beings created by the human loss of trust or faith in God. All the bad behavior that flows from non-faith comes out of the condition of separation in which human beings are focused on themselves instead of on God and God's will.

The work of salvation, in addition to bringing reconciliation to individuals, is a process for the group known in the Bible as the people or household of God. It begins with the call to Abraham and covenant with him, which is extended to his descendants who live by faith. Salvation continues through the exodus of the Israelite slaves combined with the revealing of God's nature and will. This work of salvation reaches a climax in the sending of Jesus Christ, the Savior of the world, who does the work of reconciliation through his death and resurrection. Then the work of salvation continues "in the last days" that Christ introduced and is proceeding to this day as the gospel spreads around the world. The reconciling work of Christ that is central to this salvation has never stopped to this day. This leads to another term for Jesus Christ.

MEDIATOR

"Mediator" is not an often-used term, but the concept of reconciliation behind it is a central one. First, the idea of mediation is used to refer to the one, namely Moses, through whom God dealt with his people in giving them the law after he had already given them the promise through Abraham. This reference is made in Galatians 3:19–20: "it [the law] was ordained through angels by a mediator." The writer of the Letter to the Hebrews, who relies on an understanding of the sacrificial system of the Old Testament, makes the most use of the concept of a mediator in declaring Jesus as Mediator of a new and better covenant based on better promises (Heb 8:6; 9:15; 12:24).

We read in 1 Timothy 2:3–6 a very complete statement of the mediating work of Jesus Christ. The faithful are urged to pray for those in high positions, so that Christians

> may lead a quiet and peaceable life in all godliness and dignity. This is right and is acceptable in the sight of God our Savior, who desires everyone to be saved and to come to the knowledge of the truth. For there is one God; there is also one mediator between God and humankind, Christ Jesus, himself human, who gave himself a ransom for all—this was attested at the right time.

It is very likely that the sentence beginning "there is one God" is part of a hymn sung by early Christians. This would mean that the term "mediator" was well known to Christians and sung in their worship services. Notice the importance of the mediator being a human.

The Letter to the Hebrews develops the basis for the mediating work of Jesus Christ in its outline of his priestly function, foreshadowed by the sacrificial system in the Old Testament, of offering himself as a sacrifice on behalf of the sins of people. Because of the mediating role of Christ, a "new and living way" was opened so that those with faith could boldly "approach the throne of grace" (Heb 4:16). The separation caused by sin was bridged by

Jesus Christ through his once-for-all sacrificial death. Jesus Christ had offered "for all time a single sacrifice for sins," and he is now seated at the right hand of God waiting "until his enemies would be made a footstool for his feet" (Heb 10:12–13). The old "dominion language" ("footstall for his feet") is applied not to the conquest of an earthly kingdom, but to the conquest of human hearts—the goal of God. "Enemies," of course, are not simply people who overtly resist God, but all human beings (we might especially include Christians), who have a built-in resistance to God, as we have seen.

The Apostle Paul, without using the term "mediator," expresses the language of the work of mediation or of bridging the gap of separation between God and human beings. Speaking of God's new creation in Christ, Paul adds in 2 Corinthians 5:18–21:

> All this is from God, who reconciled us to himself through Christ, and has given us the ministry of reconciliation; that is, in Christ God was reconciling the world to himself, not counting their trespasses against them, and entrusting the message of reconciliation to us. So we are ambassadors for Christ, since God is making his appeal through us; we entreat you on behalf of Christ, be reconciled to God. For our sake he made him to be sin who knew no sin, so that in him we might become the righteousness of God.

A theme of the New Testament is condensed into this paragraph with an emphasis on carrying out a ministry of reconciliation among fellow human beings. The theme of reconciliation by the blood (death) of Christ is again emphasized in Ephesians, with the twofold direction of reconciliation to God and reconciliation to others, especially between Gentiles and Jews. Thus, the mediation of Christ is carried forward by the message and acts of reconciliation of his followers.

LORD

"Lord" is a term that could be applied in New Testament times to almost anyone in authority, especially if one wanted to show subservience. It is certainly true that subservience to those of higher status was commonly expressed in ancient societies. However, in addition, "Lord" was (is) a term that was repeatedly applied to God; for example, "The Lord is my Shepherd, I shall not want . . . " (Ps 23:1). Thus, the term is ambiguous as far as being applied to God and to human beings, but it is a term that Jesus accepted, also recognizing that it could be used superficially. For example, Jesus famously stated:

> Not everyone who says to me "Lord, Lord" will enter the king-
> dom of heaven, but only the one who does the will of my Father
> in heaven. On that day many will say to me, "Lord, Lord, did we
> not prophesy in your name, and cast out demons in your name,
> and do many deeds of power in your name?" Then I will declare
> to them, "I never knew you; go away from me, you evil doers."
> (Matt 7:21–23)

Nevertheless, Jesus accepted the designation of Lord. He told his disciples after washing their feet, "You call me Teacher and Lord—and you
are right, for that is what I am. So if I, your Lord and Teacher, have washed
your feet, you also ought to wash one another's feet" (John 13:13–14). Just as
with the term *messiah*, Jesus was reluctant to accept the usual connotation
of what a Lord should be. But also just as with Messiah, Lord became the
common designation for Jesus in the early church, creating the full title,
"the Lord Jesus Christ [*Messiah*]," as in a common salutation or farewell,
"Grace to you and peace from God our Father and the Lord Jesus Christ"
(Gal 1:3) and, "The grace of the Lord Jesus Christ, the love of God, and the
communion of the Holy Spirit be with all of you" (2 Cor 13:13). At other
times, simply "Lord" or "Lord Jesus" was sufficient. "Jesus Christ, our Lord"
is used repeatedly.

In his sermon on Pentecost, Peter declared, "Therefore let the entire
house of Israel know with certainty that God has made him both Lord and
Messiah, this Jesus whom you crucified." But he went on to call on people
to repent and be baptized, adding, "For the promise is for you, for your
children, and for all who are far away, everyone whom the Lord our God
calls to him" (Acts 2:36, 39). Paul echoes these words when he says, "The
scripture says, 'No one who believes in him will be put to shame.' For there
is no distinction between Jew and Greek; the same Lord is Lord of all and is
generous to all who call on him. For 'Everyone who calls on the name of the
Lord shall be saved'" (Rom 10:11–13).

With the common use of Lord to refer to both God and Jesus Christ,
it is no wonder that the earliest confession in the church is thought to be
"Jesus is Lord." This confession is made in the last words of the hymn in
Philippians:

> Therefore God also highly exalted him and gave him the name
> that is above every name, so that at the name of Jesus every knee
> should bend, in heaven and on earth and under the earth, and
> every tongue should confess that Jesus Christ is Lord, to the
> glory of God the Father. (2:9–11)

An important result of the application of "Lord" to Jesus is that the application of this term to others has declined over the centuries, especially in the modern world. This has been accompanied by the emphasis on the equality of all human beings. If Jesus is Lord, no one else is truly Lord over our lives.

CONCLUSION

The extraordinary claims Christians made about Jesus Christ revealed in the names and titles given to him are far beyond the claims ever made for any other human being. The only possible comparison would be with claims made about mythological figures or rulers, but none of them lived up to the character of Jesus or accomplished what he accomplished, as discussed in the next chapter. Of course, classical Christianity has always claimed that he was not just a human being, although it was believed that he also was a true human being and it was highly important to affirm that. To not affirm that was actually to place oneself on the side of the opposition to Christ according to 2 John 7: "Many deceivers have gone out into the world, those who do not confess that Jesus Christ has come in the flesh; any such person is the deceiver and the antichrist!" The only course for Christianity has been to affirm the mysterious doctrine of the incarnation: that Jesus Christ is fully human and fully divine! But the claims regarding Jesus Christ are not completed in the titles used for him. There are also important claims regarding his work. In the end, as we shall see, the claims regarding Jesus Christ are self-authenticating to his followers.

Chapter 8

Christian Claims about Jesus Christ— His Work

THE CENTRALITY OF THE DEATH AND RESURRECTION OF JESUS CHRIST

THE NEW TESTAMENT NOT only contains the extraordinary claims about the person of Jesus Christ, but the claims about his accomplishments and ongoing work, much of it implied in his names and titles, are just as astounding, if not more so. The gospel accounts give a strong hint about the central accomplishment of Christ by the space they devote to his last week followed by his resurrection appearances.

A clear turning point in the synoptic gospels can be seen after the confession made by Peter in answer to the question, "But who do you say that I am?" (Mark 8:29). It is after this point in the three synoptic gospels that we begin to hear Jesus speaking of his coming death and resurrection, and we see the aim of Jesus to go to Jerusalem to finish what he came to do. This turning point is followed by the special experience of Peter, James, and John with Jesus on the Mount of Transfiguration in which the whole appearance of Jesus was changed. Following this, he was seen conversing with Moses and Elijah, representatives of the law and the prophets, and then they were told, "listen to him!" That gave the disciples the background experience with which to not be overwhelmed by what was to come. Nevertheless, they were overwhelmed with grief, but this experience was remembered in the early church (2 Pet 1:16–18).

At a key point on this last approach to Jerusalem the disciples argued once again about their future status and then were made angry by a request from the mother of James and John to Jesus that a special place be given to her sons. Jesus said, "For the Son of Man came not to be served but to serve, and to give his life a ransom for many" (Mark 10:45). Jesus knew that the climax of his ministry would be the giving of his life for the salvation of others. Furthermore, this act was to form the major model for how he wanted his disciples to act toward others, beginning with one another.

The epistles, most of which are the earliest Christian literature, very definitely emphasize the death and resurrection of Christ. In a summary of his message to the people, Paul states:

> Now I would remind you, brothers and sisters, of the good news that I proclaimed to you, which you in turn received, in which also you stand, through which also you are being saved, if you hold firmly to the message that I proclaimed to you—unless you have come to believe in vain. For I handed on to you as of first importance what I in turn had received: that Christ died for our sins in accordance with the scriptures, and that he was buried, and that he was raised on the third day in accordance with the scriptures, and that he appeared to Cephas, then to the twelve. Then he appeared to more than five hundred brothers and sisters at one time, most of whom are still alive, though some have died. Then he appeared to James, then to all the apostles. Last of all, as to one untimely born, he appeared also to me. (1 Cor 15:1–8)

Notice Paul's matter-of-fact way of expressing these major events so as to emphasize them as facts. Paul wanted to make sure the readers understood that he did not originate the gospel message containing these facts, but rather he preached a message that was the same as the message given to and conveyed by all of the apostles, including James, the brother of the Lord. James had not been one of the Twelve, but he became the major leader of the church in Jerusalem. My opinion is that he may have looked and sounded like Jesus; but whatever the case, it can be seen that at the meeting in Jerusalem in Acts 15, James had the last word. Without going into all that the death of Jesus Christ on the cross may mean, it is clear that it was directly related to the salvation of human beings from sin. The fact that Christ's death was followed by the resurrection confirmed the victory of Christ and his divinity. Bart Ehrman, from a strictly historical perspective (a perspective that he continually asserts means neutrality in belief), affirms that belief in the reality of the resurrection of Jesus was the central belief of early Christians; without it there would be no Christianity.[1]

At the same time, along with the resurrection, an emphasis on the death of Christ and its meaning is maintained throughout all the letters of the New

---

1. Ehrman, *How Jesus Became God*, 204.

Testament. In 1 Peter 2:24-25 it is affirmed, "He himself bore our sins in his body on the cross, so that, free from sins, we might live for righteousness; by his wounds you have been healed. For you were going astray like sheep, but now you have returned to the shepherd and guardian of your souls."

The Letter to the Hebrews places special emphasis on the sacrificial death of Christ, who acted as an eternal high priest in offering, not an animal sacrifice like ordinary priests, but himself to become a means for human beings to be able to approach the presence of God. Among the many passages referring to his sacrifice, we read in 9:11-14:

> But when Christ came as a high priest of the good things that have come, then through the greater and perfect tent (not made with hands, that is, not of this creation), he entered once for all into the Holy Place, not with the blood of goats and calves, but with his own blood, thus obtaining eternal redemption. For if the blood of goats and bulls, with the sprinkling of the ashes of a heifer, sanctifies those who have been defiled so that their flesh is purified, how much more will the blood of Christ, who through the eternal Spirit offered himself without blemish to God, purify our conscience from dead works to worship the living God!

Using the metaphor of the sacrificial system that preceded the coming of the Christ, in this and many other passages the writer makes clear that the death of Jesus Christ serves as a means for believers to enter into the presence of God.

The First Letter of John makes a clear reference to the central importance of the death of Jesus Christ in the life of believers: "My little children, I am writing these things to you so that you may not sin. But if anyone does sin, we have an advocate with the Father, Jesus Christ the righteous; and he is the atoning sacrifice for our sins, and not for ours only but also for the sins of the whole world" (2:1-2).

The Gospel of John places more emphasis than the synoptic gospels on the mystical union of Jesus Christ with his followers, but this mystical union is made possible by the death of Jesus. It is made clear according to John that Jesus saw his coming death as the means by which he would provide eternal life to believers. When Greeks came seeking him, Jesus saw this as a sign of his coming death. Among other things, he said, "And I, when I am lifted up from the earth, will draw all people to myself." John adds, "He said this to indicate the kind of death he was to die" (John 12:32-33).

Luke reported in one of the resurrection appearances (Luke 24:24-25) that Jesus has an extended conversation with two followers on the road to Emmaus. In this conversation Jesus says, "Oh, how foolish you are and how slow of heart to believe all that the prophets have declared! Was it not necessary that the Messiah should suffer these things and then enter into his glory?"

The death of Christ is closely linked repeatedly to his resurrection, as seen in the important passage quoted above from 1 Corinthians 15. In one of the few examples of a sermon to Gentiles, the Apostle Peter states to a group of Gentiles at the home of the centurion Cornelius:

> You know the message he [God] sent to the people of Israel, preaching peace by Jesus Christ—he is Lord of all. That message spread throughout Judea, beginning in Galilee after the baptism that John announced: how God anointed Jesus of Nazareth with the Holy Spirit and with power; how he went about doing good and healing all who were oppressed by the devil, for God was with him. We are witnesses to all that he did both in Judea and in Jerusalem. They put him to death by hanging him on a tree; but God raised him on the third day and allowed him to appear, not to all the people but to us who were chosen by God as witnesses, and who ate and drank with him after he rose from the dead. He commanded us to preach to the people and to testify that he is the one ordained by God as judge of the living and the dead. All the prophets testify about him that everyone who believes in him receives forgiveness of sins through his name. (Acts 10:36–43)

In the only other sermon to Gentiles in Acts (not counting the interrupted sermon to Gentiles in Lystra; 14:15–17), Paul gives special emphasis to the resurrection of Jesus Christ as evidence of God making him the standard by which humanity is to be judged (17:22–31). Although being raised from the dead implies the death of Jesus, there is good reason to believe that this sermon was cut short like the one in Lystra or at least only summarized. We know from Paul's writings that he had much to say about both the death and resurrection of Jesus. However, there is an additional theme found especially in both the Gospel of John and in Paul's writings. This leads to the next consideration. I like to emphasize that both Peter and Paul (very high authorities) in approaching Gentile unbelievers are complementary to them and do not emphasize their sin. They bring good news!

MYSTICAL UNION OF BELIEVERS WITH JESUS CHRIST

The new life lived in relationship with God, made possible by the death and resurrection of Jesus Christ, would not be possible without Christians' experiencing a continuing mystical union with Christ in his death and resurrection. This continuing access to God established by Jesus is maintained through an ongoing mystical union with Christ. The Gospel of John especially reflects the importance of this union in the passage from chapter 6, in which Jesus uses the difficult words referring to eating his flesh and drinking his blood. He makes clear that this refers to a continuing mystical union: "Those who eat my flesh and drink my blood abide in me, and I in them." This mystical union made possible by Jesus is again made a central part of the mission of Christ to his followers when we hear Christ say, "Abide in me as I abide in you. Just as the branch cannot bear fruit by itself unless it abides in the vine, neither can you unless you abide in me" (John 15:4).

Before John's gospel was written, the Apostle Paul emphasized the mystical union of believers with Christ. In a number of passages he describes the union with Christ as an experience of death followed by life. In Romans 6:3–11 we read:

> Do you not know that all of us who have been baptized into Christ Jesus were baptized into his death? Therefore we have been buried with him by baptism into death, so that, just as Christ was raised from the dead by the glory of the Father, so we too might walk in newness of life. For if we have been united with him in a death like his, we will certainly be united with him in a resurrection like his. We know that our old self was crucified with him so that the body of sin might be destroyed, and we might no longer be enslaved to sin. For whoever has died is freed from sin. But if we have died with Christ, we believe that we will also live with him. We know that Christ, being raised from the dead, will never die again; death no longer has dominion over him. The death he died, he died to sin, once for all; but the life he lives, he lives to God. So you also must consider yourselves dead to sin and alive to God in Christ Jesus.

Paul speaks of his own personal experience of death and life in Christ in Galatians 2:19–20: "For through the law I died to the law, so that I might live to God. I have been crucified with Christ; and it is no longer I who live, but it is Christ who lives in me. And the life I now live in the flesh I live by faith in the Son of God, who loved me and gave himself for me." The fact that the mystical experience of death and resurrection with Christ are simultaneous or undivided is expressed by Paul when he writes about his goal in life in Philippians 3:10–11: "I want to know Christ and the power of his resurrection and the sharing of his sufferings by becoming like him in his death, if somehow I may attain the resurrection from the dead." Note that knowing "the sharing of his sufferings" is actually placed after knowing "the power of his resurrection," showing that resurrection and suffering with Christ are simultaneous experiences.

The mystical experience of death and resurrection with Christ in this life is a preparation for the final experience of death and resurrection. Although physical death is not considered good in the New Testament, as well as in the Hebrew Scriptures (consider Jesus raising people from the dead), neither is it dreaded or feared (Heb 2:15—believers are freed from slavery to the fear of death). The dreaded death in the New Testament is the death from sin that means separation from God. This is the death from which we are saved by the death of Christ. The resurrection or new life that results from this experience is a foretaste of the final resurrection after our physical deaths. Notice that we have already been raised and seated with him in heavenly places, but this is only the beginning. Paul states in Ephesians 2:4–7:

> But God, who is rich in mercy, out of his great love with which
> he loved us even when we were dead through our trespasses,
> made us alive together with Christ—by grace you have been
> saved—and raised us up with him and seated us with him in
> the heavenly places in Christ Jesus, so that in the ages to come
> he might show the immeasurable riches of his grace in kindness
> toward us in Christ Jesus.

Paul exults at the end of his great "resurrection chapter" (1 Cor 15:54–57), "Death has been swallowed up in victory. Where, O death, is your victory? Where, O death, is your sting? The sting of death is sin, and the power of sin is the law. But thanks be to God, who gives us the victory through our Lord Jesus Christ."

THE ONGOING WORK OF CHRIST—THE MEANS

Jesus Christ finished the work he came to do when he died and rose again; his death does not need to be repeated. Paul states, "The death he died, he died to sin, once for all; but the life he lives, he lives to God" (Rom 6:10). The Letter to the Hebrews reinforces this truth by saying:

> But as it is, he has appeared once for all at the end of the age to
> remove sin by the sacrifice of himself. And just as it is appointed
> for mortals to die once, and after that the judgment, so Christ,
> having been offered *once* [italics mine] to bear the sins of many,
> will appear a second time, not to deal with sin, but to save those
> who are eagerly waiting for him." (9:26–28)

According to John 19:30, Jesus himself on the cross declared, "It is finished!" According to the New Testament, there is no need for Jesus to die again for the sins of the world. Many people do not understand that this is the basis for the doctrine of the "sufficiency of the Bible." It is not necessary to add more to the Bible because the Bible itself is dependent on the "once for all-ness" of the death and resurrection of Christ and its sufficiency for our salvation. We do not need another death and resurrection from Jesus Christ.

Having said this, it is also clear from Scripture that Christ himself recognized he was leaving a great work to be done, and he would not leave the work only to his unaided followers. He himself would be present with them and working in them. That was his promise stated after giving the Great Commission in Matthew 28:18–20: "And remember, I am with you always, to the end of the age." Little mention has been made so far of the third person of the Trinity, but in the Gospel of John (14:15–18, 25, 26; 15:26, 27; 16:12–15) Jesus speaks extensively about the Holy Spirit that will be sent to the disciples. Again in Acts 1:5, 7, 8 the disciples are told to wait in Jerusalem until they receive power from the baptism of the Holy Spirit. In fact, the baptism of the Holy Spirit with fire had already been mentioned at the baptism of Jesus (Mark 1:8; Matt 3:11).

The Holy Spirit is mentioned throughout the Book of Acts and the epistles. Paul refers repeatedly to the Holy Spirit in chapter 8 of his Letter to the Romans. Christians are to live according to the Spirit. The mystical union of Christ with believers in which death and resurrection are experienced is made possible by the Holy Spirit. In Romans 8:11, 13–14 Paul states:

> If the Spirit of him who raised Jesus from the dead dwells in you, he who raised Christ from the dead will give life to your mortal bodies also through his Spirit that dwells in you . . . for if you live according to the flesh, you will die; but if by the Spirit you put to death the deeds of the body, you will live. For all who are led by the Spirit of God are children of God.

It is important to remember that in this passage and others "the flesh" and "the body" are not simply the physical body, but rather the fallen nature that is directed away from God. In other words, "the flesh" does not refer simply to what we call "the sins of the flesh," although they are included. This misunderstanding has plagued Christians throughout history. It is highly important to remember that Jesus was rejected and killed by "good religious people," and religious people continue to be at the center of the Opposition to the kingdom (the capital O representing evil on a large scale), as I have written about elsewhere.[2] The most effective work of evil in opposing God is when opposition comes from the people of God or the church.

One of the most important works of the Holy Spirit in the church according to the Apostle Paul is to produce "fruit," which is the kind of life that witnesses effectively to Christ. In his letter to the Gentile Galatians, Paul contrasts the works of the flesh, many of which were manifest in contemporary Gentile life ("fornication, impurity, licentiousness, idolatry, sorcery, enmities, strife, jealousy, anger, quarrels, dissensions, factions, envy, drunkenness, carousing, and things like these"), with the fruit (singular) of the Spirit, which is "love, joy, peace, patience, kindness, generosity, faithfulness, gentleness, and self-control" (Gal 5:19–23). The works of the flesh obviously include sexual sins so often thought of as sins of the flesh, but they clearly are much broader, and an emphasis can be seen to be on attitudes and behaviors that are hurtful to the Christian communal life. The mystical union is mentioned again in connection with the Holy Spirit: "And those who belong to Christ Jesus have crucified the flesh with its passions and desires. If we live by the Spirit, let us also be guided by the Spirit. Let us not become conceited, competing against one another, envying one another" (Gal 5:24–26).

The concern of Paul for the life of the church as an effective witness to Jesus Christ is shown especially in his discussion of the gifts of the Spirit in 1 Corinthians 12 and 14. Diversity in the church should be expected and not allowed to become a basis for competition or envy. In fact, the Holy Spirit gives diverse gifts to the church so that its work and witness will be many-faceted and effective. Nevertheless, in the remarkable (beautiful and poetic) 1 Corinthians 13 chapter, Paul makes clear that if the primary fruit of the Holy Spirit, which is love, is not manifested in and through the gifts used in ministry, then whatever gifts people may have are useless—even worse than useless. Having the fruit of the Spirit is thus more important than having a gift of the Spirit used in ministry. One of the most important verses for the Christian community, in which there are many educated and talented people, may be Paul's word to the Corinthians, "Knowledge puffs up, but love builds up" (1 Cor 8:1). In the end, it is only love, which is the power of the Holy Spirit, that can bring diverse Christians and diverse denominations together, as stated at the end of chapter 6.

The New Testament does not hide the fact, and certainly Christian history plainly shows, that although Jesus Christ completed his work for our salvation and for the inauguration of the church in the world through the special outpouring of the Holy Spirit, human history is the arena in which God continues the work of redeeming the world in the *missio Dei*,

2. Montgomery, *Real New Age*, 71.

the mission of God. The means by which God is carrying out this work in the world, then, is through the Holy Spirit working in the followers of Jesus Christ, who are appointed as witness to Christ. But what is the goal of God's work in the world?

THE ONGOING WORK OF CHRIST—THE GOAL

The Letter to the Ephesians 1:9–10 announces the goal of God: "He has made known to us the mystery of his will, according to his good pleasure that he set forth in Christ, as a plan for the fullness of time, to gather up all things in him, things in heaven and things on earth." Paul uses the phrase "fullness of time" in a historic sense in Galatians 4:4: "But when the fullness of time had come, God sent his Son, born of a woman, born under the law, in order to redeem those who were under the law, so that we might receive adoption as children." Thus, the fullness of time in which Christ came inaugurated the fullness of time in which we live, characterized by the gathering up of all things. This fits with the eschatological message of the New Testament that Christ introduced the last period of history or "the last days." Hebrews 1:2 announces, "in these last days he [God] has spoken to us by a Son." We are in the last days in which God is accomplishing his purpose and these last days have existed since Jesus Christ came, in other words, about two thousand years ago.

Jesus announced at the first of his ministry, "The time is fulfilled, and the kingdom of God has come near, repent and believe the good news" (Mark 1:15; compare Matt 4:17). The kingdom of God is not something only for the next world or at the end of our present time. At his hometown, Jesus in Luke 4:18–19 announces, "The Spirit of the Lord is upon me, because he has anointed me to bring good news to the poor. He has sent me to proclaim release to the captives and recovery of sight to the blind, to let the oppressed go free, to proclaim the year of the Lord's favor." Jesus Christ is speaking of what is to begin taking place with his ministry and continue in the kingdom of God that he brought.

After the confession of Peter, Jesus told his disciples, "Truly I tell you, there are some standing here who will not taste death until they see that the kingdom of God has come with power" (Mark 9:1; compare Matt 16:28; Luke 9:27). At the Last Supper, Jesus announces to his disciples, "Truly I tell you, I will never again drink of the fruit of the vine until that day when I drink it new in the kingdom of God" (Mark 14:25; compare Matt 26:29). In Luke 22:18 it is, "For I tell you that from now on I will not drink of the fruit of the vine until the kingdom of God comes." In fact, Jesus did eat with his disciples during his resurrection appearances and in one case at least, it was during a repeat of the Last Supper that two of his disciples recognized him (Luke 24:30–31).

Some say that Jesus had a misunderstanding in thinking that the end of history would come immediately after his resurrection, leading his followers to expect his early return to earth. Certainly many disciples did have that expectation. However, I have no problem in believing that neither Jesus nor his followers knew when the end of history would arrive, just as we do not! (Mark 13:32). However, I believe on the basis of both the sayings of Jesus and other passages in the New Testament that the kingdom of God has come in history, beginning with the coming of Jesus Christ, followed by the coming of the Holy Spirit and the spread of the gospel. I believe this was the expectation of Jesus that was fulfilled, is being fulfilled, and will be fulfilled in "realized eschatology." The problem is that many interpreters of Jesus' last sayings do not see this ongoing fulfillment. If we take a long-range view of human history, as I do, there is no problem in seeing the two thousand years since Jesus came as a very short time. Learning the great length of human history in recent centuries and even years does not make this difficult.

It is clear to me that with the spread of the gospel under the Holy Spirit over the relatively short period of the last two thousand years, something very special has been taking place and will continue to take place in history. In the next chapter I will seek to deal with some important details of the history since the coming of Jesus Christ, but I will add something here about a central thrust or purpose of the work of God in history.

In Ephesians 2:17 it is stated, "So he came and proclaimed peace to those who were far off [the Gentiles] and to those who were near [the Jews]," the goal being to "create in himself one new humanity, in place of the two, thus making peace" (2:15). In another important passage (2 Cor 5:17—6:2) that considers all humanity, we read:

> So if anyone is in Christ, there is a new creation: everything old has passed away; see, everything has become new! All this is from God, who reconciled us to himself through Christ, and has given unto us the ministry of reconciliation; that is, in Christ God was reconciling the world to himself, not counting their trespasses against them, and entrusting the message of reconciliation to us. So we are ambassadors for Christ, since God is making his appeal through us; we entreat you on behalf of Christ, be reconciled to God. For our sake he made him to be sin who knew no sin, so that in him we might become the righteousness of God. As we work together with him, we urge you also not to accept the grace of God in vain. For he says,

"At an acceptable time I have listened to you, and on the day of salvation I have helped you." See, now is the acceptable time; see, now is the day of salvation!

I use this long passage, some of which I quoted above, to sum up the goal of God ("reconciling the world to God's self"), which is being carried out in history by God's "ambassadors." Accomplishing the goal is based on what Jesus Christ accomplished, but God is now acting through the Holy Spirit in using the followers of the Human One to carry on the work of reconciliation throughout the world. Obviously, there is much more to do!

CONCLUSION

The claims regarding the person and work of Jesus Christ require a decision. One can ignore and walk away from them. This means that to such a person the claims are delusional and in the end are irrelevant to life. Secondly, one can merely outwardly assent or agree to them, becoming a Christian in name but go on living without change. Jesus spoke of various forms of superficial acceptance of the Word of God (Mark 4:1–20). Thirdly, one can go beyond mere agreement and respond with personal commitment to Jesus Christ and active obedience to the Lord of love. The commitment and work of Jesus on our behalf requires our commitment and work in thankful service.

The contents of this and the previous chapter are relatively familiar subjects to many people. My purpose is to place these chapters on the claims regarding Jesus Christ in the context already discussed in the first five chapters. The claims regarding Jesus Christ are the most complete fulfillment that has ever existed of the human longing for incarnation (tangible presence) and atonement (compassion) of God. Chapters 5 and 6 serve as a warning that while human beings (particularly us) yearn for the incarnation and atonement of God, they (we) also resist God's efforts to reach out to human beings in the life and work of Jesus Christ, a work that is being carried forward through human beings. I have not discussed the great work of service uplifting human life that is going forward under Jesus Christ and the power of the Holy Spirit. It is important, therefore, to broaden the context of the incarnation and atonement to include what has happened since the coming of Jesus Christ some two thousand years ago. The following chapter will begin to do this by considering what has happened regarding the Human One in these years.

Chapter 9

Jesus Christ in Subsequent History

THE IMPERFECT WITNESS TO JESUS CHRIST

AFTER CONSIDERING THE CLAIMS made by the early believers regarding Jesus Christ, we are ready to consider Jesus Christ in subsequent history, as well as in ongoing human life in the present and future. In one respect, the approximately one third of the world's population that indicate they are followers of Jesus Christ (divided though they be) shows the enormous impact of Jesus Christ in his incarnation and atonement on human beings over the last two thousand years. On the other hand, it might also be asked, "Since he is the incarnate Son of God who atoned for human sin, why has the response to Jesus Christ not been greater?" The resistance in all human beings to God's self-disclosure is certainly one of the major reasons for the still-limited response to the outreach of God in Jesus Christ. However, I believe it is especially the resistance from the followers of Christ that has had the most negative effect on the spread of Christ's gospel. It is clear from the Bible, especially from the final words of Jesus (Matt 28:18–20; Acts 1:7, 8), that Jesus expected his followers to represent him in the world in such a way that peoples throughout the world would also become his followers, living as he taught and lived. I say "peoples" because Jesus spoke of "nations" or *ethne*, which refers to peoples, not nation-states, becoming his disciples. It happens that in human history, beginning in Europe, modern nation-states were formed. The reference to "peoples" shows that, in spite of our individualistic emphasis, discipleship is not simply an individual affair. From the beginning, disciples were in a communities called into existence by God through Jesus Christ. Even more, we cannot escape the fact that receptivity and non-receptivity to the gospel of Christ has often been shown by sociocultural groups. Unfortunately, rulers and the groups have made alliances to create monopolies out of particular versions of Christianity that are then made "official" religions.

The New Testament makes it clear that Jesus and his first followers saw the coming of Jesus as introducing the last age of history, in which the kingdom of Christ was to spread to all people by human witnesses acting under the power of the Holy Spirit given to them. However, the Opposition to Jesus Christ in the world has had the greatest success in opposing Christ through his followers by distorting their representation of him to the world. The distortion has been especially effective when the "principalities and powers" represented in sociocultural forces have influenced large groups of Christians to bring suffering and death to others or at least to be associated with those who caused suffering and death. This has taken place because of the association of Christianity with coercive power—a temptation that Jesus rejected—that began in the fourth century with Christianity being made the official religion of the Roman Empire. This association of Christianity with coercive power has lasted into the present, most notably with state churches and with Western colonialism. Nevertheless, in spite of the imperfect witness of Christians, the gospel of Jesus Christ spread and continues to spread up to the present. In viewing the time since Jesus Christ was on earth, it is important to place it in the context of God at work in history carrying out the *missio Dei*. In short, Christians need to have a philosophy of history.

A CHRISTIAN PHILOSOPHY OF HISTORY

The Bible is not a scientific book or strictly a book of history, but it clearly has a philosophy or, better yet, a theology of history. The eschatological message of Jesus seen in the light of the Hebrew Scriptures (the Old Testament) and interpreted by the whole New Testament is at the foundation of the Christian theology of history. It requires taking an overview of the Bible and human history. At the beginning of the biblical story of salvation, God made promises to Abraham, Isaac, and Jacob of blessing to their descendants and through them to the whole world. In a further and fuller revelation of God's character, especially God's compassion for the suffering and oppressed, God delivered the people of Israel from slavery in Egypt. This act was remembered throughout the history of Israel and is remembered by present-day people needing liberation—the slaves in the United States being a notable example.

The exodus from Egypt meant that throughout the history of Israel and the Bible as a whole there would an understanding of justice, particularly in the messages of the prophets, as basically meaning deliverance of the poor, oppressed, and those least able to help themselves (widows, orphans, and strangers). Note that in James 1:2 practicing this kind of justice is defined as "true religion." Justice must involve changed physical conditions, but in the Bible it is placed in the context of a relationship with God. After the exodus came the Ten Commandments and life in a covenant relationship with God. This means that those who find deliverance from physical oppression through the influence of the gospel should find true fulfillment in a life of faith and obedience to God in a covenant relationship together with God's people. However, beginning in the wilderness itself, the people of Israel were repeatedly unfaithful to God through idolatry and perpetuating injustice, a picture of how God's people have acted to the present as seen in the numerous examples of unfaithfulness of Christians. The supposed conquest of the promised land had only limited success. In the period of the judges and the succeeding kings, the Israelites were highly influenced by surrounding paganism and went through periods of outside domination. They determined they wanted to be like other nations. The nation project requested by the people (1 Samuel 8) turned out to be a failure in the history of Israel. After the rule of David and Solomon, the kingdom divided. Both kingdoms continued their disobedience and suffered much, leading up to the national destruction of both kingdoms, which included the destruction of Jerusalem and the temple, the center of life for the remaining Southern Kingdom (the Northern Kingdom had already been destroyed and the people removed). Nevertheless, through the national experiences of decline and destruction, combined with the messages of the prophets, God actually worked to purify the faith and life of the people of God and preserve a "faithful remnant." Thus, being a nation was not the core purpose and reality for the people of God; it was their selection by God to be a people who would display the glory of God to the world and become a blessing to the whole world (Gen 12:3) by fulfilling God's requirement "to do justice, and to love kindness, and to walk humbly with [their] God" (Mic 6:8). As noted, the emphasis on care for the weak, as in Psalm 82, is very strong in the Hebrew Scriptures (and has continued as a strong emphasis of the Jewish people in history and in the United States). Following the restoration to the land by Persia, the one experience of Israel after the fall of Jerusalem as an independent nation under the Hasmoneans (initiated about 140 BC), which followed their gallant resistance to the domination of Syria, ended in failure with the conquest of Rome in 63 BC. In short, becoming or attempting to become a nation-state became a hindrance to Israel fulfilling their calling to be the people of God as a "light to the Gentiles."

The prophets, in addition to explaining the suffering of Israel as due to its unfaithfulness, established an expectation of a Messiah who would bring deliverance to the people, often if not primarily seen in political terms. The promise of a Messiah together with images of the Son of Man (see chapter 1) became part of the development of both an eschatological ("last days") expectation and apocalyptic literature. Both the expectation of an end to history with the coming of the Messiah and apocalyptic literature, in effect a kind of code language depicting the judgment of all earthly empires and the triumph of God in history, contribute to the bedrock of the Christian theology of history. In this theology God is active and in charge of history in order to accomplish God's purpose: the redemption of humankind that will finally be accomplished in uniting all things in Christ (Eph 1:10). Unfortunately (remembering the misuse of truth and the good), the violence expressed symbolically in apocalyptic literature contributed to the misunderstanding by Jews, Christians, and Muslims that God works in history through their violent revolutions. Secular versions of this violence were developed in recent history in the French Revolution and Communism. Apocalyptic thought has made people unnecessarily warlike, thinking they could "help" God or history (in secular versions) by establishing an ideal realm. It is significant that of all the peoples Rome conquered around the Mediterranean, the Jews were the only one to mount revolutions. Apocalyptic thought may even have contributed to Judas betraying Jesus with the hope that Jesus would then display his power and lead in defeating Rome. It is also significant that Western history has been characterized by numerous revolutions. Nevertheless, an important point is that the fall of nations depicted in apocalyptic literature is brought on themselves through their own worship of power and use of violence and coercive power. God's people need only watch the repeated fall of human pretensions to power. My theological interpretation based on the whole Bible and especially Jesus Christ is that God has created human beings so that individuals and societies caught up in evil and the practice of injustice bring on their own downfall, but the practice of justice is self-rewarding to individuals and societies. Given the frustrated experience of the people of Israel in establishing a lasting nation, it is understandable that the expectation of a Messiah would become distorted by the view that the Messiah would re-establish a kingdom on earth that would dominate other nations and peoples. Sadly, for many this expectation eclipsed the vision that Israel should become a "light to the nations [peoples]" (Isa 42:6; 49:6; 60:3). There were no "nations" as we usually understand them today; the reference here is to the Gentiles or to all the peoples of the world.

Since Jesus and the apostles exerted no coercion to gain followers and claimed no earthly kingdom or territory, it is important to understand the complex relation of coercion to God's work and judgment in history. It is helpful to distinguish God's basic work and God's judgment in history even though there is some ambiguity (Where have we heard that before?) in the meaning of judgment. The Bible presents a God who is very active both in the affairs of the world, including political affairs, and among individual human beings, but God has the very difficult task (let us call it a "problem") of winning the hearts of human beings without force. God could obviously coerce people to believe (in the sense of admitting the reality of) in God's existence, but people cannot be coerced into believing in and loving God or another human being (a message humorously conveyed in the movie *Bruce Almighty*, when Jim Carey as God could not make his girl friend love him). Coercion would not produce what God seeks—faith and love—but instead fear and an imitative coercive action toward others. Typically, people who believe in an authoritarian God become authoritarian themselves. Also typically, people who emphasize a judgmental God become judgmental themselves. It is obvious that Jesus Christ did not coerce anyone into following him. In fact, people applied coercion to him in crucifying him.

The early church that we see in Acts and in the first three centuries was certainly not in a position to coerce people into membership. Yes, there is coercion of a kind by God that is built into the nature of the universe and of human history that creates respect and humility toward nature and the realization of human limitations and mortality. In human societies and between societies there is a place for coercion to prevent harm to people (Rom 13:1–7), but that coercion does not solve basic problems within human hearts and in societies. Over time in human history, the proud and the unjust bring down themselves, although it may take place too slowly to avoid terrible suffering, for example, Hitler and the Holocaust. What is important for Christians to know and believe is that coercion does not lead to faith. But human conflict and destruction of "the kingdoms of the world" may create new opportunities for life to flourish again and for grace to work leading to faith and love.

In addition to purifying the church and the Christian witness, the historical process since Jesus Christ came has resulted in the gradual spread of justice in the world. Christians can believe, as Martin Luther King Jr. stated, "The arc of the moral universe is long but it bends toward justice." It is true that human beings have moral natures and recognize justice when it appears, but it also had a specific revelation in the exodus of the Israelite slaves, followed by the covenant made with them. As noted above, this established the definition of justice repeatedly mentioned in the Bible. In

Christian history, justice in terms of "exodus" or deliverance has repeat-edly appeared and continues to appear to the present, though admittedly with numerous setbacks, including by Christians. Quiet evidence of justice is seen in the deliverance brought to millions, beginning with nursing in the Christian communities in the Roman Empire, which eventually through many centuries led to health care through modern medicine. Another quiet development of justice is the deliverance from ignorance through literacy and education leading to modern educational institutions for all ages. More dramatic evidence of the bent of history toward justice is seen in deliver-ance of the oppressed in the form of the recognition of human rights, the rise of democracy, establishment of freedom of thought and expression, the abolition of slavery (very like the original exodus), the raising of the status of women, and, most recently, the growing acceptance of LGBTQ persons and equality in marriage. All of these "exoduses" (deliverances) and other expressions of justice involve the change of actual physical circumstances for the formerly oppressed. This historical bent toward justice is part of the witness to the gospel and the love of God for all humanity.

Sometimes this may be when God's people are defeated in the nation or society they sought to dominate even more than when they are victorious. God works through the conflict that comes from human self-destruction to protect people from oppressors, including oppressors among God's own people, although this protection may appear to the suffering to be slow in coming. The American Civil War, during which slavery (supported by many Christians) was abolished, is a good example. The destruction of Western power and Western colonialism (associated with "Christian nations") as a result of World Wars I and II, after which the gospel greatly expanded, is another example. Colonialism created great opposition to Christianity; consequently, I believe, it was high on God's list for judgment. Just as As-syria and Babylon brought judgment on Israel, so I believe Japan was used to bring about the collapse of colonialism in the Far East, which in the end brought Japan's colonialism to an end. Such judgments give new opportu-nities for faith among those who recognize and accept God's judgment in history. It can hardly be denied, as noted above, that the collapse of West-ern colonialism brought a new openness to the gospel, especially in China, which was no longer associated with Western power. Nevertheless, faith basically comes from the work of God's grace and the spread of the gospel, even though the opportunities for grace to be perceived and received may come from the coercive judgments of God in history. Faith may come more easily because of favorable conditions, but the support of political authori-ties for Christianity may help to make faith superficial and become primar-ily a matter of ethnic or national identity. This is seen in the history of Israel in the Hebrew Scriptures, but even more in Christian history, especially since the fourth century and coming to the present, as seen in many nations where there are "official" state churches. This rise and fall of nations serves as a judgment on nations who participate in the injustices of the world. Of course, believers in nations may suffer as whole nations are judged, but they can also learn of the ways of God that have been written into human history. Thus, throughout messy human history God is continually working to purify and strengthen the faith and love of God's people and to bring justice to an ever-widening number of people.

Governments have a single responsibility: to execute justice for all.[1] Psalm 82 makes this very clear when the rulers of the world are condemned for not rescuing the weak and needy. People of faith, especially when they are a majority of the population, can seek to influence governments toward increased just actions on behalf of all people. But governments historically have sought to support those with wealth and power and to dominate and exploit people of other nations. This type of injustice is subject inevitably to God's judgment. The disciples of Jesus shared the distorted expectation held by those looking for an earth-conquering Messiah. It took the whole life, death, and resurrection of Jesus to change this expectation and create the faith community that would carry the gospel into the world. This was the work of God to win the hearts of people not through coercion, but through the sacrificial death and triumphant resurrection of Christ. It brought forgiveness and new life to those oppressed by the sin that often accompanied oppression of various kinds, revealing the justice of God (Rom 1:16–17). Even then, the disciples showed only a partial understanding of the purpose of Jesus in the world when they asked just before his ascension, "Lord, is this the time when you will restore the kingdom to Israel?"(Acts 1:6). In this question and throughout the Bible (and to this day), human nature seems to long for an outward display of God's power (working for themselves, of course), but faith and love toward God does not view God or the world this way, as Jesus demonstrated on the cross.

---

1. Using the words of the U.S. Constitution, for those who feel that I am overemphasizing "establishing justice," I would include "insuring domestic tranquility, providing for the common defense" as an overall part of "establishing justice." I would also note that "promoting the general welfare" and "securing the blessings of liberty," especially the former, are also important parts of justice. The Declaration of Independence stresses establishing "liberty and justice for all." It is true that liberals tend to stress justice over other moral foundations for society, as Haidt (*Religous Mind*, 295–309) has pointed out, and this can and has led to unintended mistakes and failures of some policies; but I still believe that a society is best served by seeing all its policies in the overall light of "justice for all." That seems to me a message of the Bible.

A basic fact is that Jesus did not act in such a way that people would have to admit his divine origin and external power over people. The temptations he faced just after his baptism were exactly in line with the possibility of making his ministry into such a display of supernatural power that his divinity would be undeniable and people would flock to him. They did flock to him, but Jesus' popularity did not retain their loyalty. Although a charismatic leader and the initiator of the "Jesus Movement," Jesus backed away from the efforts to make him a political leader. He tested their loyalty as seen in John 6 with the difficult sayings about "eating his flesh and drinking his blood." It is extremely important that the most dramatic and overawing event in Jesus' life, namely, his resurrection, was made known *only* to his followers.

What if Jesus had gone to the council that condemned him or to Pilate and Herod and said to them, "You tried to kill me, but here I am; you failed to kill me, but you will never be able to stop my message"? Their response— in fear—would have been, "Oh, Oh, we understand now. Okay, okay, now we will believe you." They would then probably ask him to raise soldiers from the dead when they fought the Roman oppressors so that they could continue fighting (a belief propagated by some historical groups who fought oppressors). It would have been a similar response if he had come down from the cross, as he was told to do, in order for people to believe in him. But a little thought about this option for Jesus is sufficient to let us know that this is not the kind of faith and relationship that God the Father and Jesus Christ wanted to establish with human beings. In fact, it would not be faith, but a kind of assent with fear, the kind mentioned sarcastically in James 2:19: "You believe that God is one: you do well. Even the demons believe— and shudder." The implicit demand of people now for some proof of the existence of God or the divinity of Jesus is a demand for God to act against God's nature, and the result would not be faith and love, but fear only. Thus, to believe in the existence of God is not the issue, as many think. Many deny the existence of God as conceived in their minds, not the God and Father of Jesus Christ. Nevertheless, the fact that God is non-coercive means that in regard to creating faith God created a world in which people can get along without God, living apparently "normal" lives; hence the spawning of unbelief and, most recently, modern secularism as a way of life.

Having said all of this, I believe remarkable events have taken place in history since the time of Christ that give the followers of Jesus encouragement and support in their belief that God is working in history. This is seen in the spread of justice describe above. I take Mary's song of praise (Luke 1:46–55) as an expression of joy in seeing God at work. My argument is that although faith is not based upon reason or historical evidence, faith is nevertheless reasonable, and through faith we can see God at work in history.

In other words, although faith is not based upon proof, there are empirical supports for faith that make sense even if they cannot be put together in a way to convince unbelievers. It simply makes sense that a Creator God would love all creation and would seek to redeem it, namely, bring it all into a harmonious relationship with God's being. In addition, it makes sense that God would want to improve the living conditions of his creatures. The problem for God, of course, is exactly the same as that faced by Jesus Christ and the church, discussed above, of using coercion or any inducements or outward demonstrations to gain followers. Although Jesus and the apostles showed "signs and wonders," Jesus would not use signs to gain followers, as he was asked so often to do; people would then have to believe in him out of fear or awe (Mark 8:12). I have always thought it was highly significant that, as far as we know, none of the twelve disciples was healed of sickness, and Paul was specifically not healed of a physical ailment even though he prayed for healing (2 Cor 12:7–9). The story of the people of Israel and of Jesus the Messiah, discussed above, and the subsequent history of the followers of Christ, though full of failures, is exactly the kind of activity in history that a loving God would use in order to bring human beings to salvation through faith and love. Nevertheless, these and other developments that have taken place since Jesus Christ came make sense as the activity of God in human history. While not convincing those who do not want to believe these developments as the advance of justice or do not want to believe in Jesus Christ, what has taken place can be an encouragement to those who want to believe or do believe in him and also believe in the advance of justice in history.

Above we dealt with the complex subject of God's activity in history—perhaps not to the satisfaction of everyone, but we do have the evidence that Christianity is the most widespread religion in the world, which, according to my studies discussed in chapters 3 and 4, tells us something about the widespread appeal of Jesus Christ. Jesus Christ and his followers were certainly non-coercive and proclaimed a gospel of grace that is non-coercive. Certainly in the first three hundred years of the history of Christianity the gospel of Christ spread without coercion. Nevertheless, the tendency of Christianity, like all religions, to follow ethnic and national lines as it spread is seen in its early spread to Syrian city-states, Armenia, and Ethiopia and the tendency for different versions of Christianity to develop in different sociocultural areas. This tendency would be reinforced through the centuries as Christianity was expressed in the Roman Empire by such groups as Syrians, Greeks, Egyptians, Latin speakers, and Goths. Many scholars do not recognize how Christianity helped to revive the culture in these various groups and areas. Then Christianity spread northward to the other European tribes ("barbarians") that became the European countries.

AN OVERVIEW OF HUMAN DISTORTION OF AND ACCEPTANCE OF GOD'S RULE

One of the most careful and helpful studies of Christianity in world history was made by the Dutch missionary-theologian Arend Th. van Leeuwen.[2] His study extends our understanding of a Christian philosophy of history discussed above. At the core of his argument is the contrast made between the ontocratic state that was based on the religions of the old civilizations and the kind of societies growing (not without great struggle) out of the Jewish and Christian contexts that came into existence primarily in the West. Ontocracy refers to the attempt of the first civilizations to make rulers to be at the apex of an earthly reality that extends upward and makes contact with the cosmic powers believed to surround and dominate the earth. The pyramidal structure, or sacred mountain, seen in most ancient civilizations symbolized this view of reality in which rulers were seen as an extension of the cosmos. This ideology was used to support oppressive and violent systems dominating large numbers of people under divine or semi-divine rulers.

The challenge to this view of the state and society begins in the Old Testament stories of creation, the tower of Babel, and the subsequent salvation history of Israel. Although Israel was tempted to follow the pattern of surrounding societies with their ontocratic pattern, it was prevented from doing so. Even though the Davidic kingdom was elevated as highly favored by God, it was not ontocratic like other kingdoms because divine judgment fell alike on both throne and altar. Van Leeuwen uses the term "theocratic" in contrast to "ontocratic." Theocratic is the biblical understanding of God's rule, in which the ruler is not divine, but rather came under God's continuing corrective judgment. Acceptance of God's judgment by rulers is crucial for the non-ontocratic government.

The great crisis in Christian history, as I have noted, took place in the fourth century with regard to whether the ontocratic pattern would become dominant with the adoption of Christianity as the official religion of the Roman Empire. The contrast between the old ontocratic pattern and the one introduced by the Bible and Christ in particular is described, according to van Leeuwen, in Augustine's *City of God*. Here we see the eschatological tension between all earthly rule and the kingdom of God brought by Christ. He writes, "Augustine's vision, brought to birth at a moment of change and crisis in the history of the world [soon after the fall of Rome in AD 410], has continued to lie like a charge of dynamite beneath all the theologies and ecclesiastical

2. Leeuwen, *Christianity in World History.*

concepts of the Western Church."[3] Basically, the "revolutionary character" of Western civilization was established by the kingdom of God introduced in the Hebrew Scriptures and brought by Jesus Christ—a kingdom present and yet ever coming, a kingdom in the world yet not of it. In spite of the church's pretensions to authority and power following the fourth century, the ontocratic pattern could not succeed. Van Leeuwen writes:

> So it was that during the Middle Ages those forces which were to shatter the edifice of the *Corpus Christianum Romanum* and were destined to open the way through to modern civilization were gathering their strength. The mediaeval order had to give way, because it proved impossible to build a truly Christian order to an ontocratic pattern. It would be an unfair and one-sided judgment of the mediaeval West simply to say that it set out to reproduce, in the realm of ecclesiastic and political affairs, the sacral pattern of the Roman Empire. If that were the case, the Middle Ages in the West would have done no more than prolong, under a new guise, the ancient ontocratic pattern of the great primary civilizations. What was really unique about its history during this period was the dramatic fashion in which the ontocratic order disintegrated—not under pressure of external forces nor through any inherent principle of senile decay; it was exploded from within by an intolerable pressure, by the force of the collision between the two powers, each of which claimed the sole authority over it.[4]

This description of the failure of political Christianity is consistent with my view expressed above that the use of coercive power by the church distorts the gospel and ultimately brings destruction to the church and any society that claims to be Christian. The Reformation introduced new experiences and concepts of the powers of religion expressed in the church and the secular power of the state. However, the Protestant churches continued the old state church pattern, but with some new and different emphases. Added to the Roman Catholic notion of the subjection of the state to the church was the Lutheran notion of the state as guardian of the church and the Calvinistic experience and notion of the joint relationship of church and state based on a common allegiance to the Word of God.[5] Coercion was left to the state, but was to be used justly. This meant that in the Calvinist-influenced systems religious people would become "meddlers" in social and

3. Ibid., 281–82.
4. Ibid., 287.
5. Ibid., 305.

political affairs, a common phenomenon that was expressed later in the United States. It meant that Calvinists could become involved in overturning governments, although some would add that this would be as citizens, not as the church as such. This may be too fine a distinction for many people to make, but with establishment of individual rights and democracies, especially in the United States, change in governments could be made peacefully by coalitions of individuals, with explicit involvement of the church not allowed. In any event, the dynamic "revolutionary history" of the West accelerated with the unleashing of numerous new religious, social, and political forces by the Reformation along with nationalistic movements. These forces were already at work in the Middle Ages. They included the rise of secularism, nationalism, individualism, capitalism, institutionalized science, and democratic organizations. These forces marked the beginning of the "modern era" in which they extended their influence around the world, breaking "religious canopies" as they had in the West. Within these modern forces, as already noted, were also movements toward greater justice. These movements were often led by Christians or had the involvement of Christians, but also were opposed by Christians. Movements for greater justice were also led by many from the public at large, including many non-Christians or anti-Christians, for example, French Revolutionists, Fascists, and Marxists with their own versions of justice. The movements for "greater justice" have divided societies in the West between the "left" and "right" and, among Americans, particularly Christians, "liberals" and "conservatives." Conservatism has roots in Britain, particularly among those supporting the monarchy (Tories) versus those supporting Parliament (Whigs). Conservative ideology also has special roots among those in opposition to the extremes of the French Revolution and favoring established institutions. In America the liberal/conservative line can be fuzzy, but tends to divide between those supporting the Democratic and Republican parties.

This development is related to an additional important additional force: the process of secularization, which on the one hand was supported by Christians, especially in the United States, but on the other hand opened the way for the anti-religious force of secularism, a philosophy and lifestyle in which God is considered irrelevant. Thus, after the sociocultural forces listed above began to take shape in the sixteenth and especially the seventeenth century, the eighteenth century added the beginnings of the anti-religious movement of secularism, particularly among intellectuals, which has continued up to the present and has also extended around the world. However, the Enlightenment of the eighteenth century was only partly anti-religious, with France as the major source of the anti-religious movement, followed in the nineteenth century by Germany. The process of disestablishing organized religion from its authority and power was pursued by both anti-religious *and* religious groups. The result was that secularization, as this process was labeled, had both an anti-religious and a religious component; and supporters of the latter were often not recognized by the former. This complex combination was expressed most clearly in the United States, where the various religious groups prevented one another from obtaining official government sponsorship. I do not want to enter the debate regarding the various meanings given to the terms "secular," "secularism," and "secularization" except to point out that what they represent has been part of the dynamic and complex product of the "revolutionary West." Specifically, the secularization movement, as broadly understood, was an unintended result of the Protestant Reformation that challenged religious authority. The point I am making here is that the removal of religion from governmental power has both anti-religious or non-religious and religious supporters. This was especially true in the United States, where religious people wanted to be free from domination from any one religion, largely due to their bad experiences under religions allied with governments in Europe. At the same time, some Christians seem to hanker after gaining political influence. With the dethroning of organized religion, the old partly ontocratic system in Europe was challenged and set aside. It had dominated societies for ages and it had continued its influence into the sixteenth and seventeenth centuries under the "divine right" of kings, but was seriously challenged by the French Revolution and the later revolutions in Europe in the nineteenth century.

If the basic Christian philosophy of history is that God is working in history so that the gospel of Jesus Christ may be known and God's "will may be done on earth as it is in heaven," what are we to make of the complex changes that have taken place at an accelerating rate? These changes introduce two great unintended effects: first, an effect of religious change, and second, an effect on religions change.

RELIGION BECOMES AN OPTION

With the at least partial self-destruction of the ontocratic system in Europe, religion lost its place as a canopy over life in much of the West, and the effect of this breaking of the religious canopy is spreading around the world. In the West particularly, religion became an option alongside non-religion or irreligion. Recently, some social scientists have pointed to this development.[6] A variety of religions and non-religions are increasingly becoming

6. Beck, *God of One's Own*, 78–81; Joas, *Faith as an Option*, 78–91.

apparent for most people in many parts of the world. Thus, although an unintended effect of the Protestant Reformation was the initiation of the secularization process, an unintended effect of the secularization process has been the clarification of the faith option.

Human beings have always had secular aspects to their lives simply because they live in the created world. These include such mundane activities as eating, sleeping, marrying, having children and raising them, and various forms of labor, such as hunting and gathering and later farming and carrying on trade. All of these activities can be seen and often were seen as taking place under God or some supernatural influences. In this sense, there was no purely secular realm for most people in traditional societies. But this is still the case for many religious people, including both Christians and Muslims today, since we believe that God is in all things and active in all things. However, with religion and non-religion as options in the modern world, religious activities take their place alongside of non-religious or secular activities. Rather than being a negative development for faith, the conditions that make religious choices voluntary seem to be exactly in line with what we believe God desires: to be chosen by us, or rather, for us to discover that we are chosen because faith is a gift of grace.

For religious people, as noted, their mundane secular activities can be seen as taking place under God and to be carried out as offerings to God, thus making them sacred. On the other hand, the opportunity (the temptation) to ignore God became more possible than ever before. For some people, religion and the secular became compartmentalized so that they could move between their secular activities and their religious activities. This was seen in chapter 6 under "Resistance through Apathy." For other people, sadly, the secular becomes a total lifestyle and the religious "compartment" either disappears or practically disappears—reserved only for holidays. In the old religious canopy days this seems to have taken place for many people. In other words, religion became primarily an outward observance followed in order to be socially and even legally accepted.

Another option developed with secularization, which is often been ignored by those who adopt and universalize the secular as their lifestyle, philosophy, or worldview. This other option, adopted by many religious people, is to recognize and use the secular as a methodology to be understood and used within a larger faith perspective and commitment. In two major areas this option of using the secular as a methodology becomes clear: one is in the pursuit of knowledge, particularly through science but also in general education; the other is in the political realm of government. In other words, the secular, for example, in science or politics, for believers actually becomes a means for exercising their faith in service to others. Modern medicine is an area employing scientific methods that can be seen as a service to God. It only takes a little thought (and a strong faith) for the Christian to apply this to all occupations, in fact all realms of life. This extends from plowing fields to brain surgery. Each is a secular field that can be infused with faith. That is the faith option. At the same time, a secular methodology can be shared by those with or without faith. It gives all people a basis on which to interact. It is up to believers to show that they can use a secular methodology in science, government, medicine, education, business, and physical labor as well or better than anyone else. Doing an excellent job in using a secular methodology is a form of witnessing to God, who calls the people of God to faithfulness in using God's creation for the benefit of all.

Looking at science specifically, it uses the secular methodology because no reference can be made to God as a causative force. Consciously using the scientific method means that the searcher for knowledge is consciously not seeking religious reasons for understanding events in nature (the natural sciences) or in human behavior (the social sciences). The value of this methodology is that it protects the searcher for understanding nature from the premature injection of religious explanations, all of which include fallible and biased human thought (remembering total depravity). The term "bias" became a technical term in science (instead of simply being equivalent to "prejudice" in common language) to refer to all human thought that is not controlled by the special techniques used in scientific studies. Because of the universal "infection" of bias (like the scientific equivalent of sin), scientific studies require imposition of special controls, as well as the need to be open to criticism, replication, and constant modification and elaboration.[7] This is the technical (not necessarily personal) "humility" required of scientists.[8] From this perspective, the secular method of science and other types of search for knowledge, as in historical studies, can and should be incorporated by believers into a larger religious faith perspective. The secular becomes a tool to protect human beings from false religious ideas as well as, of course, advancing knowledge in the secular world, which, from a faith perspective, was both created by God and is good, though affected by evil. Most importantly, knowledge is to be used to benefit humankind and to care for God's whole creation.

Another area where the secular has proven to be very useful as a methodology is in the area of government. The world, or at least much of it, has had its fill of bad religion, including bad Christianity, which has been used

7. Montgomery, "Bias in Interpreting Social Facts."

8. Merton, "Normative Structure of Science"; Montgomery, "Bias in Interpreting Social Facts," 288.

to bring death, destruction, and oppression to numerous people or has been influenced by or been associated with such behavior. (We may be in an era when the Muslim world is slowly learning the negative effect of religion in government, as much of the Western world learned it in the sixteenth and seventeenth centuries.) A secular government avoids the use of religion or the name of God as justification for its actions. In principle, the role of government becomes simply the enactment of justice for its people. Of course, what is justice is always debatable and continually contested, but in a secular government God's name is not to be used as a rationalization for government action. This is not only a protection from the injection of bad religious rationalizations, but it is also a protection for those in government from breaking the third commandment, which prohibits taking God's name in vain. This appears to be completely forgotten by many religious people who constantly seek to express their religious ideas as justification for their political actions and on that basis to impose through government action their moral views on others—although, once again, religious people in government, just as in science, are free to act (and should act) on the basis of their religious faith because all of life is under God to whom they are responsible. The rightness of political views should be made to stand the test of practice over time and not be based on a professed knowledge of God's will.

Of course, with faith as an option, secularism as a lifestyle or philosophy also becomes an option. Belief in and love of God has always been an option, a choice that human beings need to make but do not have to make, because God is non-coercive in relation to faith. The making of religion or non-religion as options in life has taken place in the last few centuries under what may be termed the "secularization process." In this process, organized religion and religious language have been taken out officially from the public sphere, although, as any observer of politics can tell, religious language is still used unofficially by politicians. This is deemed to make religious people "comfortable." While many religious people decry secularization as "taking God out" of government and various public institutions, it does help to clarify the call of the non-coercive God to a life of faith and love. Of course, God is not "taken out" of anything because God is always present, especially in the hearts of the people of God. But, as we know from experience, God's people are far from perfect. Religious people are still free to express their personal faith, but not in ways that impose their faith on others. Some people feel that this is an attack on their faith. In some cases this may seem to be true if their faith is weak and depends on a vague religious aura and the public affirmation that religion is a good thing. However, the removal of religious language from official spaces opens the opportunity to express one's personal faith, especially in "deeds of love and mercy" and in the way one carries out the calling to serve others. The expression of one's personal religious experience is permissible as long it is emphasized humbly as being personal and imperfect. Political leaders should never impose their faith. The clarification of the secular as a methodology that protects against the misuse of religion, even if it offers the option of no religion to some, may be considered a call to Christians to be living witnesses to Jesus Christ. That witness is to be made increasingly clear in human history, so that the world will come to see Jesus Christ as the revelation of God. Even if it takes many centuries, it will be a short time in human history.

FOLLOWERS OF JESUS CHRIST IN WORLD HISTORY, A MIXED STORY

This book does not claim that the many good things that have happened in history have come only from followers of Jesus Christ or from Christianity. For example, although Christians were active in the development of science and democracy—especially in the early stages in the sixteenth- and seventeenth-century developments that came before the touted Enlightenment of the eighteenth century—it is clear that both science and democracy have been supported and advanced by non-Christians, even anti-Christians. In fact, as time has passed many scientists, especially social scientists, have been non-Christians. This is consistent with the belief set forth in the Bible that human beings were created in the image of God and are capable of recognizing and carrying out many beneficial activities. Human beings were created to have a sense of right and wrong and therefore have the ability to recognize justice and injustice. In theology this is called "common grace." At the same time, Christians can hardly avoid recognizing some of the terrible ideas and activities carried out and justified by Christians as being an expression of human weakness and failings. This can be recognized as the result of "total depravity," meaning that sin infects the total person, especially her or his ideas, some of them religious ideas. Although recognizing the great contribution of Christianity to the development of modern science and democracy, Rodney Stark has written persuasively of the capacity of Christians for both good and evil, such as terrible persecutions.[9] In other words, much good in the world developed without Christianity or certainly with the participation of non-Christians. Also, good has been accomplished by Christians or Christian influence even along with evil. In regard to beneficial influence in spite of associations with the evils of colonialism, Robert Woodberry has demonstrated that Protestant missions especially contrib-

9. Stark, *For the Glory of God*, 201–88.

uted to the establishment of democracies in many parts of the world. God clearly works through or alongside human sinful acts to accomplish good.[10]

The development (not the origin) of two aspects of modern life that have come to benefit humanity on a wide basis can be attributed to a great extent to the activities of many Christians in the Western world. One of these is modern medicine benefiting numerous people, and the other is education on a broad (public) level, very much because of emphasizing literacy of the Bible. These are areas that have also become highly secularized, partly because they were quickly recognized by members at large in societies as beneficial for all people and societies. The result has been the adoption by governments throughout the world of policies to promote the practice of modern medicine on a large scale and the offer of education as widely as possible. Whether one wants to admit the large influence of Christians in initiating both movements (modern medicine and mass education) in the world, both movements are certainly consistent with the life and ministry of Jesus Christ and as representing what the loving Creator God of the Bible desires for all human beings. Certainly, wherever Christian missions have gone, they have sought not only to proclaim the gospel and build churches but have almost always sought to establish hospitals and schools. I cannot help but add that both classical music and Christian hymnody have been carried around the world by Christians, inspiring millions. I would also add that jazz was greatly stimulated by the triumphant parades after Christian funerals, so different from the attitude of most of the world toward death.

Apart from both the harmful and beneficial activities that can be attributed to the followers of Jesus Christ, the fact remains that after two thousand years the name of Jesus Christ has become the most widely known of all names, and those who claim to follow Jesus Christ are more numerous than the followers of any other religious founder. The purpose here is not to convince anyone through argument that Jesus Christ is the Savior of humankind, even though that is my belief, but to point out that human beings are faced with the challenge more clearly than ever before to believe this. If there is a direction in history, as I believe there is, among the most important results of history so far, subsequent to the coming of Jesus Christ, is that there is greater clarity of who Jesus Christ is and a greater opportunity or freedom to believe in him than ever before. Nevertheless, there is still considerable confusion about Jesus Christ, certainly in large part due to Christians themselves and the so-called Christian nations or Christian West; and there is still neither universal opportunity nor freedom to believe in and follow him. But history marches on and at an increasing pace, so

10. Woodberry, "Missionary Roots of Liberal Democracy."

that it appears to be running.[11] A major development since World War II that may be seen as the working of God in history is the disestablishment of "Christendom" in the West, which accompanied the collapse of Western colonialism. The positive effect on the spread of the gospel in China and Africa has been dramatic.

CONCLUSION

While many people look at history subsequent to Jesus Christ as simply a natural flow of events, Christians see the triune God—Creator, Redeemer, and Enabler—as active in the world working primarily through the people of God (the designated witnesses to Jesus Christ), but also carrying out judgments on human injustice in societies and nations while maintaining human existence. Judgments have fallen on societies that claimed to be Christian, as well as on the so-called Christian West as a whole. In fact, these judgments have been the most important judgments since they helped to bring corrections to God's people and clarify the gospel of Jesus Christ. Through it all, an advancement is seen in the spread of the gospel of Jesus Christ through four stages: (1) the first three hundred years, primarily in the Roman Empire and small societies to the east; (2) the period to 1500, when Christianity spread to the European tribes with some outreach to the India and China; (3) the missionary movement accompanying colonialism up to World War II; and finally (4) the postcolonial era since World War II. In this perspective of periods in the spread of the gospel, we have just begun the fourth period of the spread of the gospel. There are divergences or exceptions of spread beyond the first two geographical areas (the Roman Empire and the Western world), but these two areas represented the places of the most outward success in the spread of Christianity. However, the periods since 1500 have seen the globalization of Christianity attending the general accelerating globalization process.

It is the subjective spiritual perception through faith that "sees" God at work even though the particular views of Christians (including mine) may be mistaken about what God is doing in particular instances and places. Nevertheless, it is difficult, even from a secular historical perspective, not to give credit to Christianity for contributing to the many advances in the West. The diversity of faith and viewpoints that is in the Bible, has been present throughout history, and is widely expressed in the United States is now seen

11. Friedman, *Thank you for Being Late*. Friedman makes clear the accelerating change in the three areas of technology, globalization, and nature (climate change), but also points to the growing great need for cooperation and mutual trust.

increasing throughout the world. At the same time, rejection of or apathy toward any faith has become a clear option for increasing numbers of people around the world. And this rejection of faith as a movement began in the "Christian West"! In spite of this latter fact, there continues a strong and vital sensibility of God among many people and a variety of expressions of Christian faith alongside secularism. Believers and non-believers work together in using secular methodologies, especially in the search for knowledge about the world through science and in the advancement of democracy in government. In fact, secular methodology makes it possible for believers and non-believers to interact and work together, although there are tensions.[12]

To state it again, it is true that in the history of the West, where the most Christians have lived since the beginning of the second millennium until recently (although in much of the first millennium there were more Christians in the Middle East) and where Christianity was foundational to the civilization, many positive developments ensued in what has been called the "revolutionary West." One development often overlooked is the development of nationalism, easily noticed by any perusal of a map of the Euro-Asian land mass. The European tribes moved to nationhood without having to go through the domination of an empire, although there were attempts (Charlemagne, the Holy Roman Empire—neither holy nor Roman, Napoleon, and Hitler). This was arguably because the gospel came to the tribes in the early stages of the development of Western civilization with the message of the worth of each distinct tribal or language group. Of course, a terrible downside to the development of nationalism was that accompanying the stimulation to national creative initiatives were the many conflicts resulting from national rivalries and competition, which came to a terrible climax in the last century with World Wars I and II. Let us hope that the European Union represents the efforts of those of good will to follow of a path not dominated by national rivalries.

---

12. Christian Smith in *The Sacred Project of American Sociology* (7–8) discusses the almost religious commitment of many sociologists to a sacred project of "realizing the emancipation, equality, and moral affirmation of all human beings as autonomous, self-directing individual agents (who should be) out to live their lives as they personally desire, by constructing their own favored identities, entering and exiting relationships as they choose, and equally enjoying the gratification of experiential, material, and bodily pleasures." As someone not deeply involved in the social scientific community, I have been aware of those who exhibit an anti-Christian perspective, but at the same time I have found others, including Smith, who do work that supports Christian perspectives and openly admit their Christian faith. In the end, I am encouraged that the social sciences as a discipline must adhere to the objective principles of scientific investigation, and in spite of the over-valuation of autonomy and self-expression studies can show that self-centered thought and action are in the end self-destructive.

While Christians contributed to many of the developments in the revolutionary West, such as political and religious freedom, individual rights, science, abolition of slavery, and widespread education and medical work, they also opposed many of these advances. I like to add as a contribution of Christianity, with the support of non-Christians, the development of glorious music in the West. At the same time, Christians supported or failed to block terrible persecutions, wars, imperial domination of many lands, and, most tragic of all, the terrible Holocaust in the last century. Finally, Christianity is breaking free (largely involuntarily) from identification with the West and increasingly from association with dominating economic and political power. In fact, a development—the "leveling of the nations"—is helping to detach Christianity from any dominating power in the world, thus helping to reduce the former prejudice against Christianity in many traditional societies.

I want to close this chapter on Jesus Christ in history subsequent to his first coming with an undeniable fact. In all the disagreements over the various causes for changes in history, how many have been caused by Christianity, and when and where there will be more changes for good or for bad, it can hardly be denied that there has been an acceleration of change in the world. I have already pointed out that the New Testament makes clear that Jesus Christ introduced the last days of human history. Recent scientific work has shown how literally true this seems. John Haught illustrates the great age of the cosmos by comparing it to thirty volumes with 450 pages in each book.[13] Anatomically modern human beings appear on the bottom fifth of page 450 in the last volume. This is a very short time in terms of the history of the cosmos, but still a long time in terms of modern history. In other words, human beings have existed on earth for well over fifty thousand years, perhaps over one hundred thousand years. The speeding up of change began most clearly less than ten thousand years ago with the development of agriculture, called the Neolithic Revolution. Following this came the early civilizations that were based on agriculture. Agriculture was able to support the development of cities, along with commerce, writing, central governments, and organized religions, but also very oppressive empires. Needless to say, not all human beings were caught up in these urban-based civilizations; many continued to live as hunter-gatherers and horticulturalists, often at a healthier standard of living than the people living in the misery of crowded cities, toiling people on farms, and under the cruel rule of "god-king" tyrants in various kingdoms and empires.

13. Haught, *Science and Faith*, 1–2.

Whatever may be said about the changes stimulated by Christianity, the religion that arose from the followers of Jesus Christ, it is undeniable that Christianity has spread throughout the world only in the last two thousand years. In this short time, Jesus Christ has drawn the love and loyalty of more people than any other historical figure. Now, after the collapse of Western colonialism in the middle of the last century, Christianity has entered a new era in which all kinds of changes are accelerating, affecting human consciousness in ways yet to be fully understood.[14] At the very least it has given many a sense that the people of the world must learn to live together and that the promise in Ephesians 1:9–10 was never more relevant: "He [God] has made known to us the mystery of his will, according to his good pleasure that he set forth in Christ, as a plan for the fullness of time, to gather up all things in him, things in heaven and things on earth." Being a follower of the Human One means beginning to participate in this great gathering up.

14. Friedman, *Thank You For Being Late*, discusses three great accelerations taking place in technology, globalization (the market), and climate change. Following his discussion of these dizzying changes, he discusses at length the great necessity of people on every level, from the local to the international, to learn to work together based on mutual trust.

Chapter 10

The Human One in Personal and Communal Life

COMPREHENDING JESUS CHRIST IN LIFE

As ALREADY NOTED, THE secular scientific method is a valuable tool in understanding not only nature, but also human behavior. The latter is the particular subject of study for the social sciences. Christians and all people need to open themselves to examination by methods that seek to control for bias in order to reveal areas that need correction and improvement. Many social scientists, however, are often not sufficiently aware of the limitations the scientific method places upon them. Of course, the scientific method cannot examine God directly, but there are aspects of human inner life that are related to God that can only be studied indirectly. Emotions, commitments, motivations, and many other inner states of minds and wills may be (and often are) studied but only through a variety of indicators or external expressions. The brain itself is increasingly being studied scientifically. The effects of changes in human perception or consciousness can be observed through external indicators or brain scans, but the perceptions or the consciousness of God itself cannot be observed. This kind of perception or consciousness is spiritual because it extends from an inner state of mind to God and in a different way from one person to the inner states of mind in others. This perception or consciousness is a "sensibility" because it is able to recognize the inner sense of others or at least aspects of it. When this sensibility is of God, then clearly it is a "spiritual sensibility" or "spiritual perception." Of course, human spiritual sensibility is imperfect (possibly false) and always in need of support and the leading of God's Word and Spirit. We can identify with the father who said to Jesus, "I believe; help my unbelief!" (Mark 9:24). It goes without saying that my view of the existence of an inner spiritual life is a faith perspective that is not empirically demonstrable, even though the eyes of both faith and science may see empirical effects (including brain waves) of the spiritual life. It also goes without saying that given human fallen nature, it is wise to be humble about the content of spiritual consciousness or sensibility.[1]

The call in the Bible is to hear and to see what God is doing. The prophet Isaiah is sent out to the people with the message, "Keep listening, but do not comprehend; keep looking, but do not understand" (Isa 6:9). This is obviously a challenge to the people of whom Isaiah (1:3) earlier stated, "The ox knows its owner, and the donkey its master's crib; but Israel does not know, my people do not understand." Jesus takes up this theme from Isaiah in connection with speaking in parables. He tells his disciples, "To you has been given the secret of the kingdom of God, but for those outside, everything comes in parables; in order that 'they may indeed look, but not perceive, and may indeed listen, but not understand; so that they may not turn again and be forgiven.'" (Mark 4:11–12). Thus, the parables of Jesus are a challenge to gain spiritual perception.

Again, the Apostle Paul uses the Isaiah passage (after debate with local Jewish leaders) when he states:

> The Holy Spirit was right in saying to your ancestors through the prophet Isaiah, "Go to this people and say, You will indeed listen, but never understand, and you will indeed look, but never perceive. For this people's heart has grown dull, and their ears are hard of hearing, and they have shut their eyes; so that they might not look with their eyes, and listen with their ears, and understand with their heart and turn—and I would heal them." (Acts 28:25–27)

This way of repeating God's commission to Isaiah is meant to be a challenge to "understand with the heart and turn."

Another case referring to spiritual sensibility (perception or consciousness) is when the disciples of John the Baptist were sent by him to ask Jesus if he was "the one who is to come, or are we to wait for another?" Jesus answered them, "Go and tell John what you have seen and heard: the blind receive their sight, the lame walk, the lepers are cleansed, the deaf hear, the dead are raised, the poor have good news brought to them. And blessed is anyone who takes no offense at me" (Luke 7:20–23).

---

1. I mentioned the philosophy of critical realism, associated especially with the philosopher Roy Bhaskar (1944–2014), in connection with Christian Smith's book *What Is a Person?* I believe that the concept of spiritual sensibility or consciousness is consistent with the fact of non-empirical causation.

The biblical passages above show that spiritual sensibility or perception is based upon or in the end is a result and expression of faith. It can only be by faith that we perceive God's presence and work in the world. This faith is not simply the faith of direct trust in God but also of the experience of God working both within the self and among others in the world. It is the perception of God in the spiritual fulfillments of worship (joy, peace, challenge, inspiration, etc.), but it is also a perception of God working in the many deeds that lift human beings from suffering and oppression. The disciples experienced the presence of God with Jesus Christ, seeing his work and hearing his words. Of course, as already noted, this spiritual perception based on faith is a subjective human experience and therefore partial and fallible: "For we know only in part, and we prophesy only in part" (1 Cor 13:9).

Many people do not see and hear the presence and work in the world of the triune God—Father, Son, and Holy Spirit, or Creator, Redeemer, and Enabler. As Isaiah, Jesus, and Paul said, they are blind and deaf, but this has been experienced by all human beings, including most believers. Some have grown up in the church or around believing people but have not perceived the work of God all around them. Others are either apathetic toward or actively oppose any belief in God. However, rather than judge one another's ability to sense God at work in the world, humility requires recognition that all of us as human beings are afflicted with spiritual blindness and in need of healing. Our vision of God at work will always be only partial. All Christians need to struggle against becoming like the Christians in Laodicea—"wretched, pitiable, poor, blind, and naked."

As one who obtained an advanced degree in the social sciences, I see on the one hand an attempt by some scholars to seriously study the inner life of human beings, including their moral decisions, as difficult as this study is.[2] On the other hand, some scholars seem to focus, for example, primarily on outward events and activities related to Jesus Christ and the subsequent history without taking into account the impact of the person of Jesus on both the inner individual and the social life of the expanding group of followers in the years after his resurrection. This includes the powerful emotions generated in the new faith communities and the compassion they showed to others. As an example, I found the historical analysis of Bart Ehrman of "how Jesus became God" very helpful in tracing the major events and influences in the period during and after the life of Jesus among his followers and the outward expressions of their faith, but I missed an account for the impact of Jesus as a person on their inner life both during and

2. Collins, *Interaction Ritual Chains*; Smith, *Moral, Believing Animals*; *What Is a Person?*

after his ministry.[3] This will be considered more explicitly in the rest of this chapter.

THINKING OF JESUS TODAY

This book affirms that Jesus Christ fulfills the human longing for incarnation, which for Christians means a personal and envisioned, though not tangible, contact with and continual access to the transcendent God, the Creator and Ruler of the universe. Even more important, Jesus also fulfills the longing for atonement based on his compassion and his sacrificial death for all, but especially for oneself personally. This means that although we cannot now see Jesus, we can know by faith that he came; lived on earth; was physically close to other human beings, especially his followers; and then died a literal death for the sins of the world, followed by his resurrection and appearance to his followers. We can envision him in all these aspects of his life on earth among people.

We believe the tangibility of Jesus through the words of his followers, an especially clear example of which we read in 1 John 1:1–4:

> We declare to you what was from the beginning, what we have heard, what we have seen with our eyes, what we have looked at and touched with our hands, concerning the word of life—this life was revealed, and we have seen it and testify to it, and declare to you the eternal life that was with the Father and was revealed to us—we declare to you what we have seen and heard so that you also may have fellowships with us; and truly our fellowship is with the Father and with his Son Jesus Christ. We are writing these things so that our joy may be complete.

Even though we cannot now see Jesus in the flesh, we are especially comforted by the words of blessing said to "doubting Thomas" in John 20:29: "Blessed are those who have not seen and yet have come to believe." Nevertheless, the question remains for all the followers of Jesus since he ascended from the sight of his disciples: how are we to think of Jesus, both in our devotional life or lives of prayer and in our life with other believers?

There are many pictures and statues of Jesus that have been extremely important in Christian art history, but I am one of those who do not find them helpful. To me they only show what Jesus did *not* look like. The fact that there is no description of Jesus in the gospels is an indication to me that his physical appearance is not important. We only need to know that now it

---

3. Ehrman, *How Jesus Became God.*

is a glorified human appearance as described in the transfiguration and the resurrection appearances, which we will someday be like. Even in the resurrection appearances, his glorified presence seems to have been sufficiently like that of the Lord the disciples had known so that they recognized him, even though several times not at first. Mary in the garden was slow to recognize him. We also remember the two on the road to Emmaus who did not recognize him until he blessed and broke the bread in their presence. The tangible Holy Communion service continues to be a time when Christians sense the presence of Christ by words spoken, by physically eating together, and by the inner work of the Holy Spirit. The enactment helps us realize that Jesus is as real as the food we ingest, his sacrifice just as real as the cup poured out, and communion with him as real as the people partaking with us. We realize that we are participants in a mystical way in the sacrificial life and work of Jesus through the body of Christ, the church.

There is still more that must be said about thinking of Jesus. Because Jesus did live on earth among human beings and interacted with many people, especially with a group of followers to whom he was very dear and often puzzling, it is possible for many Christians today to imagine Jesus with them. Some may think of Mary, sister of Martha, sitting and listening at the feet of Jesus and place themselves mentally in a similar position. Some may think of Thomas kneeling before Jesus at the sight of his nail-pierced hands and the wound in his side and also think of themselves as doing the same. Many may think of themselves as conversing with Jesus like the two on the road to Emmaus. I must add that there are those who dream about Jesus. This has been mentioned by people who converted from Islam and by a well-known writer, Lauren Winner, who converted from Judaism.[4] Whatever one may think of the dreams some have reported, the basic fact is that Jesus the person may be envisioned because people believe that he walked the earth and kept close company with people and deeply enjoyed that company. When a Christian is in a social context that is opposed to Christianity or a situation of oppression or suffering, some kind of personal encounter with Jesus the person may be a major means of comfort and encouragement. Jesus may break through the mental opposition or reservations as he did with Paul on the road to Damascus. We know that African-American Christians, most of whom personally know discrimination and danger, are especially active in imagining Jesus and praying to him in all the circumstances of life.[5] The contact of these and others with Jesus is very personal, but at the same time communal.

---

4. Kraft, *Searching for Heaven in the Real World*; Winner, *Girl Meets God*.
5. Shelton and Emerson, *Black and Whites in Christian America*.

I will mention that being called by Jesus to follow him is a guide in prayer. We can think about where Jesus would go if he were in our community and world. We can then follow him in our prayers as we go with him to people and places we have come to know Jesus would visit and touch. The people and places are too many for us to always go to in our prayers and yet we can go in prayer to many of them and know in our hearts that we are following the Human One, who is God with us and the world. We may find that we are physically able to go to some of those places to represent Jesus Christ, who went before us.

JESUS AND THE TRIUNE GOD

Christians believe in Jesus as the second person of the Trinity. It does not mean that we believe in three gods, but it does raise the question of how we relate to the Trinity in our devotions. I believe that in our devotions and even in fleeting moments it is helpful to think of Jesus as with us as he was with his disciples in many settings. It is also very helpful to remember that God the Holy Spirit is with us helping us to pray "with sighs too deep for words" (Rom 8:26). Even though the thoughts about Jesus and the Holy Spirit are helpful in devotions, in relation to the triune God, Jesus taught us to pray to God the Father: "Our Father, who art in heaven . . . " Jesus had a way of drawing attention to God the Father rather than to himself. When the rich young ruler called him good, Jesus said to him, "Why do you call me good? No one is good but God alone" (Mark 10:18). This is a healthy reminder to those who may focus only on Jesus Christ as opposed to the Trinity of Father, Son, and Holy Spirit. In his temptation, Jesus said to the devil, quoting Scripture, "Worship the Lord your God, and serve only him" (Luke 4:7). In the garden of Gethsemane during his temptation, Jesus prayed, "Abba, Father, for you all things are possible; remove this cup from me; yet, not what I want, but what you want" (Mark 14:36). On the cross Jesus cried out, "My God, my God, why have you forsaken me?"(Mark 15:34). He also prayed, "Father, forgive them; for they do not know what they are doing" and then finally, "Father, into your hands I commend my spirit" (Luke 23:34, 46). In no way can it be said that Jesus wanted to hinder or block any direct prayer to God the Father. In fact, he wanted to do just the opposite: to facilitate and encourage prayer to God the Father. In short, the judgment of his followers is that Jesus is the Mediator, who gives us "confidence to enter the sanctuary by the blood of Jesus, by the new and living way that he opened for us through the curtain (that is, through his flesh)" (Heb 10:19). It is important to remember that Jesus is not the Mediator between us and an angry and condemning God. No, it is our hearts that are cold, apathetic, and consciously or unconsciously hostile to God. He wins our hearts and draws our hearts to God, whom he taught us was like the father of the prodigal son—rushing out to embrace us. One of the clearest words on praying to God the Father is found in John 16:26–27: "On that day you will ask in my name. I do not say to you that I will ask the Father on your behalf; for the Father himself loves you, because you have loved me and have believed that I came from God."

Having said all this, Jesus did invite people to come to him: "Come unto me, all you who are weary and are carrying heavy burdens, and I will give you rest" (Matt 11:28). Of course, "follow me" was the continuing call of Jesus to people. In John, he called on people to be united with him in a very intimate way ("Those who eat my flesh and drink my blood abide in me and I in them", 6:56; and "Abide in me as I abide in you," 15:4). John also presents a strong discussion of the work of the Holy Spirit, who "will guide us into all the truth" (16:12). Also, in Luke 1:8 Jesus tells the disciples, "But you will receive power when the Holy Spirit has come upon you." Thus, the focus on God the Father as the focus of prayer does not leave out the important work of the Trinity in the work of redemption.

It is true that people pray to Jesus at times, some more than others and perhaps in some churches more than others. However, it appears to me that while we may be thinking of him as walking with us and envision him as seated "at the right hand of God," our prayers should usually be directed to God the Father. It seems to me that this is what Jesus wants us to do and the Holy Spirit helps us to do. We have words in John that encourage us to think of Jesus and God the Father together. There are the words to Philip, "Have I been with you all this time, Philip, and you still do not know me? Whoever has seen me has seen the Father. How can you say, 'Show us the Father'? Do you not believe that I am in the Father and the Father is in me?" (John 14:9–10). Then there are the powerful words in the "high priestly prayer" of John 17, in which Jesus identified himself with God the Father. He begins the prayer:

> Father, the hour has come; glorify your Son so that the Son may glorify you, since you have given him authority over all people [flesh], to give eternal life to all whom you have given him. And this is eternal life, that they may know you, the only true God, and Jesus Christ whom you have sent. I glorified you on earth by finishing the work that you gave me to do. So now, Father, glorify me in your own presence with the glory that I had in your presence before the world existed. (17:1–5)

These words from the New Testament seem to me to encourage us to think of Jesus and God the Father together. But then also we have the more hidden and quiet, but highly important, work of the Holy Spirit mentioned above, which we must not forget. We are to be open to the work of the Holy Spirit throughout life. The work of the Holy Spirit is referred to in the words of Jesus, "I have said these things to you while I am still with you. But the Advocate, the Holy Spirit, whom the Father will send in my name, will teach you everything, and remind you of all that I have said to you" (John 14:25–26). The Holy Spirit will even lead us "into all the truth," but it will be the truth that is both new and yet thoroughly consistent with what we know from Jesus (John 16:12–15). I take this to mean that we are to seek the wisdom and love that comes from the Holy Spirit as we deal with the many conditions of life that unfold in our individual lives and in human history, especially those in those conditions not previously encountered. However, it is important that the Holy Spirit is not a private gift to us as individuals, but is God's self-gifting to the church, the whole people of God. We should seek the guidance of the Holy Spirit given to the whole people of God, not just to us as individuals or even to our own Christian fellowship or denomination only. Surely the Holy Spirit inspired the many new forms of worship, music, architecture, and art developed in the church, but also much that developed outside of the church, often by the activity of Christians, but also by others: education, science, medicine, and many social services together with the concepts of human rights and democracy that have unfolded in history. Nevertheless, the core inspiration of the Holy Spirit was the mission outreach that began formally from Antioch (Acts 13:2) and continues to be inspired from countless places to this day.

Regarding the work of the Holy Spirit, Paul placed special emphasis on it in Romans 8, which includes the words, "When we cry, 'Abba! Father!' it is that very Spirit bearing witness with our spirit that we are children of God, and if children, then heirs, heirs of God and joint heirs with Christ—if, in fact, we suffer with him so that we may also be glorified with him" (Rom 8:15–17). He adds, "Likewise, the Spirit helps us in our weakness; for we do not know how to pray as we ought, but that very Spirit intercedes with sighs too deep for words. And God, who searches the heart, knows what is the mind of the Spirit, because the Spirit intercedes for the saints according to the will of God" (8:26–27). From what is said in these various passages, it is clear that Jesus Christ leads us in our ongoing spiritual life (including both devotional times and spontaneous and constant "thought prayers," but also in our fellowship and worship with others) into a living relationship with the triune God. Christ is the Mediator as we pray to the Father and live in the Spirit.

JESUS AND PERSONS

On the one hand, Jesus Christ directs us toward God the Father and identifies himself with the God toward whom he directs us. At the same time, Jesus Christ also identifies himself with human beings, both by his favorite name for himself, the Human One, and by words that refer to acts of kindness to human beings in need as being the same as acts of kindness to him. Now we see why we are not told what Jesus looked like: we are to see Jesus in each person we meet. If anything, we should see Jesus and even the church as whole, at least at times, as in Isaiah's prophesy, "so marred was his appearance, beyond human semblance and his form beyond that of mortals" (Isa 52:14); "he had no form or majesty that we should look at him, nothing in his appearance that we should desire him" (Isa 53:2). As he taught us himself, Jesus wants us to see him in the suffering people we meet or, more likely, people whom we often ignore or are hidden from us. It is not just God the Father he is showing us; it is others, many of whom we have a natural aversion to, but who are God's creations made in God's image.

In all three of the gospels, Jesus identifies himself with children or "little ones," who are welcomed by him, but in that identification he also associates God, who sent him: "Whoever welcomes one such child in my name welcomes me, and whoever welcomes me welcomes not me but the one who sent me (Mark 9:37; compare Matt 18:5 and Luke 9:48). His clearest identification with those in need is stated in Matthew 25:31–32, 34–36:

> When the Son of Man [the Human One] comes in his glory, and all the angels with him, then he will sit on the throne of his glory. All the nations will be gathered before him, and he will separate the people from one another as a shepherd separates the sheep from the goats. . . . Then, the king will say to those at his right hand, "Come, you that are blessed by my Father, inherit the kingdom prepared for you from the foundation of the world; for I was hungry and you gave me food, I was thirsty and you gave me something to drink, I was a stranger and you welcomed me, I was naked and you gave me clothing, I was sick and you took care of me, I was in prison and you visited me.

When the righteous expressed surprise because they did not remember doing these things for Jesus, they are told by the king, "Truly I tell you, just as you did it to one of the least of these who are members of my family, you did it to me." Those who are separated to the left, who are condemned to "the eternal fire prepared by the devil and his angels," are told that when they did not act on behalf of those in need they were not acting on behalf of the king, who is the Human One (Matt 25:40–41). Others may not agree, but I take "eternal fire" as metaphorical, namely as experience in this life, which in our spiritual dullness we may not even be aware of. I believe one of the great conditions of spiritual blindness is to underestimate the self-destructive power of sin, of which we are often unconscious. At the very least, the words of Jesus show the great seriousness of what he is talking about.

These passages that speak of encountering Jesus as we encounter people, especially those in need, make us realize that we can hardly meet Jesus by himself. We meet him with others and in others. It is a truism to say that Jesus loved people, but one of the most important overlooked characteristics of Jesus was his sociability. If we could only have seen the expressions on his face and heard the various tones of his voice, we might have a better understanding of how much Jesus loved being with and interacting with people. When we first see him after his baptism, he is interacting with Andrew, Peter, Philip, and Nathanael. After they met and came to know him, Jesus later issued his call to Peter, Andrew, James, and John on the shores of Lake Galilee, followed by other calls and the establishment of the formal group of the twelve apostles.

Jesus is repeatedly invited to meals and therefore must have been seen as a convivial and animated guest, as well as one who would make interesting, if sometimes sharp, comments. We know that he was "full of stories." His hosts were sometimes those who seemed to invite him out of curiosity, as in the case of Simon the Pharisee (Luke 7:36–50). The gospels note how he was criticized for eating—dare we say partying?—with tax collectors and sinners (Luke 15:2; Matt 11:19). It is hard to imagine that a "serious and solemn" person would have done such things. On more than one occasion, people were with Jesus in an isolated area for a longer period than usual. Instead of sending people away, Jesus in effect said, "Let's have a picnic." People, especially children, are very perceptive and children would not have been brought to him unless Jesus was known as someone who paid attention to children and enjoyed them. I do not know that embracing children is reported of any other religious founder. There are many songs about this.

In John 15:14–15 we are amazed to hear Jesus, the Son of God, call his disciples "friends": "I do not call you servants [slaves] any longer, because the servant does not know what the master is doing; but I have called you friends, because I have made known to you everything that I have heard from my Father." We believe that Jesus felt the weight of the sins of the world during his prayer in the garden of Gethsemane (Mark 14:32–42), but it would be consistent with what we know of him that part of his great sorrow was that he did not want to give up physical fellowship with his friends, which would be made necessary by his death. He was able to go forward because he knew that his death would be the basis for creating a whole new human community with which he would have an ever-widening fellowship.

After the resurrection, Jesus came back to his disciples and obviously enjoyed the reconnection he was able to make with them. We can hear his heartfelt word, "Greetings!" (Matt 28:9). He chose to have an extended discussion with two relatively unknown followers while walking on the road to Emmaus (Luke 24:13–35). The promise of the triumphant Christ to his followers was, "And remember, I am with you always, to the end of the age" (Matt 28:20). Our great joy and comfort is his abiding presence!

JESUS THROUGH THE ARTS

In chapter 9, on "Jesus Christ in Subsequent History," I did not include a section on the influence of Jesus on the arts—written, visual, dramatic, and musical. This would require many books. The world would look and sound very differently without the coming and presence of Jesus Christ. Beyond that, some or all of the arts have a great effect on the personal and communal life of faith in Jesus. With me it is especially music that affects me emotionally and makes me feel close to Jesus. The visual arts related to Jesus have not affected me as much, but the incarnation and atonement have had an enormous effect on the visual arts in several Christian traditions and on many people. Lauren F. Winner, author and historian, and a convert from Orthodox Judaism, writes:

> I've filled my bedroom with pictures of Jesus. Icons and paintings and church fans and other Jesuses dance all over my walls. Everywhere you turn, there He is, peering at you. Sometimes with a halo, sometimes on a cross, sometimes knocking at a door. When I don't much like Christianity, or when I can't remember why I am doing any of this, I look at these pictures of Jesus. Often I talk to them. I talk to them when I am too distracted, otherwise, to pray, and I talk to them when none of my friends are home and I am bored and alone. Eastern Orthodox Christians have an elaborate and sophisticated theology and practice of icons: they somehow enter into the icons, the icons become a window through which to see Him. My thinking about icons is a little more rudimentary. My icons are sort of like imaginary friends, only Jesus isn't imaginary.[6]

She goes on to express what I am trying to say about the longing of all human beings and the core of the Christian life:

6. Winner, *Girl Meets God*, 73.

In my more pompous moments, I describe myself, my Christianity, as *radically incarnational* [italics hers]. The incarnation, that God took flesh, is the whole reason I am not an Orthodox Jew. The incarnation is the whole reason I am not lighting a menorah at this time of year. I am a Christian because being a Christian gives me a picture of God to talk to during all these moments when, without the picture, I would forget that God exists. My old professor can't imagine how it can possibly be true that God became a man, he can't imagine how I can possibly make sense of it, but I no longer know how to make sense of God, or anything else for that matter without it.[7]

CONCLUSION

Jesus Christ was related closely to God the Father, but he also identified closely with human beings. We see him enjoying a warm relationship with his followers, whom he called "friends," in spite of their lack of understanding and "slowness of heart to believe" (Luke 24:25). This twofold relationship shows Jesus as the perfect Mediator—the one who makes the depth of God's love known to human hearts and the one who leads us patiently by the hand into the presence of the one who otherwise would be hidden in holy mystery. We know that God is "high and lofty" (Isa 6:1), that we should "take off our shoes" in his presence (Exod 3:5), and that to touch his holy mountain from which the law goes forth is highly dangerous (Exod 19:23); but as the great writer of the Letter to the Hebrews says,

> But you have come to Mount Zion and to the city of the living God, the heavenly Jerusalem, and to innumerable angels in festal gathering and to the assembly of the firstborn who are enrolled in heaven, and to God the judge of all, and to the spirits of the righteous made perfect, *and to Jesus* [italics mine], the mediator of a new covenant, and to the sprinkled blood that speaks a better word than the blood of Abel. (12:22–24)

Because of his compassion and love of persons, Jesus Christ is a highly appealing and attractive personality. There are numerous verses and hymns (not always the best music) celebrating the personal relationship that people feel for Jesus: "Blessed Assurance Jesus Is Mine," "I Walk in the Garden Alone," "I Want Jesus to Walk with Me," "Jesus, Priceless Treasure," "Jesus, Thy Boundless Love to Me," and on and on. I do not reject a certain amount

---

7. Ibid., 73, 74.

of sentimentality, certainly of emotion. At least, there is a place for a sense of a very personal connection to Jesus Christ. Paul expressed such a sense when he said, "I have been crucified with Christ; and it is no longer I who live, but it is Christ who lives in me. And the life I now live in the flesh I live by faith in the Son of God, who loved me and gave himself for me" (Gal 2:19–20). Nevertheless, it is very clear that we cannot meet Jesus Christ and be with him without at the same time meeting and being with both God the Father and the Holy Spirit and *also* at the same time with other people. Given human emotional nature, it is certainly possible to have an overly romantic picture of Jesus. But we know that Jesus in the power of the Holy Spirit brings us, like the prodigal son, "to our senses" (Luke 15:17) and then brings us into the arms of God the Father (15:20). At the same time, we are constituted as part of his earthly body, which is the church, the community of God's people, where the eternal celebration begins (15:22–24). As already noted, historians, in trying to explain the spread of Christianity, especially while noting the famous church figures in those first three hundred years, often forget the personal power and joy found in the presence of Jesus Christ by ordinary Christians, often spoken of as the work of the Holy Spirit. And then there are the many communities of believers where, in a unique way, unlike the usual experience of human beings, people learn to put up with each other and care for each other because they have a common Lord to whom they belong in one body.

Chapter 11

The Authority of the Human One

THE HIGHEST CLAIM OF JESUS CHRIST

THE DIVINITY OF JESUS Christ is not based on a direct or unequivocal claim by him to be God or divine. It was not his way. His way was to draw out faith in himself and to wait for recognition of faith in others of himself. His way was to demonstrate who he was as he did in answer to the question by John the Baptist regarding whether he was the "one who is to come" (Matt 11:3; Luke 7:19). Ultimately, Jesus counted on recognition by those who would be his followers, not those who were not his followers. However, a very sweeping claim was made by Jesus to his followers after the accomplishment of his death and resurrection and just before returning to the Father. At that time he said, "All authority in heaven and on earth has been given to me" (Matt 28:18). "Heaven and earth" means the total universe and so this was a claim of universal cosmic authority. This is certainly equivalent to a claim to divine authority, but authority is not established by simple affirmation. Authority exists by right and ultimate authority belongs to God, but it only exists for human beings when it is accepted. The recognition of the cosmic significance of Jesus Christ is given clearly in very early Christian literature, possibly part of an early hymn, already quoted in chapter 7, in the Letter to the Colossians 1:15–20.

While this clear assertion of divinity has been the belief of classical Christianity, it is a belief that cannot be forced, but must be willingly, lovingly, and joyfully received, although it may be preceded by a struggle of the heart. Notice that the assertion of the divinity and cosmic authority of Jesus Christ in the Colossians passage ends with "the blood of the cross." This is how the now transcendent Human One wins the hearts and loyalty of human beings, which includes the recognition of his authority.

One insight into the nature of the authority of Jesus Christ is given in the incident when the religious leaders asked Jesus, "By what authority are you doing these things? Who gave you this authority to do them?" (Mark 11:28; Luke 20:1–7). Jesus did not answer them but asked them a question about John the Baptist: "Did the baptism of John come from heaven, or was it of human origin?" (Mark 11:30). After arguing among themselves, they refused to answer the question and so Jesus did not answer their question. This incident shows that Jesus expected his authority to be recognized intuitively by faith, from the heart. This is consistent with the meaning of authority; it must be recognized as belonging by rights to those who have it.

THE NATURE OF AUTHORITY

"Authority" is sometimes confused with "power." Power can be exercised without any reference to the thought or views of those on whom it is exercised. Governments need to have a monopoly of power in a given territory. However, governments realize that to rule by the exercise of raw power can be very expensive and is not sustainable in the long run. This is why governments seek authority based on the recognition by those ruled of the right of the ruler or government to rule. Interestingly, although some may not like to express it this way, God faces the same problem as all governments: how to establish authority. God does not want to rule by raw or coercive power, but rather through loving acceptance of God's authority, through which personal transformation takes place. The whole Bible, and especially the account of what Jesus did for us, tells us the story of what God has done to win our recognition of God's authority expressed through Jesus Christ. "Authority," unlike "power," is a relational term. This makes the claim to universal authority by Jesus very understandable, because his goal is to establish a relationship with all human beings in every time and place.

After making the claim to universal authority, Jesus immediately mandates his followers to go everywhere and "make disciples of all peoples," baptizing them and teaching them to obey him. Nothing could be more personal than giving and receiving publicly the mark of being a follower of Jesus Christ through baptism and then undertaking a permanent effort of obedience to the way of Jesus Christ. Jesus and his disciples must have understood that, since identification as a member of the household of God was henceforth not to be by ethnicity or by descent, as with Jews, but rather the sign of baptism would become the mark of followers. Becoming a disciple of Jesus Christ became open to anyone. In spite of disagreements among Christians about the meaning and mode of baptism, giving this sign has become the universal practice of the universal church.

The difference between authority and power is the major reason why governments have almost universally sought to become linked to religion. They want to make sure that they obtain legitimacy based on a divine or supernatural authority. Since religion and ideology are closely linked, in the modern world, in which the authority of religion has been challenged and set aside, secular ideologies have gained in importance. This is seen particularly in the twentieth century, when Fascism and Communism gained quasi-religious status and were used to demand loyalty from large populations. Christianity has even sought to be an ideology or a counter-ideology by being linked to political parties, for example, "Christian Socialists." Such names have been avoided in the United States, but people sometimes oppose political enemies by accusing them of secular humanism or even godless secularism. They may also be accused of socialism because of its known link with a secular approach in government and even as taking a step toward atheistic Communism. Probably one reason the term "Christian Socialist" is used for the name of a political party in Europe is in order to deny a link to Communism. Whatever the case, we see those with or seeking political power typically use some kind of ideology to support their authority. Even in the United States there exists a "civil religion" that is used in expressions of patriotism. It has overtones of religion, but fortunately at its core is the declaration of human equality and many checks to authoritarianism. Patriotism becomes dangerous when it becomes like a religion and is used as a cover for carrying out injustices. That is why I would rather speak of the American "civil covenant" or even "civil ideals." Every nation needs a basic agreement to certain values and morals to maintain unity. For Christians, the best legitimization of political authority is when governments act justly, which includes governing with the consent of all the people, especially of those with the least power. Our civil ideals are best expressed in the Declaration of Independence (which mentions God as the Creator) and the Constitution (which does not mention God) as the ongoing attempt to practice democracy. Ideology or religion, including Christianity, should not be used as a tool to gain and maintain political authority and power, as is too often the case. Martin Luther King Jr.'s challenge to America to live up to its ideals is the best way to advance justice in America.

DERIVATIVE AUTHORITIES

There are many authorities in the world, the first authority one encounters being the authority of parents. This authority is affirmed in the fifth commandment. However, it is well known that this authority was relativized by Jesus when he placed loyalty to him above loyalty to parents and family (Matt 10:35–37; 12:46–50). At the same time, he condemned those who used the law to avoid responsibility for their parents (Matt 15:3–9). The point is that the authority of parents, like all human authorities, is under God or derived from God, but not above God or above Jesus.

Governments are an obvious source of authority, but just as with all the authorities other than Jesus Christ, the authority of governments is derivative. Jesus recognized the right of those in authority to tax people under them (Matt 17:24–27; 22:15–22). Although Paul openly recognized that the authority of governments was given by God (Rom 13:1–7), in the Book of Revelation, Roman authority and power is seen as being used for evil, showing that governments may misuse their authority. Christians have considered Paul's words as a valid argument for normal obedience to governments, and some have used his words to support governmental suppression of resistance. At the same time, Christians historically have not believed that the Bible rules out all resistance to governments. Peter's word to those in authority has proven useful to resisters of oppression: "We must obey God rather than any human authority" (Acts 5:29).

The working out of the principles of democracy has taken many centuries and the suffering of many people who resisted the misuse of government and church authority. The principles of democracy have been to seek to ensure that the authority of government is based on the consent of the governed. In the last few centuries, it has even been recognized that since religion has often been misused by governments to support their power, democratic governments should be made secular. This is still being debated, since many do not realize that making governments secular does not mean that those in government may not be inspired and motivated by their religious faith. It only means that religion is not used to justify governmental actions. Christians believe they should be motivated in all things by their faith but that they should not use the name of God to justify the policies that they support. In all the debate about governmental authority, most Christians along with most other people, with the exception of anarchists, recognize that human beings need some type of governmental authority both for protection from evil actions and for promotion of peace, justice, and the welfare of minorities and those unable to provide for themselves. But, of course, authority may be misused.

In human societies, there are many forms of authority under which people live, for example, the authority of the organizations for which they work, such as businesses organizations and educational and healthcare institutions, and also the authority of the many other organizations to which people belong. Religious institutions, which for Christians are represented by the church, have their own form of order and authority. The movement toward democracy of the last few centuries has both influenced and been influenced by Protestant congregations, which gave people experience in democratic processes. To say that the kingdom of God is not a democracy as a justification for authoritarianism or non-democracy in the church is silly to me because the church of Jesus Christ is not equivalent to the kingdom of God. Churches have been less strict in exercising their authority in recent centuries or, rather, have focused more on spiritual authority than on the physical control of lives. Individualistic ideology, fostered especially by Protestantism, has been misused by individuals to let them feel free to withdraw from churches they did not like and to form their own churches, usually considered more spiritual or orthodox than older churches. Many simply decide to remain unrelated to any church out of an anti-authoritarian or anti-organizational spirit. These often consider themselves "spiritual" but not "religious."

Religions, including Christianity, have relied on the authority of religious leaders and of religious scriptures. These two sources of authority are seen in the contrast between the old churches (Orthodoxy and Roman Catholicism), which tend to look to properly authorized religious leaders, and Protestant churches, which emphasize the authority of the Bible as interpreted by church assemblies, but more recently by "Spirit-inspired" or charismatic leaders. The need for a sense of security and certainty in life is seen especially in the reliance in Roman Catholicism on the authority of the pope and in the reliance of some Protestants on an "infallible" or especially an "inerrant Bible." Christian Smith has pointed out the intellectual "impossibility" of this kind of biblicism in much conservative Protestantism.[1] Biblicism has typically been associated with literalism in interpreting the Bible. A similar reliance on infallible authority is also seen in other fundamentalisms, especially in Islam, where the Qur'an is believed to have been dictated by God to Muhammad (similar to the view of the Bible by some Christians). With the failure of Fascism and Communism (at least in the West), highly authoritarian ideologies have lost influence, but the human attraction to authoritarianism is still evident, especially in what are termed "radical" groups, such as hate groups in the West and similar groups in

---

1. Smith, *Bible Made Impossible*.

Islam. Such authoritarianism seems to satisfy some deep human sense of insecurity. Unfortunately, when people feel insecure in chaotic and corrupt societies, they tend to accept authoritarian rulers.

In addition to human authorities or the authority of human institutions, there has always been a kind of authority associated with powers in nature that is wise to recognize. For example, human beings cannot ignore the power of gravity, the power of a lightning strike or an earthquake, or the power of a charging lion. In recent centuries, the systematic investigation of nature conducted by science has yielded many kinds of knowledge of the powers in natural events and processes. As a result, scientists gained authority as interpreters of nature, and those who are trained to use technology learned from science gained authority in their fields of expertise. They have gained and even surpassed the authority of those with specialized knowledge gained from study of some subject, such as law or literature. In fact, it can be said that the authority of scientists and science has become equal to or surpassed the authority of religious leaders and the Bible.

It is interesting that Jesus recognized the dependable aspects of nature that provided a kind of security and evidence of the Creator God's care for human beings (Matt 6:25–30). He saw that the dependability of nature (God through nature) provides an opportunity for human beings to concentrate on serving in the kingdom of God (Matt 6:31–33). There are even powers within nature that are self-improving or self-renewing if allowed to work. What is encouraging is that the order and the patterns found in nature, as well as the many exceptions to prevailing patterns, have enabled human beings through science to alleviate much suffering and to bring numerous benefits to the world. At the same time, as with all of God's gifts, human beings have used science and technology to exert power over others and bring suffering and destruction to many people. Nevertheless, the misuse of nature brings a certain judgment on those who misuse it, sometimes after much time. Climate change, especially since the Industrial Revolution, is a good example.

SPIRITUAL AUTHORITIES AND POWERS

In chapter 2 I described the natural and supernatural nature of human beings—the supernatural being in the God-given capacity of human beings to recognize their relationship with God, communicate with God, and live eternally with God. Human beings are subject to influence by God, but they are also subject to the influence of evil, given the susceptibility to temptation of human beings. The Lord's Prayer itself, with "And do not bring us to the time of trial, but rescue us from evil [or the evil one]" (Matt 6:13), indicates the ever present danger of influence from evil. However, as made clear in the Bible, evil has been defeated by Christ.

The primary means of influence that God has chosen is the relationship of faith and love that God establishes with the redeemed. This is clear from the story of Israel, but especially in the life and work of Jesus, in which he draws out faith and love from his followers rather than seeking to coerce faith. Although a gift from God, faith and love emanate from an inner or subjective source within human beings responding to the grace of God. This inner source is the inner self that is also a source for thought, feeling, and intuition or sensibility that find expression in everyday life, especially in human relationships. Since the inner self is expressed in various observable ways, it can be studied as a human phenomenon. For example, human motivations and attitudes that emanate from the inner self can be studied by ordinary observation of outward indicators. While these may well be (*should be* for Christians) influenced by faith and love toward God, they are also influenced by external sociocultural factors, which are almost always mixed with good and evil elements paralleling the good and evil within human beings. Evil is able to act upon individuals primarily because it finds a response within the sinful human heart. At the same time, evil works from outside upon individuals through sociocultural forces that are a part of all human life, given the social and creative nature of human beings. This is the area of the "authorities" or "principalities and powers" recognized by the Bible, namely, the forces that act upon human beings from the outside. They gain special power through coming under the influence of evil.

People from preliterate societies and most traditional societies recognized and typically feared unseen authorities and powers. These "supernatural" powers were worshipped in order to gain various favors. The Bible comes out of this ancient world and recognizes that there are such fearful authorities and powers, but that they are subject to God. Psalm 82 is an example in which it is asserted that God's authority and power is over other authorities and powers and, furthermore, that the other authorities and powers are temporary or mortal, like human beings. However, it is in the New Testament, especially in the writings of Paul (1 Cor 2:2–8; Rom 8:38–39; 1 Cor 15:24–28; Col 1:16; 2:9–10, 13–15; Eph 2:1–2; 3:10; 6:12), that we see a more advanced understanding of the nature of the spiritual authorities and powers, which are greater than individuals and exert great influence on human life. The work of Wink in drawing attention to the "principalities and powers" has already been mentioned in chapter 2.[2] In interpreting the various phrases found in the Bible, Wink states:

> We found ourselves to be dealing not with analytically precise categories used consistently from one passage to another but with terms that cluster and swarm around the reality they describe, as if by heaping up synonymous phrases and parallel constructions an intuitive sense of the reality described might emerge. So we discovered series, strings, and pairs of terms used with a kind of consistent indiscriminateness, and within this field of language, a genuine power-reality that comes to expression.[3]

My view is that in many respects the social sciences that were developed in the last few centuries have reaffirmed what the Bible recognized long ago: that forces above and beyond individuals exist in human societies that powerfully affect how human beings think and act, often with little consciousness in themselves of the reality and influence of these forces. In fact, the social sciences can be a great aid in gaining some understanding of the invisible forces that affect human thinking. The principalities and powers of Paul are not simply equivalent to sociocultural forces, because Paul recognizes a supernatural element working in them, but there is a certain similarity between them. Both principalities and powers and sociocultural forces are beyond individuals and they can be good, bad, or neutral in effect. What is important for Christians to recognize, as well as others who are willing to acknowledge human frailty, is that all human beings come under forces that are beyond individuals and societies and that influence basic thinking, including beliefs, values, motivations, and attitudes. (I do not care for the term "worldview" because I feel that it is too encompassing, used too indiscriminately, and used as if it is more unchanging than it really is.) The influences on our thinking from the invisible world of sociocultural forces begin in the generations before us and come to us through our first authorities, our parents, but then these influences soon influence us through our communities and the larger social contexts in which we live. These influences are all the more powerful because we are largely unconscious of them. The term "white privilege" refers to one of those forces of which white people are largely unconscious. It is at this point that Christians should recognize the need to wrestle with these influences (Eph 6:12). Nevertheless, as powerful as the principalities and powers are, they are not as powerful as the force of God's love. Jesus Christ has undercut their power through his victory on the cross.

2. Wink, *Naming the Powers*; *Unmasking the Powers*; *Engaging the Powers*.
3. Wink, *Naming the Powers*, 100.

I would like to point to the useful work of Haidt in developing a "moral foundations theory" to help explain why liberals and conservatives have such difficulty in agreeing or even dialoguing.[4] Basically, he points to how they (and libertarians) all have moral bases for their views, but tend to emphasize different moral bases. His studies found that conservatives emphasize a broad set of six moral foundations, whereas liberals tend to emphasize the one moral foundation of justice and libertarians the one basis of liberty. I have not done his theory justice, but its important contribution is to encourage liberals, conservatives, and others to take time to listen to each other. Another contribution is to make clear that human beings have moral natures and that any system of government should make its moral bases as clear as possible. In a democratic society, moral bases should be chosen to act upon through democratic debate and decision. Thankfully, in America there are competing forums to debate which way society should proceed (for example, political parties and the free press) and different powers in government (the three branches and state governments). All are fallible and historically the American government has alternated between different parties emphasizing different moral bases. My perspective is the bases that have been emphasized are, on the one hand, general welfare (Democratic Party) and, on the other hand, individual responsibility (Republican Party), both of which have value and both of which can be misused and made to have unintended consequences. As I have considered the various moral foundations identified by Haidt, I have come to believe that the message of the Bible makes the moral foundation of justice the most comprehensive moral foundation, capable of incorporating the others.[5]

WRESTLING WITH AUTHORITIES AND POWERS

The authority of parents, organizations, governments, and churches in both their divine and human aspects are all derived from and subject to the authority of the Cosmic Christ. However, in addition to human organizations and institutions, as we have just seen, there are various powerful invisible spiritual and sociocultural authorities and powers more powerful than institutions that influence our thinking, emotions, and volition. They are also part of the created world of human life, which is under the overall authority of Jesus Christ, but they easily become instruments of evil because of their hidden yet taken-for-granted nature and the presence of sin within humans making them receptive to evil. They are closes to human inner life with its

4. Haidt, *Righteous Mind*.

5. Ibid., 295–309.

thoughts, beliefs, values, motivations, and attitudes, and we can believe that these influences reach into the depths of the unconscious. This is the part of human life that Christ seeks to rule most directly and that believers need to struggle with in order to place it under the authority of Christ. How can we be subject to the proper human authorities and live in human cultures and subcultures, which are an inescapable aspect of human life, and yet not be merely conformed to forces of the world (Rom 12:2)? As Christians we should continually examine and question the sociocultural forces of the world and allow God to continually transform our thinking from the inside out. This is what Paul calls "the struggle," which is not against human beings ("flesh and blood") but against "spiritual forces."

This struggle is demonstrated for us by Jesus before Pilate. Jesus recognized what Pilate was not willing to admit or take seriously: that his authority as governor had been given to him—"You would have no power over me unless it had been given you from above" (John 19:11). (This recognizes the legitimacy of human governmental authority and power, but also that it can be misused.) Jesus also told Pilate that the kingdom Christ brought into the world is "not from this world"—"not from here." He went on to say, "You say that I am a king. For this I was born, and for this I came into the world, to testify to the truth. Everyone who belongs to the truth listens to my voice." Pilate then asked what people have asked ever since: "What is truth?" (John 18:37–39). The truth was standing before him, but without faith he did not recognize it. Jesus brought before Pilate a perspective with his very body that completely undercut the perspective of Pilate and also challenged him to become sensitive to eternal truth. Pilate, like many people, did not do this, although apparently his wife realized that something greater than an ordinary life was at stake.

In describing how we are to wrestle with the spiritual forces that would dislodge us from our faith, Paul names the tools we are to use as pieces of armor. The first one is truth. Related to and overlapping with truth are righteousness, the gospel of peace, faith, salvation, and finally the Word of God. All of these are closely related. They are closely connected to what Christ told Pilate was the truth he represented. This leads us to what is the greatest conundrum for the Christian and the church of Jesus Christ, one faced especially by Protestants who have reduced human authority in the church. Of all the authorities derived from and dependent on the authority of Jesus Christ, the authoritative source for truth by which our thoughts and all that is related to them should be influenced is the Bible, the written revelation of God. But one glance at historic and contemporary Christianity tells us that interpreting the Bible, and especially living by the Bible, has been the most difficult task for Christians. Yet the Bible, interpreted by the

Holy Spirit (given to the church, not just individuals), is for Christians the primary path to truth that liberates a person to live the life of faith.

It is highly important, therefore, that Christians consider how to approach and use the Bible. It would be more accurate to say, "how to let the Bible speak to us." Immediately after describing the "armor" of Christians, Paul says, "Pray in the Spirit at all times" (Eph 6:18). This is a reminder that the great Interpreter of the Bible is the Author of the Bible, namely, the Holy Spirit of God. What is not emphasized by many, especially Protestant Christians, is that the Holy Spirit was given to the church of Jesus Christ and is not just a private link to God. This is an immediate clue that interpretation of the Bible should be done in the context of the whole church and not by individual Christians who ignore the work of the historic church from its earliest days. This is the basis for denominations, which carry traditions of interpretation of the Bible. It is also why wise Christians look to denominationally trained ministers for guidance in interpreting the Bible rather than to those who emphasize their own independent and private spiritual connection to God or do not recognize the authority of a recognized Christian theological tradition. Speaking for myself, I follow the Reformed tradition of interpreting the Bible, but I recognize that all Christian traditions should and can learn from each other. I also believe that we have much to learn from secular studies, even though some are anti-Christian in presupposition and purpose. We are still in the early stages of listening and learning from each other. Furthermore, we should not shut out the larger world, but listen to what other religious traditions are saying to understand the deepest human longings and how they may be following the Way of Jesus Christ without knowing it (Rom 1:14–16).

CONCLUSION

The claim to universal authority may be the most audacious claim ever made, but this claim by and for Jesus Christ (Matt 28:18) is at the center of the Christian faith. It is consistent with the statement in John 1:1–3 that Jesus as the divine Word was "with God, and was God." Furthermore, "all things came into being through him, and without him not one thing came into being" (Col 1:15–20). The expanded statement given by Paul regarding the Cosmic Christ has already been mentioned. Interpretation of the troubling passage for some people in John 14:6 that Jesus is the only Way to the Father should be interpreted in the light of these passages. This Way is beyond all human thought and words. It is the Way that all things were created, especially human beings and the "Way" all things are being brought together in God (Eph 1:10).

What is most important to realize regarding the universal authority of Jesus Christ is that the exercise of this authority by Christ is for one purpose: the salvation of human beings and the bringing together of all things in heaven and on earth. Following the claim to universal authority in Matthew 28 is the Great Commission: "Go therefore and make disciples of all nations [peoples]" and it is even specified, "baptizing them in the name of the Father and the Son and of the Holy Spirit, and teaching them to obey everything that I have commanded you. And remember, I am with you always, to the end of the age" (28:19–20). The everlasting divine Word in John "became flesh and lived among us, and we have seen his glory, the glory as of a father's only son, full of grace and truth" (John 1:14). Paul states that the one in whom all things hold together is the head of the church and that in him "God was pleased to reconcile to himself all things, whether on earth or in heaven, by making peace through the blood of his cross" (Col 1:18–20).

There are other legitimate authorities under the overall authority of Jesus Christ. Although legitimate and necessary for human life, such as parental, organizational, and governmental authorities, they are often misused by human beings, as at the crucifixion of Jesus by Roman authorities and the persecution of Christians by the Roman Empire, but then the long persecution of Jews by Christian authorities and people. These human authorities, including parental authority, can always be improved or corrected or, as we know, overthrown. The development of democratic principles has been one of the great improvements in governmental authority. Human beings, including Christians, had to learn that governmental authorities claiming to be Christian often misused their authority and were necessarily judged. It was best when governments become secular in order not to misrepresent God. I call this using the secular as a methodology. It is also true that all human institutions are temporary and are judged by God over time. The church of Jesus Christ, though having a spiritual authority above any other human institution, is also a human institution and has historically misused its authority. It too is under God's judgment, even more than other institutions because of the requirement placed upon it to represent ("witness to") Jesus Christ in the world.

Because the rule of Christ and his kingdom is over the hearts and minds of human beings, the forces that affect the hearts and minds of people are the most important and capable of the most harm in their effect. These forces are affected by evil that is in the universe and are greater than any individual human power. However, they have been defeated by Jesus Christ through his death and resurrection. One way that these super-individual forces affect human beings is through the sociocultural context of normal human life. The most important means available for human beings to resist the evil forces of life is through the knowledge gained from the Bible combined with prayer through the Holy Spirit and life in the church. This is not simply intellectual knowledge or repeated words of prayer, but the knowledge that comes with faith, love, and communication with God through Christ and the Holy Spirit in fellowship with other believers. Paul in 2 Corinthians 10:3–6 writes:

> Indeed, we live as human beings, but we do not wage war according to human standards; for the weapons of our warfare are not merely human, but they have divine power to destroy strongholds. We destroy arguments and every proud obstacle raised up against the knowledge of God, and we take every thought captive to obey Christ. We are ready to punish every disobedience when your obedience is complete.

Paul is speaking about particular problems in the church in Corinth and claims to have an authority in the church given to him by Jesus Christ. This is a reminder that then and now there needs to be some recognized order and authority in the universal church and the many churches. The church and every Christian is under a discipline, which in its best form brings self-discipline, but there is also the discipline of the Christian community. In the end, however, Paul rests upon the power of truth with love to lead the church, not simply his formal authority as an apostle. In the same way, every Christian and the church today needs the derivative authority of both the Bible and the church. When they are both placed under the Holy Spirit, then Christians can grow into Jesus Christ, representing him increasingly clearly, because they will be hearing "the truth in love" (Eph 4:15). The truth carries authority in itself and is best known when presented in love. This may mean openly challenging misused human authority as Jesus did. It is the truth in the person of Jesus Christ that defeats every "principality and power" operating through sociocultural forces that bring harm to human beings.

Chapter 12

Who Do You Say That I Am?

THE CRUCIAL QUESTION

We come in this chapter to the most important question that ultimately is posed to every individual: "Who do you say that I am?" This is the question of the identity of Jesus that points to the meaning of his life, death, and resurrection, but also to our own identity as a follower of Jesus or not. This question is more crucial than the question of whether there is a God. Jesus Christ is a historical figure and the claim regarding him is that he is the central figure for God's redemptive work of humankind and all creation. In short, can we accept the claims made about him by his earliest followers based on their experiences with him (in the case of Paul a vision of him)? Who is he and is he the ultimate "good news" for human beings and all creation that his followers declared him to be?

According to David Bosch, "it is important that we should not delineate the content of our evangelism too sharply, too precisely, and too self-confidently."[1] I agree with this when referring to our Christian formulations and presentations of the gospel. The four gospels themselves, with the rest of the New Testament and Jesus Christ himself, give us many ways of expressing the gospel of what God has done for us. Some do not like this "lack of clarity." However, I am proposing that evangelism in the largest and basic sense can be seen in relation to bringing the world to face and answer the crucial question Jesus asked his disciples. This is the task God has undertaken, the *missio Dei*, but Christians are to be involved under God in bringing the world to face it. Furthermore, beyond evangelism, Christian education can be seen as bringing growth in the realization of what it means to an-

1. Bosch, *Transforming Mission*, 420.

swer this question truthfully and to live into its implications, which means becoming disciples of the Lord of life. Both evangelism and education are part of the *missio Dei* of "making disciples of all peoples" (Matt 28:19).

Isn't it an amazing fact is that Jesus asked his disciples the question, "Who do you say that I am?" This is God asking human beings for their opinions! What dignity is granted to us! This shows the great humility of God, and especially God's desire to be chosen. The desire of God for human fellowship was first shown in Genesis 3:8 in the amazing verse that speaks the deep theology of God "walking in the garden" while humans hid from God among the trees. This is the story of humanity: God seeking and human beings hiding. The question of who Jesus is shows the great weight that is placed on our thoughts and decisions, particularly the response we give to the special person God sent into the world. This is the "faith option" that is becoming ever clearer in the world.[2]

The joint evangelistic and educational tasks are both simple and complex. On the one hand, the answer to the question of who Jesus Christ is requires simple faith and love, as expressed by Peter and later by Thomas: "My Lord and my God!" (John 20:28). On the other hand, enabling people to see Jesus for who he is can be quite difficult and requires great effort on the part of the followers of Jesus. There is certainly resistance in each individual and group, as discussed in chapters 5 and 6, and this resistance can take a powerful form as the "principalities and powers" of sociocultural forces that unconsciously dominate individuals along with small and large groups of people from families to nations. If we look at history and our own experience in families and churches, we see that we Christians have greatly hindered people, including our own children, coming to recognize Jesus for who he is and what he did. At the same time, parents should not necessarily blame themselves for not being able to counter some outside influences. It helps to know that without fully understanding who he was and where he was going, the disciples stayed with him or, at least, after scattering returned to be regathered by him. After Jesus accomplished the purpose for which he came, the disciples were enabled to continue their journey of faith with the gift of the Holy Spirit. So we Christians must continue our faith journeys even after our "scatterings" and failures to follow Jesus.

I will always carry in my heart and mind the special evidence of the wholehearted acceptance of the gospel of Christ by the aboriginal people in Taiwan. My studies since then of the spread of the gospel of Christ in the world and throughout history have only strengthened my conviction that many people, in spite of a natural resistance, will accept who Jesus Christ is

2. Joas, *Faith as an Option.*

and what he did (chapters 7 and 8) *when the conditions are right.* This draws our attention to macro factors such as geopolitical as well as national and community conditions and relationships. The right conditions are when Christians, as individuals and in their institutions and organizations, have not and do not set up barriers for others to believe in Christ and instead have represented effectively the love and compassion of Christ for all people. As I am emphasizing, this kind of representation of Christ applies not only to individuals but also to families, to groups, and to societies in which Christians make up a large proportion. Providentially, the West and the United States after the collapse of colonialism are not perceived as representing Jesus Christ as much as they once were. Secularization is helping to distinguish Christianity from the societies in which it exists. In addition, with globalization a leveling of the nations is taking place. Nevertheless, Christians still have the responsibility of seeking to extend justice wherever they live, often cooperating with non-Christians. This is especially true in societies like the United States where Christians form a majority of the population. People cannot help but connect Christianity with some of the national actions of such a nation. Germany, perhaps in reaction to a reputation inherited from World War II, has graciously accepted more refugees than other nations.

If one thinks about it, it is amazing how people will believe the gospel coming from strangers with nothing to commend the strangers except that they came to tell them the good news about Jesus Christ. This has taken place over the centuries. It is helpful, of course, if the strangers are perceived positively (as Christians often have not been) and in some measure (sometimes a very small measure) as representing what the one they speak of is like. Wherever the gospel comes from, the goal and methods of evangelism and education should be to draw out faith, as Jesus did, not to aggressively seek to force faith or even to threaten people if they do not have faith, as some have done. It also means not giving an overemphasis to words alone. Some Christians, especially Protestants, place an overemphasis on correct or orthodox verbal statements. Peter had the right words with which to answer Christ, but he did not grasp their meaning, as became evident by what he said in response to Jesus' words about his coming death (Matt 16:21–23). In general it should be noted that regarding the spread of the gospel after its initial introduction to a new people from the outside, the most effective work of evangelism and education is done by those in the receiving group or society who become believers. They are the best evidence of the power of the gospel to change lives. This may be noticed from the spread of the gospel among the European tribes to its present spread in China and Africa.

ON THE ROAD AGAIN

It is significant that the question regarding the identity of Jesus took place "on the road." The people of God have been "on the road"—a journey of faith—since Abraham. They were not at their best when they settled down and became "people of the land." Is not the Old Testament a demonstration of this fact? This was true even after the exile when they were brought back to the land where they previously lived. I believe it is still true in regard to a "Jewish state." Jesus remained on the move from the time he began his ministry and he never intended that his kingdom should be a "settled kingdom" or identified with a place. Now we see why God does not want the identification of Christianity as a "Western religion" or an "American religion," as history has been demonstrating.

The question of Jesus to his disciples marked a stage in their journey of faith. His question and Peter's answer establishes forever that the faith God seeks to establish is a journeying faith, the basic characteristic of which is following Jesus. It was to continue on to the cross, the resurrection, the gift of the Holy Spirit, and the going forth to the ends of the earth. Each follower makes the journey of faith throughout life, as the Apostle Paul declared: "Not that I have already obtained this [knowing Christ] or have already reached the goal; but I press on to make it my own, because Christ Jesus has made me his own" (Phil 3:12). The confession of Peter, though not understood by himself and the disciples, established that the disciples would continue to follow Jesus and at the same time established the basis for all future faith: following Jesus as the Messiah, the Fulfiller of human longing and flourishing.

It is important, I believe, that Jesus did not spring the question of who he was on his disciples at the very first and never asked the question to those who were not already following him. He invited his disciples to join him and even to participate in his mission of catching people (Mark 1:17), but mostly he showed them, as in the case of his answer to the question of John the Baptist (through John's disciples) as to what his kingdom would look like (Matt 11:2–6). This is the "soft evangelism" of Jesus. ("He will not break a bruised reed or quench a smoldering wick"; Matt 12:20). We know that friendship evangelism and network evangelism are the most effective forms of evangelism.[3] They are what Jesus practiced. Our job as followers of Jesus is to allow Jesus to attract people, as he said, "And I, when I am lifted up from earth, will draw all people to myself" (John 12:32).

---

3. Stark, *Rise of Christianity*, 73–94.

Clearly the words and acts of Jesus did not require the full understanding of his followers in order for them to go forward, nor does it require our full understanding. Nevertheless, the weak and fallible faith of Peter and the disciples was evidence of God's work in them ("flesh and blood has not revealed this to you, but my Father in heaven"). It also provided a foundation on which the future invincible household of God on earth would be built ("on this rock I will build my church, and the gates of Hades will not prevail against it" (Matt 16:17, 18). From this point forward, Christ's work of salvation through the cross and resurrection began unfolding. We learn from this central turning point in the ministry of Jesus how crucial the personal human response was to him and to us. As seen in chapter 9, the response of faith since Jesus Christ lived on earth, as weak and fallible as it is, has spread around the world to all peoples. What is important now is that the accelerating changes in the world are making the question of who Christ is increasingly inescapable. One response is to deny the claims made about Jesus Christ by his followers as we have them in the New Testament. Another way is to avoid the question by becoming busy with matters of personal concern. This is like turning down the invitation to the great feast described in Luke 14:15–24. The third option is to "hang in there" by faith, as the disciples did, aided by the Holy Spirit.

There is an important point to add about answering the question of Jesus Christ, "Who do you say that I am?" In answering the question, we are also saying something about ourselves. If we answer the question as Peter did—"You are the Messiah [Christ] of God"—then we are saying about ourselves, "I want to be a follower of yours." We are also accepting the designation of "witness"—"I will be one of your witnesses in the world." Although our answer is personal, it is not private. We are identifying ourselves as part of a special people, the people from every race and tongue who are marked by baptism. This is made very clear in the New Testament. We are accepting the designation of being part of the household of God, "built upon the foundation of apostles and prophets, Christ Jesus himself as the cornerstone" (Eph 2:20); and even as said in 1 Peter 2:4–5, we are built into the "spiritual house" of Jesus Christ like "living stones" ourselves, becoming a "holy priesthood." There is a whole set of rich biblical words to describe what it means to be a follower of Jesus Christ. It is far from a private affair, but rather it is a corporate experience. This has been true from the beginning of the creation of God's people on earth and has been true from the beginning to the present of the ministry of Jesus Christ and the gift of the Holy Spirit at Pentecost.

The question of who is Jesus Christ is a question that will become increasingly insistent and clearer as times passes, but we should not make it an oppressively loud. The question will become increasingly insistent and louder as people get an ever clearer vision of Jesus Christ. For some people in the world, for example, in Muslim lands where open witnessing to Christ is difficult or forbidden, the encounters with Jesus may be actual visions or dreams about Jesus.[4] But it is Christians, particularly those who respond to Christ in receiving societies, who will make it most possible for people to see what Jesus Christ is like. This is the kind of evangelism we see in the Book of Acts, where, for example, Paul says to King Agrippa and all assembled with him, "Whether quickly or not, I pray to God that not only you but also all who are listening to me today might become such as I am—except for these chains" (26:29). This supports the definition of evangelism given by D. T. Niles: "Evangelism is one beggar telling another beggar where to get food."[5]

People can believe the claims about Christ; people can reject those claims; or people can avoid answering the question, at least for a time, but avoiding an answer can become an answer itself. It is also true that those who accept the claims about Christ may deny them by their lives.

CREEPING DEAFNESS TO THE CRUCIAL QUESTION

As we review the history (long in terms of centuries, but short if we consider the tens of thousands of years of human life on earth) from God's special revelation in Jesus Christ to the present, we see an important pattern in human response to God's revelation. Before Christ, the Old Testament prophets spoke clearly of this pattern. The pattern is that after people have received the revelation of God and the blessings that come with it, a certain spiritual deafness and blindness afflicts them. They see life as an ordinary routine and take the many blessings of God for granted. God's revelation of himself and his blessings lose their extraordinary character. Spiritual dullness, which is really a basic lack of faith in the reality of God's presence and action, leads to a certain self-centeredness and callousness toward others and their needs. Self-maintenance becomes the major goal in life and greed soon dominates life.

The New Testament also recognizes the old pattern of spiritual dullness as an affliction that overtakes God's people throughout history. The Letter to the Hebrews in the New Testament is directed especially to Christians who appear to have become tired in following Christ: "Therefore lift your drooping hands and strengthen your weak knees, and make straight paths for your feet, so that what is lame may not be put out of joint, but rather be healed"

4. Kraft, *Searching for Heaven in the Real World*.
5. Niles, *That They May Have Life*, 96.

(12:12–13). The readers are urged "to provoke one another to love and good deeds, not neglecting to meet together, as is the habit of some, but encouraging one another, and all the more as you see the Day approaching" (10:24–25). In the words to the church at Ephesus among the seven churches in the Book of Revelation, it is written, "But I have this against you, that you have abandoned the love you had at first" (2:4). The church at Laodicea was designated as "lukewarm" (3:16). In fact, most of the seven churches in the first three chapters of the Book of Revelation had serious problems of faith. In probably one of the last books to be written in the New Testament, we read: "First of all you must understand this, that in the last days scoffers will come, scoffing and indulging their own lusts and saying, 'Where is the promise of his coming? For ever since our ancestors died, all things continue as they were from the beginning of creation!'" This leads to the conclusion: "But do not ignore this one fact, beloved, that with the Lord one day is like a thousand years, and a thousand years are like one day. The Lord is not slow about his promise, as some think of slowness, but is patient with you, not wanting any to perish, but all to come to repentance" (2 Pet 3:3–4, 8–9).

In light of what we now know about the age of the earth and of humanity, it has indeed been a very short time since Jesus Christ came and called people to be his disciples. For this reason, I believe we need to interpret the meaning of Jesus "coming soon" or the exhortations to be ready at all times for his coming as a challenge to see Jesus in everyone we meet, particularly those with special needs. Many have great needs that are not obvious. Some Christians, particularly some Protestants, like to say that Jesus might come with the end of the world possibly tomorrow or at least in the next few years. I do not believe that is consistent with God's will to save all people, including the two thirds of the world that have not believed in Jesus Christ. What about those who have not perceived the gospel largely because of the failures of Christians? Paul told the Athenians, "God has overlooked the times of ignorance," but then added, "now he commands all people everywhere to repent" (Acts 17:30). This puts the responsibility of Christians to witness faithfully and lovingly and not to be judgmental of those who have not believed. Paul witnessed but did not argue. In fact, Paul had complementary and encouraging words, as Peter before him to Cornelius, to unbelieving Gentiles. I believe we should emphasize that we are going to meet Christ in unexpected ways when we meet other people. We have to be ready to meet Jesus in every person until we see Jesus face to face! Just as Jesus was not recognized as the Messiah the first time he came, we should expect him not to be recognized in his coming now.

All of this is simply to remind us that Christians should expect to have spiritual problems and insensitivity in our individual Christian lives and in our Christian communities. The source of spiritual dullness is closely related to the concern for self-maintenance and self-indulgence. This not only afflicts individuals but also organizations, institutions, and whole societies. We see this both in ancient Israel and in the history of the church of Jesus Christ. The pattern we see is that after the revelation, salvation, and blessing of God upon God's people, life takes on a taken-for-granted nature. What religious life there is takes on a routine character in which one "fulfills one's duty" and maintains important social connections. A callousness toward others creeps into thinking. The suffering of others is seen as due to their failures and even the judgment of God. The most important activity in life becomes the advancement of oneself and one's group. This may well involve the mistreatment and oppression of others or at least overlooking their needs.

This spiritual dullness or the avoidance of "really hearing and seeing" God at work overtook Israel and has repeatedly overtaken the church. This is seen clearly in the history of the West in the ongoing struggle in the church to exhibit or witness to who Jesus Christ is. As I struggled to answer the question of why so many peoples in the world have been able to avoid answering the question of Jesus' identity or have outright rejected him, I came to believe that the "principalities and powers" referred to in the Bible, especially in Paul's writings, hold a key to explaining the great variety of responses to Jesus Christ. Today, it is helpful if we think of the "principalities and powers" as very much like the "sociocultural forces" into which we are socialized and which have such a strong influence over our lives. The trilogy by Wink on "the powers" gave me the clue to the parallel nature of "principalities and powers" to "sociocultural forces."[6] We can be hardened through these influences into which we are born and which seem to come from "above and beyond" ordinary human life. I describe in a number of my writings how these forces gain domination over large Christian populations, leading non-Christians to have distorted visions of Jesus Christ because of Christianity, the religion of Christians.[7] I will not repeat my arguments in detail, but rather attempt a brief description of how these forces have worked, repeating some points made in chapters 5, 6, and 9.

---

6. Wink, *Unmasking the Powers*; *Naming the Powers*, *Engaging the Powers*.

7. Montgomery, "Spread of Religions and Macro-Social Relations"; *Diffusion of Religions*; *Lopsided Spread of Christianity*; *Why Religions Spread*; *Real New Age*; "Conversion and the Historic Spread of Religion."

BLESSINGS WITH DEATH AND DESTRUCTION IN THE
HISTORY OF THE WEST

Looking at the second stage of the spread of the gospel after the fourth century (the first stage being the first three hundred years), when the tribes
of Europe were "Christianized," a flowering of civilization took place. The
distinctive identities and gifts of individual people and of the various ethnic groups were affirmed through the influence of the gospel of God's love.
The basis for the development of nationalism was established. Look at a
Euro-Asian land mass map and the flowering of individual societies into
nations in Europe will be obvious. Great philosophy, architecture, literature, art, music, and science were produced and eventually the Industrial
Revolution raising standards of living. Consciousness of human rights grew
strong. However, the institution of the church, which had become pervasive
among the different peoples, sought to maintain its power through alliances
with the various rulers, becoming state churches. Creative competition
developed between the nations, but also wars of attempted conquests and
empire building. In spite of the domination of church and state and numerous distortions of the gospel, the seed of consciousness of individual and
group value in God's eyes was planted and continually produced opposition
movements to dominating powers, which were often cruelly suppressed.
The Jewish people were harshly persecuted and a series of military invasions
of the Middle East undertaken. Worldwide imperialism was undertaken by
the European powers beginning about 1500, followed by colonialism, which
was later joined by the United States.

Stepping back, numerous church divisions took place around theological controversies at the church councils. The churches of the East
(Nestorian and Monophysite Christians) separated or were driven from the
church in early centuries. A major schism took place between the churches
of the Eastern Orthodox and the church in the West in 1054. I believe Islam
came into existence largely because its founder and succeeding leaders met
a so-called Christian empire—the Byzantine Empire—instead of networks
of Christian communities living and humbly serving the needs of people
in the various lands. Islam, rather than Christianity (embodied in the en-
emy Byzantine Empire), was seen as offering the best means of bringing
disparate tribes and peoples together. In the sixteenth century, another
great schism took place between Roman Catholic and Protestant churches,
which tended to follow a division between northern and southern Europe.
The various opposition movements in the church were greatly supported
by the development of nationalism or the desire for distinct national sover-
eignties of people in particular areas. The competition among nations was

accompanied by the flowering of seeds planted by the learning and experiences of earlier periods. The classical civilizations of the Mediterranean had a great influence, but the biblical heritage that placed special value on individuals and human rights under God was an even more powerful influence. The coming together of these influences led to the further flowering of civilization in science and democracy in the seventeenth century.

Because of the domination of churches, whether through claims to being the "true church" or through alliances with national governments, or both, there developed individual and organized resistance to religious domination. A secularization movement developed that was partly anti-Christian and irreligious, but partly led by Christians seeking to escape the domination of other Christians. Most irreligious people adopted science and the autonomous individual as their secular idols. The Industrial Revolution brought unprecedented wealth to the nations of Northern Europe in the eighteenth and nineteenth centuries and fired their conquests outside of the West following the earlier explorations and conquests from southern Europe. A general sense of well-being and of superiority developed among the European nations, ironically the former barbarians to the Greco-Roman civilization. It became the aim of European nations to bequeath the "blessings" of Western civilization on the "benighted peoples" of the world. Religious self-concern and self-maintenance became dominant concerns of individuals, groups, and nations. This created spiritual dullness among the people of the state churches and a callousness toward the suffering that accompanied the perceived advancement of industrialization, imperialism, and colonialism.

As an "accident of history" (providential to Christians) the newly founded United States was able to find freedom from domination by one religion (or version of Christianity) that was allied with the state, the typical pattern in Europe. The United States also entered an unprecedented period of growth, prosperity, and national power. While enjoying resulting benefits of growth and trade, the nation inflicted terrible suffering on both indigenous peoples and slaves brought from Africa. Its internal struggle in the Civil War also brought great suffering to countless numbers of people. Although that war brought a partial correction in the suffering inflicted on the slaves, oppression was soon continued under the system of racial segregation. The United States joined the colonial powers at the end of the nineteenth century in taking over the Philippines, helping to prolong the domination by the West of the Philippines for a brief half a century. Women went through a period when they were denied the right to vote as well as advancement in leadership in government, business, and the church, and the struggle for equality goes on. However, just as the alliance of religion and government was (providentially) broken with the founding of the United States, with its mixed peoples and religions, so the domination of nations over other nations through colonialism was (providentially) broken or at least greatly reduced with the defeat of Western nations by Japan and by and the collapse of the power of the European nations in Africa. (They had exhausted themselves in the wars.) Then in turn the Japanese Empire was brought down. The "leveling of the nations" began as the five-hundred-year reign of European powers came to an end, followed by the rise of the Asian "tiger" nations, especially China.

The complicated mix of blessings and evil in the history of the West on the one hand enabled Christians to present Jesus Christ to the world, but at the same time distorted his image in the world, making it difficult for many to hear and answer, "Who do you say that I am?" I had the privilege of seeing a Christian movement among the aboriginal people of Taiwan. They had not experienced Western domination, but rather domination from Japan and the majority Taiwanese population, and could therefore perceive Jesus Christ unassociated with domination or coercion. However, for many peoples of the world, including people within the Christian context of the West, Christ became associated with domination or an imposed faith.

With the end of Western colonial domination of the world, there has been an explosion in answering the question of Jesus, "Who do you say that I am?" with, "We believe you are the Savior of the world," especially in China and Africa. Nevertheless, many still have a distorted image of Christ and of the gospel of his kingdom. Islamic nations in particular have a distorted image of Christianity going back as far as the Byzantine Empire and later Western aggression. At the same time, many followers of Buddhism have a compassionate figure in Buddha to follow, not unlike Jesus Christ, who, unlike Buddha, is associated with the "intruding" West. Christians in Buddhist and Hindu majority societies have their job cut out for them to present a clear picture of who Jesus Christ is and what he has done, a picture that will come more from what Christians do than what they say.

RECOGNIZING JESUS CHRIST IN THE NEW WORLD ORDER

The new world order is still being born and some of its characteristics are only barely appearing, if at all, in some nations. I admit that it may be premature to call it an "order," but certain broad outlines seem to be appearing. One of the basic characteristics of the New World Order that appeared first was the demand for freedom and dignity on the group and national levels.

This follows the spread of a nationalistic spirit that had developed in Europe. The nationalistic spirit developing in non-Western nations did much to bring about the loss of domination by the West. The additional demand that has barely appeared in many areas is for freedom and dignity on the personal level. Nationalism was not accompanied by democracy, except in name. It should be remembered that personal freedom was gained in the Western world after long struggles with many setbacks. Recently, the Arab Spring came as a sign of the demand in some of Islamic nations for greater freedom and participation of the people in some Islamic governments. However, a reversal toward autocratic rule has taken place in most countries. China also experienced a demand for greater freedom, but it was not successful, although human rights lawyers continue patient work under great difficulties. Although the results of the movements for greater freedom have not brought the desired goals, it could be said that "the cat is out of the bag." The demands for freedom will only increase around the world, but nationalism and the revival of traditional religions, mixed with reactions to perceived outside domination, will also likely create many reverse developments by elevating local authoritarian rulers. Nevertheless, the worldwide advances in communication, transportation, economic development, and also population movements will ensure that the demand for freedom cannot be stopped in the shrinking world.

The increase in freedom on the national, group, and personal levels, along with the shrinking of the world brought by technology, brings about an increase in diversity of all kinds. Populations become mixed ethnically and also religiously as people travel and migrate domestically and internationally. Socialization to limited perspectives in families is modified as growing children are confronted with much greater ethnic and religious diversity than previously. Ethnic and religious intermarriages increase. The increase in personal freedom with the resulting diversification of populations means that personal choice gains greater new weight. People must choose schooling, jobs, marriage partners, and locations to live. The choice of religion also appears in the mix of choices to be made. Parental influence and other social influences remain important, but an emphasis shifts to individual responsibility for choices. However, it must be mentioned that greater individual autonomy and individualism has enabled many people to make self-destructive choices in drugs, alcohol, and crime. In this shift toward individualizing and personalizing, human beings continue to need and seek community, involving helpful contacts, lasting relationships, and support from others, as well as communities offering false promises and anti-social behaviors, such as gangs or hate groups.

In the New World Order of increasing freedom, individualization, and diversity, there will inevitably be an increasing focus on the content of religions in terms of their beliefs, their practices, and the experiences they offer. "Comparative religion" will move from being a college course to being the exercise of individual observation, thought, and experience. The contents of religion and non-religion consist of both experience and ideas that people will choose. Religions (providentially) cease from being simply national, ethnic, or even family traditions. However, I would stress that it is important to remember that the personalization of religion in the modern world is sometimes spoken of as the "privatization of religion." It may take that character with some people, particularly intellectuals and academics, but it is more accurate to speak of the "communalization of religion." Jesus Christ gathered a community around him, and it was a community of believers that became the church at Pentecost. It is clear that Jesus wants the question of who he is asked and answered in a community formed by the Holy Spirit because, as he pointed out, the right answer has to be given by God (Matt 16:17). This means that people need to be loved into fellowship, starting from childhood and extending throughout life, where they can then hear and answer correctly the question, "Who do you say that I am?" This is what Jesus did for his disciples, and this is what his followers must do for others.

CONCLUSION

Jesus' question "Who do you say that I am?" is the most crucial question anyone can answer. Jesus did not force the answer to this question but drew it out of his disciples. He asked it after they had been with him for a while. And still their answer, which on the surface was correct, needed much development in understanding. The answer that Jesus is the Messiah needed filling out through his favorite name for himself, the Human One (the Son of Man). This is the name he used at his trial to point to his future revelation with redeemed humanity based on the eschatological vision in Daniel 7. Jesus Christ was deeply interested in the salvation of humanity. It was the basis of all that he did, which is why he saw himself as fulfilling the role of the Human One (the Son of Man) and why he sent his followers out into the world.

The goal of Jesus should be the goal of our outreach to the world. If evangelism is one beggar telling another beggar where to get food, then the witness of Christians is that Jesus is the "true bread of heaven" and "the bread of life," who should become internal to our lives as truly as bread becomes part of our lives (John 6:32, 48). This may be a hard saying for some people, but coming to Jesus and staying with him is the way to know that he is "the way, the truth, and the life" (John 14:6). Our best witness as Christians is the witness of hospitality in which people realize, often gradually, that when they are with Jesus and Jesus is with them they are truly "at home," and they are nourished with the "bread of life." It is clear when we review our lives and when we review Christian history that the followers of Jesus are on a journey of faith that has often been interrupted and misdirected corporately and individually. Just as Peter and Paul both realized, there were always surprises and new insights to be gained as they followed Jesus. The brother of Jesus becoming head of the church in Jerusalem was certainly unexpected from what we know of the disciples, from which fellowship James was apparently absent before the death and resurrection of Jesus. The selection of Paul, rather than one of the twelve apostles, was a new turn in the road of God's people, not really predictable by what has been previously known by the followers. Peter had to learn lessons through a strange dream, the encounter with a Roman centurion, and a dispute with Paul about whether to eat with Gentiles. These are only illustrations of the many changes and turns that have been taken by individuals and the people of God to the present. In the light of the long history of humanity and the large number of people who have not yet answered successfully and satisfactorily the question of who Jesus is, it is not hard to believe that we Christians have only begun to make Jesus Christ known to the world.

Chapter 13

The Great Circle and Little Circles of Love and Life

LONGING FOR UNITY

EARLY IN THE BOOK I discussed the human longing for a tangible contact with God and for compassion from God. I interpreted this longing as being completely fulfilled in the incarnation and atonement of Jesus Christ, even though we Christians, as well as all people, never cease resisting God in ways often unknown or unrecognized by us, thus misrepresenting Jesus to the world. As I come to the end of the book, an important aspect of human longing needs to be seen in a larger perspective. The longing for unity with God and the transcendent incorporates also the longing for unity of the self and unity with other human beings. We see this in the powers of religions to create communities and to elevate self-esteem, experienced as a sense of wholeness in identity. The three most widely spreading religions, discussed in chapters 3 and 4, have demonstrated these powers especially through their founders, Buddha, Jesus, and Muhammad, as they have been interpreted by their followers. I believe that, above all, Jesus Christ has been able to fulfill this longing for unity with God, self, and others in the most complete and fulfilling way.

Coexistent with the religious propensity of human beings, the social propensity of human beings for some unity with others is almost impossible to ignore. At a very obvious level, human beings are raised and socialized into groups. They normally gather with others throughout their lives, and in large modern complex societies people will form numerous voluntary associations, if allowed. (This is especially obvious in the United States with its freedom of association that was spurred by Christian experience in congregations.) Important periodic gatherings took place among early hu-man beings, as shown by the gatherings of people who have preserved many of the characteristics of early groups, such as the Australian aboriginals. The gatherings of clans such as the Scottish clans and other such groups in which people are part of the same gene pool are well known. In early American society, camp meetings were a common occurrence, especially on the frontier. In most modern societies there are numerous occasions in which people gather for reasons related to religion, sociability, professional associations, political causes, entertainment, and sports. These gatherings often function as "rites of intensification," in which people reaffirm their common beliefs and values; but religious gatherings especially become such rites. In fact, one of major characteristics of religions, long recognized, is their power to create cohesion among people, sometimes large numbers of people. This has been a major part of the appeal of Islam from its beginning among the separate Arab tribes and later among other groups. The growth of Islam was undoubtedly spurred by its ability to gather disparate tribes into a larger community, the *umma*.

Accompanying the strong evidence of human longing for unity with God or the transcendent and with others, there is also evidence of a desire for individual internal unity or coherence. This is related to the need to maintain relationships with others, which are difficult to maintain if a per-son does not have some internal coherence that enables a person to be rec-ognized by others and to present herself or himself as the same person over time. Of course, human beings often fail to maintain internal coherence. Without internal coherence, unity with the transcendent or God through prayer and with other human beings through genuine fellowship is made very difficult. But in the opposite direction, unity with God, as partial as it may be, and unity with others are a great aid in gaining a sense of the unity of one's personhood. Before discussing the gospel of Jesus Christ and the communion of believers that enables the satisfactory unities for which they long, we consider the failures in gaining unity.

FAILURES IN GAINING UNITY

In seeking unity with others we see two historic tendencies. The first is the tendency for some to create conformity by coercion, suppressing those that do not conform. Those within the group tend to want to conform to main-tain unity, but as groups expand through conquest coercion is applied to the new populations. Religion became one of the means of bringing about compliance to at least an outward form of unity. The early small groupings of hunter-gatherers generally showed a high degree of sharing and cooperation among themselves, as modern tribal people show. However, in insecure conditions they often could come into conflict with other groups in competition over scarce resources. The warlike Yanamano of Brazil are a clear example. Sometimes these conflicts had a ritual characteristic in which conflict between the groups was limited, as seen in conflicts between some tribes, for example, the Dana people in New Guinea. Most notably, however, as groups became larger and developed into the complex societies that were characteristic of the ancient civilizations, internal coercion and external conquest escalated. The ancient civilizations typically sought to dominate their own people and conquer surrounding peoples. The stories of these ancient civilizations are very well known with their divine or semi-divine rulers. These were (are) the ontocratic systems identified by van Leeuwen that were discussed earlier in chapter 9. In this pattern, rulers use their supposed close identification with the Divine to justify their autocratic and oppressive rule, as well as their divine right to conquer other peoples and unite them under their rule. The divine beings in the cosmos with which rulers identified themselves were often pictured as violent, helping to justify the violence of their representatives on earth. Even up to the seventeenth century in England and the eighteenth century in France, autocratic rulers claimed the divine right to demand unity under their rule—a holdover from the ontocratic system. The rulers in the secular age introduced in the nineteenth century claimed the right to exercise absolute power in the name of the state and established very coercive states with secular ideologies. In many ways, an overall downward development can be seen in civilization development that included the multiplication of gods and the general loss of emphasis on a High God. People usually submitted to coerced unity as an alternative to chaos and a means of protection from outside "barbarians."

As far as unity of the self is concerned, there is no person who can claim not to have internal tensions and conflicts. Many or most of these conflicts may be traced to childhood and to socialization into families with tensions or dysfunctions of various kinds. The experiences of conflicts by people in families are often extended into numerous conflicts with others and in the world at large. When these conflicts in families and in the world at large are strong and unresolved, they can lead to self-destructive thoughts and actions. They not only cause self-destruction, but they can cause people to bring great harm to others. In spite of the great failure of human beings to achieve unity with God, others, and the self, the good news of the gospel is that God has done what human beings could not do for themselves: create unity with God, the self, and others through Jesus Christ by creating a Great Circle of Love with many subsidiary circles of love.

THE GREAT CIRCLE OF LOVE

The Bible attests to the fact that God has bridged the gap between God's self and humanity and established a means for creating unity between human beings and God and other human beings. Furthermore, within this unity, the other unities for which human beings long (unity with the self and others) are brought into a great all-encompassing unity with God. I believe, on the basis of the Bible, this may be called the Great Circle of Love. This Great Circle is created by God's reaching down to humanity (speaking metaphorically) and making it possible for human beings to enter into a relationship with God, with others, and simultaneously with the self that is extended throughout life and completed after death in God. We can begin this unifying relationship, however weak, in this life and it will finally be accomplished with the full revelation of the Human One (the Son of Man), Jesus Christ, and redeemed humanity in him. The incarnation and atonement of Jesus Christ is the basis for the creation of the Great Circle of Love in which human beings are lifted up and brought to God their Creator. It is a Circle of Love because God is love (1 John 4:7–16) and God's love leads to the extension of the loving inner circle of the Trinity to all creation (John 3:16), which will finally be brought back into unity with God in the end (Eph 1:10). Love for the self (as loved and forgiven by God) and love for others (as also loved by God) is wrapped up in love for God.

No one on earth, other than Jesus Christ, has achieved the unity with God, self, and others for which human beings long and for which they are destined through Jesus Christ. The process begins through faith, which is a gift of God's Holy Spirit. Human beings join the Great Circle through faith and continue walking or moving in it, however partially and imperfectly, by faith, hope, and love that come through the Holy Spirit. When we join the Great Circle, we do not have to create an object or goal for our lives because it is given to us in Jesus Christ. Although all substitutes for God (idols) are ruled out, there is a lifelong struggle for the followers of Christ to give up any substitute for God as known in Christ. It has already been seen in chapters 5 and 6 that our human tendency is to resist God, even using what comes from God—God's creation, God's commands (laws), and any sacred objects, even including God's words in the gospels—to serve the self rather than God. God took the risk in coming to earth in the Great Circle of Love knowing human resistance to that love. But God came in Christ and continues to come in the Holy Spirit in spite of our resistance and is continually working to turn us away from resistance to the way of obedience to God's love in the Great Circle of Love.

THE GREAT CIRCLE MADE TANGIBLE

In Jesus Christ the Great Circle of God's love became tangible in a human being. There was a time of preparation for this making tangible of the Circle in a person by God's making a covenant with the people of Israel, a very tangible group of people. But the tangibility of the Circle in Jesus Christ did not stop at the historic time when Jesus Christ came. It continues to exist in the tangible world of people and things. We say this when we say, "I believe in the forgiveness of sins and the holy catholic church . . . " In other words, the unity with God created in Christ does exist in ourselves (forgiven) and with other people (also forgiven by the same Lord). It is not a private or only an internal unity but one that is shared with others. Walking in the Circle of Love means that we walk with others in mutual forgiveness. This shared life in the Circle of Love is what forms the church of Jesus Christ. It is where we learn to "put up with" one another and even ourselves. (I believe this experience was important for preparing the way for democratic government.) The shared life in the Circle of Love is what I believe Jesus referred to in his trial as the coming of the Human One (the Son of Man) that all will see (Mark 14:62). This passage, so important for the present book as stated in chapter 1, was Jesus' way of declaring the ongoing visible creation through him of the Great Circle of Love. This creation has just begun! His coming becomes our coming and our coming becomes his coming! In other words, his coming is also "the revealing of the children of God" (Rom 8:19). His statement at his trial was both a declaration of his identity as the Human One spoken of in Daniel 7:13–14 and an invitation to people to join him in "coming in clouds of glory."

Following Jesus Christ, beginning to be transformed, and participating in his church is a simultaneous experience, not first one and then the other. The church of Jesus Christ is both intangible and tangible, but as tangible it is the ongoing visible expression of the Circle of Love in the world. However, as we well know, we do not yet see a perfect church or a perfect Circle of Love. In fact, the tangible or visible circle has done much to drive people away from the universal Great Circle of Love. Followers of Jesus Christ have been brought into the Circle, but are also on the road in search for the perfect Circle of Love. Each believer and each community of believers has unique areas of struggle to keep walking with Christ in the Circle created through him. This requires helping each other in supporting the little circles of love that exist within the Great Circle. While the "holy catholic church" is the expression of the Great Circle, it exists in many little circles. Each grouping of believers, typically known as a "denomination" and then a "congregation," has unique areas of struggle to express and to remain in the Great Circle of Love from God. In addition to the denominations that exist in many societies, there are local congregations of believers who worship, have fellowship, and serve together in God's mission in the world. Sadly, some Christians disdain the tangible or visible church, judging themselves to be more orthodox or pure, and separate themselves from other Christians as individuals or as independent groups. Others are simply not able to "put up with" other people in an organized group and profess to be "spiritual" and "not religious." They disdain the human need for human authority under God, human organization, and mutual discipline in love. Many Christians, even those in denominations, may have little consciousness of and place little importance on the church beyond their own congregation. Some Christians show a lack of faith in the truth to prevail over time when their interpretations of the Bible are not the same as those of their church leaders. Pride and lack of love have always been a problem in the church preventing people from listening to each other and learning from one another. Nevertheless, God may use both those who continue to identify themselves with the visible church in one of the historic denominations and also those individuals and groups who separate themselves from other Christians. God judges both the denominations and the independent groups, all in order to make the witness to Jesus Christ as clear as possible. What is most important is that believers who walk in the Great Circle of Love continually forgive each other, just as God has forgiven them. At the same time, the unity given by the Holy Spirit means healthy self-love based on the acceptance of God's forgiveness and a sense of the peace and joy that God gives. Forgiveness or the acceptance of the atonement of Christ for the self and for others is what creates individual internal unity of the self, unity within the little circles of denominations and congregations, and unity within the Great Circle of God's Love.

Let me hasten to emphasize that unity in the Great Circle of Love in the church does not mean uniformity. This is obvious from the time of the twelve apostles with the additional apostles of James, the brother of Jesus and head of the church in Jerusalem, and Paul, the gifted theologian, missionary, church planter, church leader, writer, and fund-raiser. All of these church leaders expressed views and behaviors that were diverse from one another. Paul in 1 Corinthians 12–14 writes movingly of the diversity in the church represented by the various gifts given to the church. What he makes clear with the insertion of chapter 13 between 12 and 14 is that the gifts, as useful and necessary as they are, do not count for anything if love does not work through them. All of this means that in the Great Circle of Love there will always be diversity within the unity. How this will be worked out in history is a matter that is still unfolding or "coming in clouds of glory" if we open our eyes of faith. What is important for Christians to know is that the world is waiting to see a tangible expression of God's Great Circle of Love.

THE GREAT CIRCLE AND SOCIETY

The Great Circle comes into the world and is in the world, but is not of it. It exists in society in the imperfect form of the church with its many branches. The Great Circle of Love influences society in its many parts, but it is not to be identified with any part, such as the state or the family. This is a complex subject, but it is important for Christians to think about it. Augustine of Hippo thought on this subject deeply because after Christianity was made official in the Roman Empire the empire obviously began a decline in power that led to its ultimate fall, at least in the West. Where was the church in this new and confused situation? Augustine's important work *The City of God* was written shortly after Rome was sacked in AD 410 by Goths, many of whom were Arian Christians. Even though the church had become entangled with the Roman state and some blamed the decline of the empire on Christianity, Augustine made a clear distinction between the two "cities," in which the City of God is clearly distinguished from the City of Man by its direction toward God and eternity, whereas the City of Man only finds fulfillment on earth and is shot through with human, selfish goals. Unfortunately, the subsequent church was not able to live with this eschatological perspective because it sought to encompass the state and society as a whole (the ontocratic pattern).

Following the changes in the West that accompanied the Renaissance, the Reformations (Protestant and Roman Catholic), the scientific movement, and the Enlightenment, the overall domination or sacred canopy of the church over societies was broken, producing the movement toward affirming the secular, often called "secularization." Martin Marty helpfully identified the "modern schism" with its three paths to the secular: the European continent moving toward utter secularity in the clash of doctrines, the British Isles moving toward mere secularity in "everydayishness," and America moving toward "controlled secularity."[1] In America, where the legal separation of organized religion from government was made most clearly, the church (and religion generally) with its many denominations and organizations became compartmentalized from the rest of society. But at the same time, religion as a force in people's lives—as the "religious part" of their lives—actually increased for many people.

The Secular Revolution, edited by Christian Smith, details the many different realms of American society that have broken from control or even major influence from the church, beginning primarily in the 1870s.[2]

1. Marty, *Modern Schism*, 18, 59, 95.
2. Smith, *Secular Revolution*.

The overlapping realms or fields described include education, science, psychology, law, journalism, and medicine. Nevertheless, in America, where the secular did not and does not carry the anti-Christian implications that it does on the European continent, Christians have freedom to maintain their faith personally and communally in the secular societies in which they live and work. Although Christians may not feel free to express their faith in the secular institutions and organizations in which they work, they are certainly free to express their faith through Christian churches, institutions, and organizations. Even in secular or nonsectarian organizations, in a setting of mutual tolerance and respect, Christians my express their faith. Nevertheless, a certain compartmentalization of religion has taken place that can have a negative effect in influencing people to compartmentalize their faith and religious practice to only certain times and places. Most churches try to address this danger. Much to the dismay of many Christians and secularists, in the United States, where the government has officially stepped away from either establishing or disestablishing any church or religion, there are Christians who want to return to what they like to call a "Christian America"—forgetting the slavery, segregation, and disadvantages to women in the so-called Christian America of the past. They also forget that to try to make America be representative of Christianity is really to distort the gospel, which cannot be represented by a nation-state. While it is difficult for anti-Christians or anti-religious people to be elected to political office, church approval of candidates usually carries little weight and may even count against a candidate. It is almost expected that politicians will make references to God, such "May God bless America," but most people would not approve of a politician giving a religious rationalization for their political program. Politicians may mention their religious affiliation but not make it a criterion for electing them. Thus, while the schism of religion and society is in some ways more fuzzy in America than in Europe, the church as such is definitely not the bearer of an overall canopy for society, as in much of Europe, even though Christians are free to seek and do seek God's will for society and for the government in particular, especially where they see moral issues involved, as they often are.

My view is that religion in general, and the churches representing Christianity in particular, have demonstrated since the fourth century (perhaps most clearly in the religious wars of the seventeenth century) the need to divorce organized religion from political power, certainly from any fusion with government. But this is far different from divorcing faith from governmental or any other activity. History shows that Christianity as a religion can be associated both with erroneous knowledge and unjust and cruel governments. At the same time, secularism has also demonstrated its negative potential, particularly in its non-religious or anti-religious ideologies (Fascism and Communism), which were just as much or even more authoritarian than religions with political power. In the end, we see that religion and the secular are both capable of good and evil.

From a Christian point of view, there is no secular realm because God is everywhere and working in everything. However, the secular (not secularism) has proven to be an important God-given tool or methodology for gaining knowledge through scientific and academic studies and also in government for advancing just policies without the injection of religious fallible arguments. Nevertheless, people of faith can and should be motivated in their goals and actions by personal and communal faith in the secular world, knowing that their lives are not secular, but always under God.

It is important for Christians to recognize that since a large proportion of the population in the United States is made up of professing Christians, even though Christians may not like it, many people around the world are influenced in their attitudes toward Christianity by how the United States treats other nations and peoples, including its own people. As a Christian I believe there are two wills of God and two judgments of God: one will of God is for the United States as a nation and the other is for the Christian church as made up of those who profess Jesus Christ as Lord and Savior. Likewise, God judges each differently: governments for how well they carry out justice, and Christianity for how well it represents Jesus Christ (which includes his love of justice)—a much larger and weightier criteria. This provides a strong motivation for Christians to participate in political and social action in addition to serving God through the church, knowing that governments are capable of much good, but also of much evil.

Thus, the nation as an "earthly city" still has a responsibility to carry out justice, which means it has responsibility for the well-being of its citizens and of limiting the effects of evil. Without going into the long history of development of modern government, to which Christians contributed much, secular democracy has shown itself to be the most just form of government, in spite of its many failures associated with particular political leaders, as well as the weaknesses of electorates in supporting unworthy leaders and acting selfishly. Nevertheless, democracy has become widely recognized throughout the world as a goal for nations. Some forms of democracy existed with early human beings, but then declined in civilizations. However, the development of democracy accelerated with the recognition of human rights and has been a judgment of God on autocratic, corrupt, and oppressive governments. In the United States there is still constant need for improvement in establishing a more just society. The United States has certainly been judged (or brought destruction on itself) for its injustice (the

Civil War) and Europe likewise (nationalistic wars) and the West as a whole (collapse of imperialism and colonialism). God's judgment on the secular state does not bring about conversion to God, but it opens up opportunities for the gospel to spread. This may be seen in Japan bringing on the collapse of colonialism in East and Southeast Asia.

Christians still have an important role to contribute toward the goal of creating a just society, even though clearly they will not agree on the best approaches. As noted above, it must be admitted that even though the United States is an "earthly city," its behavior has had an effect on how the gospel has been received. In fact, the behavior of all of the Western nations where there are (have been) many Christians has had an effect on the reception of the gospel. Western colonialism, for example, had a very negative effect on the reception of the gospel in Africa and Asia. Earlier, the Byzantine Empire and the Crusades had a very negative influence on the spread of the gospel in the Middle East. Perhaps the United States can avoid the judgment that fell on the Roman Empire and other empires of the past that have ceased to exist, but, whatever happens to the United States (for example, losing power in relation to other nations), God's Great Circle of Love will continue in the world among all nations. I believe it will continue to spread in the world, even if in a somewhat irregular fashion, as it has ever since the Circle received the gift of the Holy Spirit ("pouring God's love into our hearts"; Rom 5:5) after the work of Jesus Christ in the world.

Like the relationship of government and society to the Great Circle in general, the relationship of the family to the Great Circle is complex, but the family can become more a part of the Great Circle of Love than the secular state. The family is a human institution that exists in all societies. Christians seek to bring their families into the Great Circle as they join the church. The family has responsibilities of transmitting the faith that the secular state cannot and should not bear. The Christian family is not going to be perfect, but it is an important means given and used by God for transmitting the faith to children, as well as a witness for Christ to others outside of the family. In the end, each individual in the family is responsible to enter and walk in the Great Circle of Love by faith. Every family whose members do that will be blessed.

Both the state and the family exercise coercive powers that are not appropriate for the church. These are necessary for the protection of people, especially children, but coercive power as such does not advance the kingdom, as we know from the example of Christ. The powers exercised in the family are mostly limited to when people are children, but in Christian families it should be clear that the powers are exercised as expressions of love. The powers of the state are much more extensive and are exercised throughout the lifetime of its citizens. Again, there has been a slow development of the exercise of powers justly in democracies, based primarily on the recognition of the dignity and rights of every individual. Nevertheless, there will always be a need for improvement in the exercise of state powers justly where there is often great variation within populations in their social, economic, and political powers. Minorities and those marginal to societies especially need protection and encouragement from the majority in societies.

In spite of the many failings of the earthly, tangible expression of the Great Circle of Love in the church, it will continue until it is fully united with the one who originated the Circle through Jesus Christ and the Holy Spirit. We can believe that the church will continue to be judged by God in order to clarify the witness to its Savior. My own belief is that the church has been judged for its long years of entanglement with the state. This was due to falling for the temptation that Christ rejected in the wilderness, which was to use earthly powers to advance himself. We can still see this judgment in the turning away of many people from Christianity for its attempt to control them and their knowledge. I also believe that secular methodology in government and in gaining knowledge can be a useful tool to avoid the wrong use of power by religious people, with which the world is all too familiar. It can also protect religious people from using God's name in vain as they break the third commandment through false references to God. A secular methodology is not the same as secularism or a style of life that ignores God. The individual government leader and individual academic or scientist can still benefit greatly by personal faith and the guidance of God. Such people should not use their faith or religion as a means of advancing their knowledge of the world or their power in the world, but rather as a means of advancing their knowledge of God in relation to God's world and their spiritual power given by God to use in the world. We are still in a period in which Christians need to come to an understanding of the right use of the secular but, as noted, I believe the right use is to regard the secular as a tool or methodology. In this way, the secular can be used to protect people from bad or incorrect religious ideas and actions and provide opportunities for the advance of the influence of faith and love found in the Great Circle of Love that comes from God.

A central concern for Christians in regard to society should be the sociocultural forces that come to dominate large numbers of people, not simply the sins of individuals. This takes place largely unconsciously. Wink links the theology found especially in Paul's writings of the "principalities and powers" to what social scientists have discovered in the last two centuries concerning the powerful influence of sociocultural forces on people.[3] As already noted, it is as though the social sciences rediscovered what the Bible recognized long ago: there are forces coming, as it were, "from above" (actually through groups of people) that influence every individual. In short, these are the views, values, and practices found in cultures and the institutions that preserve and foster them. These forces can be morally neutral, morally good, or they can bring destruction to people's lives. Christians should seek to creatively influence these forces, just as they should influence the institutions of society, but this includes recognizing and opposing destructive forces. This is the "wrestling" or "struggle" that Paul speaks of in Ephesians 6:12. It is also the "not conforming to this world" of Roman 12:2. Historically, these forces ("principalities and powers"), even though evil, have dominated large numbers of people, including Christians and many good people, for example, in the slavery and segregation systems in the United States. In general, it is helpful for a society to have a variety of subcultures to offset and stimulate each other. This is also true of the church, in which the various denominations and congregations represent subcultures. However, diversity itself is not sufficient to make a healthy society. Diversity should lead to pluralism, which is diverse groups interacting and working together. The goal of Christians should be to make their church subculture, as much as possible, a representation of the Great Circle of Love and also to work in the world to help create a context in which the Great Circle of Love can grow.

THE GREAT CIRCLE AND THE COSMOS

The discovery that the age of the cosmos is close to fourteen billion years creates exciting implications for theological thought regarding the great purpose of God to unite all things through the Human One, who is Jesus Christ. God took so much time to make it possible for us to enjoy the Grand Canyon, the Great Smokies, the Himalayas, and much, much more. The long evolutionary process has produced great diversity of life that appears everywhere, with new forms constantly being discovered, all of it creating awe-inspiring beauty and incredible interest to life. Most importantly, the patterns and regularities in nature make it possible for human beings to act on the basis of probabilities and expectations and thereby create numerous useful and effective devices, techniques, and medicines that aid human beings. However, it is also true that there are anomalies and irregularities that require numerous adjustments to life and especially thought and care for

3. Wink, *Naming the Powers*; *Unmasking the Powers*; *Engaging the Powers*.

one another and the world. As we know, changes, mutations, or anomalies made evolution and the development of humanity possible. Some Christians do not like the irregularities of nature, as they believe it implies that God made a mistake, which God cannot do. This has contributed to the opposition to the LGBTQ movement. On the other hand, creating the cosmos and nature as God has done fits exactly with the need for human beings to think responsibly and act in love for other human beings and for all creation.

I have spoken of the fact that the followers of Jesus viewed him as an eschatological prophet and as introducing the "Last Days" (Heb 1:2). Christians have tended to focus on the temporal meaning of "Last Days" instead of what is most important: the bringing together of the cosmos ("things in heaven and things on earth") in Jesus Christ. At the core of this process is human beings meeting the Human One and becoming like him, who is the image of God that we were also created to be. Jesus Christ himself taught that when we meet others with needs—and all human beings have needs— we are meeting him. We are told, "keep awake therefore, for you do not know on what day [or what hour] your Lord is coming" (Matt 24:42). In light of these teachings of Jesus, the suddenness of the return of Jesus should be associated with the suddenness and unexpectedness of meeting other human beings in need through whom we meet Jesus. There is great mystery here, but the coming together of the cosmos must be related to the coming together of human beings in the Human One. This process has started very weakly in the followers of Jesus Christ in the church, but that is the future to which we have been called. Meeting Jesus in others at any time should be the basis for our urgency, not just thinking of the calendar.

In the light of the incarnation and atonement of the Human One, we can now see that the purpose of God from the beginning, hidden for ages until only recently, is to create a new humanity to live in a new cosmos. The outlines of the life of this new humanity are now seen in Jesus Christ, but the fulfillment is unfolding in history, now accelerating with changes. The joy, excitement, and privilege of participation in the "coming of humanity" with the Human One "in clouds of glory" is offered to every person. This is life in the Great Circle of Love.

CONCLUSION

This book stated in chapter 2 the notion that human beings are both natural and supernatural, that is, they are part of nature and yet made with the capacity to think about and commune with God and also to live beyond death. Human beings have a longing for the transcendent and powers from beyond that are expressed in a tangible form. On the one hand, creation itself and the humanness of Jesus Christ expresses God's love and care for and commitment to the tangible world, and at the same time, transcendent realities of love and power are expressed very clearly in Jesus Christ and testified to by his followers. But the transcendent realities are expressed by Jesus in a way that prevents or works against the human tendency to use and manipulate others and objects in creation for selfish purposes. We see this clearly in the way Jesus Christ related to others and then died and rose again, appearing only to his followers. Jesus Christ made a Way, a road that human beings can walk that leads back to God, from whom they are estranged without him. The road came from God in Jesus Christ, but is very definitely in this tangible world, and as we follow the Human One we participate in returning ourselves to God and bringing recreation to the tangible world. That is why Christians embrace ways to prevent destruction of the environment and continually seek ways to improve the lives of people by practicing and enacting justice and mercy. This following the Human One and walking in the Great Circle of Love that comes from God catches up humanity and the whole cosmos, and leads back to God. Jesus promised to walk with us by the Holy Spirit so that we could show to the world the Way of the Circle of Love and lead them to join us in it. It is up to us in the church, the ongoing body of Christ, to give tangible expression to God's love in what we tell and show about Jesus Christ in our little circles of love that are made whole in the Great Circle seen in Jesus Christ and the whole evolving cosmos. This is the Way of fulfillment of what we were meant to be and the Way of flourishing in the consciousness of God's love in the present world, as eternal life that begins now and continues forever.

Bibliography

Alexander, Eben. *Proof of Heaven: A Neurosurgeon's Journey into the Afterlife*. New York: Simon & Schuster, 2012.

Allison, Scott T., and George R. Goethals. *Heroes: What They Do & Why We Need Them*. New York: Oxford University Press, 2011.

Beck, Ulrich. *A God of One's Own: Religion's Capacity for Peace and Potential for Violence*. Translated by Rodney Livingstone. Malden, MA: Polity, 2010.

Bosch, David J. *Transforming Mission: Paradigm Shifts in Theology of Mission*. Maryknoll, NY: Orbis, 2005.

Boyarin, Daniel. *The Jewish Gospels: The Story of the Jewish Christ*. New York: New Press, 2012.

Calvin, John. *Institutes of the Christian Religion*. Vols 1–2. Translated by John Allen. Philadelphia: Presbyterian Board of Publication and Sabbath-School Work, 1899.

Ch'en, Kenneth K. S. *Buddhism in China: A Historical Survey*. Princeton, NJ: Princeton University Press, 1973.

Chilton, Bruce. *Rabbi Jesus: An Intimate Biography*. New York: Doubleday, 2000.

Collins, Randall. *Interaction Ritual Chains*. Princeton, NJ: Princeton University Press. 2004.

Common English Bible, Everyday Outreach New Testament. Nashville: Common English Bible, 2012.

Ehrman, Bart D. *How Jesus Became God: The Exaltation of a Jewish Preacher from Galilee*. New York: HarperOne, 2014.

Ernst, Carl W. *Following Muhammad: Rethinking Islam in the Contemporary World*. Chapel Hill: University of North Carolina Press, 2003.

Esposito, John L. *The Future of Islam*. New York: Oxford University Press, 2008.

Friedman, Thomas L. *Thank You for Being Late: An Optimist's Guide to Thriving in the Age of Accelerations*. Kindle ed. New York: Farrar, Straus, and Giroux, 2012.

Froese, Paul. *The Plot to Kill God: Findings from the Soviet Experiment in Secularization*. Berkeley: University of California Press, 2008.

Haidt, Jonathan. *The Righteous Mind: Why Good People Are Divided by Politics and Religion*. New York: Pantheon, 2012.

Haught, John F. *Science and Faith: A New Introduction*. Mahwah, NJ: Paulist, 2012.

Jenkins, Philip. *Jesus Wars: How Four Patriarchs, Three Queens, and Two Emperors Decided What Christians Would Believe for the Next 1,500 Years*. New York: HarperCollins, 2010.

Joas, Hans. *Faith as an Option: Possible Futures for Christianity*. Translated by Alex Skinner. Stanford, CA: Stanford University Press, 2014.

Johnson, William Stacy. *A Time to Embrace: Same-Sex Relationships in Religion, Law, and Politics*. Grand Rapids: Eerdmans, 2012.

Kraft, Kathryn Ann. *Searching for Heaven in the Real World: A Sociological Discussion of Conversion in the Arab World*. Oxford: Regnum, 2012.

Leeuwen, Arend Theodoor van. *Christianity in World History: The Meeting of the Faiths of East and West*. Translated by H. H. Hoskins. New York: Scribner, 1964.

Lewis, C. S. *The Screwtape Letters*. London: Geoffrey Bles, 1950.

Marty, Martin E. *The Modern Schism: Three Paths to the Secular*. New York: Harper & Row, 1969.

Merton, Robert. "The Normative Structure of Science." In *The Sociology of Science*, edited by Norman W. Storer, 267–75. Chicago: University of Chicago Press, 1973.

Moffett, Samuel H. *A History of Christianity in Asia*. Vol. 1, *Beginnings to 1500*. San Francisco: HarperCollins, 1992.

Montgomery, Robert L. "Bias in Interpreting Social Facts: Is it a Sin?" *Journal for the Scientific Study of Religion* 23.3 (September 1984) 278–91.

———. "Conversion and the Historic Spread of Religions." In *The Oxford Handbook of Religious Conversion*, edited by Lewis R. Rambo and Charles E. Farhadian, 164–89. Oxford: Oxford University Press, 2014.

———. *The Diffusion of Religions: A Sociological Perspective*. Lanham, MD: University Press of America, 1996.

———. *Introduction to the Sociology of Missions*. Westport, CT: Praeger, 1999.

———. *The Lopsided Spread of Christianity: Toward an Understanding of the Diffusion of Religions*. Westport, CT: Praeger, 2002.

———. *The Real New Age and the Opposition: Biblical Eschatology for Today*. Asheville, NC: Cross Lines, 2012

———. "Receptivity to an Outside Religion: Light from Interaction Between Sociology and Missiology." *Missiology* 14.3 (July 1986) 287–99.

———. "Special Persons and the Spread of Religions." *Pastoral Psychology* 65.3 (2016) 369–93.

———. "The Spread of Religions and Macrosocial Relations." *Sociological Analysis* (now *Sociology of Religion*) 52.1 (1991) 37–52.

———. *Why Religions Spread: The Expansion of Buddhism, Christianity, and Islam with Implications for Missions*. 2nd ed. Asheville, NC: Cross Lines, 2012.

Newberg, Andrew, and Mark Robert Waldman. *How God Changes Your Brain: Breakthrough Findings from a Leading Neuroscientist*. New York: Ballantine, 2010.

Niles, Daniel Thambyrajah. *That They May Have Life*. Harper, 1951.

Noss, John Boyer. *Man's Religions*. New York: Macmillan, 1949.

Otto, Rudolf. *The Idea of the Holy: An Inquiry into the Non-Rational Factor in the Idea of the Divine and Its Relation to the Rational*. Translated by John W. Harvey. 6th impression with additions. London: Oxford University Press. 1931.

Rogers, Jack. *Jesus, the Bible, and Homosexuality: Explode the Myths, Heal the Church*. Louisville: Westminster John Knox, 2006.

Sanneh, Lamin. *Piety and Power: Muslims and Christians in West Africa*. Maryknoll, NY: Orbis, 1996.

Sayyid, S. *Recalling the Caliphate: Decolonization and World Order*. London: Hurst, 2014.

Schäfer, Peter. *The Jewish Jesus: How Judaism and Christianity Shaped Each Other*. Princeton, NJ: Princeton University Press, 2012.

Sharot, Stephen. *A Comparative Sociology of World Religions: Virtuosos, Priests, and Popular Religion*. New York: New York University Press, 2001.

Shelton, Jason E., and Michael O. Emerson. *Blacks and Whites in Christian America: How Racial Discrimination Shapes Religious Convictions*. New York: New York University Press, 2012.

Smith, Christian. *The Bible Made Impossible: Why Biblicism Is Not a Truly Evangelical Reading of Scripture*. Grand Rapids: Brazos, 2012.

————. *Moral, Believing Animals: Human Personhood and Culture*. New York: Oxford University Press, 2003.

————. *The Sacred Project of American Sociology*. New York: Oxford University Press, 2014.

————, ed. *The Secular Revolution: Power, Interests, and Conflict in the Secularization of American Public Life*. Berkeley: University of California Press, 2003.

————. *What Is a Person?: Rethinking Humanity, Social Life, and the Moral Good from the Person Up*. Chicago: University of Chicago Press, 2010.

Spiro, Melford. *Buddhism and Society: A Great Tradition and Burmese Vicissitudes*. Berkeley: University of California Press, 1982.

Stark, Rodney. *For the Glory of God: How Monotheism Led to Reformations, Science, Witch-Hunts, and the End of Slavery*. Princeton, NJ: Princeton University Press, 2003.

————. *How the West Won: The Neglected Story of the Triumph of Modernity*. Wilmington, DE: ISI, 2014.

————. *One True God: Historical Consequences of Monotheism*. Princeton, NJ: Princeton University Press, 2001.

————. *The Rise of Christianity: How the Obscure, Marginal Jesus Movement Became the Dominant Religious Force in the Western World in a Few Centuries*. San Francisco: HaperCollins, 1997.

Stenmark, Mikael. *Scientism: Science, Ethics, and Religion*. Burlington, VT: Ashgate, 2001.

Volf, Miroslav. *A Public Faith: How Followers of Christ Should Serve the Common Good*. Grand Rapids: Brazos, 2011.

Wade, Nicholas. *The Faith Instinct: How Religion Evolved and Why It Endures*. New York: Penguin, 2009.

Weber, Max. *From Max Weber: Essays in Sociology*. Translated, edited, and with an introduction by H. H. Gerth and C. Wright Mills. New York: Oxford University Press, 1967.

————. *The Sociology of Religion*. Translated by Ephraim Fischoff. Boston: Beacon, 1972.

Wink, Walter. *Engaging the Powers: Discernment and Resistance in a World of Domination*. Philadelphia: Fortress, 1992.

————. *The Human Being: Jesus and the Enigma of the Son of the Man*. Minneapolis: Fortress, 2002.

———. *Naming the Powers: The Language of Power in the New Testament.* Philadelphia: Fortress, 1989.

———. *Unmasking the Powers: The Invisible Forces That Determine Human Existence.* Philadelphia: Fortress, 1986.

Winner, Lauren F. *Girl Meets God: On the Path to a Spiritual Life.* Chapel Hill, NC: Algonquin, 2002.

Woodberry, Robert D. "The Missionary Roots of Liberal Democracy." *American Political Science Review* 106.2 (2012) 244–74.

Index